force came from the expectation that God himself was about to usher in a new dispensation of the saints. In the meantime, every member of the community should be a missionary. . . . The author himself does not come from any of the Anabaptist groups and is motivated not so much by an urge to vindicate their memory from aspersions as to assess their significance in the total life of the Church and of the American nation. This is a significant appraisal."

Said *Church History:* " At long last, the church historian has a book in his hands which will give him in a most authoritative way a reliable and rich picture of that elusive phenomenon of Anabaptism, which to most scholars has remained a dark spot up to now. One major reason for this remarkable neglect was the apparent or only assumed difficulty of getting acquainted with the original sources. The book under review is a strong proof to the contrary. . . . "

Says James Luther Adams of the Harvard Divinity School: " This is an excellent piece of work. Chapter one is a particularly interesting and valuable piece of scholarship in that it restores the left-wing heretics to their true character. Ever since the Reformation, these people have been maligned by the right-wing orthodox critics, and it has taken a great deal of scholarly research to dig up the truth about the left-wing non-conformists whose names have been blackened and whose characters have been made to seem umbrageous by those of the opposite camp, who happen to have the ear of the world."

The Anabaptist View of the Church

Franklin Hamlin Littell is professor of Church History at Emory University, Atlanta, Georgia. A graduate of Cornell College (Iowa), he received a B.D. degree from the Union Theological Seminary in 1940 and a Ph.D. degree from Yale in 1946. From 1949 to 1951 he served as a member of the religious affairs staff of the United States High Commissioner for Germany. From 1951 to 1953 Dr. Littell was dean of the chapel of Boston University. He returned to Germany from 1953 to 1958 as senior representative of the Franz Lieber Foundation, St. Paul, Minnesota, and was also chairman of the Ecumenical Committee of the German Kirchentag (Laymen's Movement). He is author of *The Free Church,* published by the Starr King Press.

The Anabaptist View of the Church

A Study in the Origins of Sectarian Protestantism

by Franklin Hamlin Littell

Second edition, revised and enlarged

Starr King Press   Beacon Hill   Boston

Library of Congress Catalog card number: 58 - 6338

This book was originally published in 1952, as the Prize Essay of the Frank S. Brewer Fund of the American Society of Church History, as Volume VIII of "Studies in Church History."

Starr King Press books are distributed by the Beacon Press, Inc.
Printed in the United States of America

1955 2

Contents

Preface to Revised Edition

This essay was submitted in its original form to the Faculty of the Graduate School of Yale University in partial fulfillment of the requirements for the degree of Doctor of Philosophy. I was then primarily concerned with forms of religious voluntaryism and lay initiative in Christian history, and was directed to the study of the Anabaptists and advised throughout by Dr. Roland H. Bainton, Titus Professor of Ecclesiastical History in Yale Divinity School. Dr. Kenneth Scott Latourette, Sterling Professor of Missions and Oriental History, was also generous with time and counsel; to him I owe some understanding of the importance of the missionary mandate in Christian history, especially as a shaping force in the life of Free Churches. From both I learned again how teaching as a vocation implies "a fellowship of teachers and students" (*universitas magistrorum ac scolarium*) as well as the mastery of one or more intellectual disciplines. To them, as well as to my father, Dr. Clair Francis Littell of Cornell College (Iowa), I wish to express deep gratitude for encouragement and assistance, without unburdening myself of responsibility for shortcomings and errors.

The Frank S. Brewer Prize Committee of the American Society of Church History saw fit to sponsor the study in revised form as the 1952 Prize Essay of the Society: Volume 8 of *Studies in Church History*. I wish to thank Professor James Hastings Nichols of Chicago, Professor William Pauck (now of Union Theological Seminary) and Professor L. J. Trinterud of McCormick Theological Seminary for seeing the first edition through publication, a duty made difficult by my residence overseas and by the sudden death of the publisher. Mr. C. H. Sprunger of Berne, Indiana, served the Society devotedly for some years; I hope this word may help to keep memory of his service green.

When *The Anabaptist View of the Church* first appeared it had the good fortune to fall into place in the midst of a revival of historical and theological interest in the Free Church way.

Interest of general students and specialists in the formative period
of what Troeltsch called "sectarian Protestantism," in the generation which was coming to be recognized as the classical era of
the Free Churches, was high. In spite of a title esoteric by
ordinary standards the book sold out almost immediately, to the
surprise of author, editors, and publisher.

Preparation of a reprint was made difficult not only by the
normal demands of administrative work abroad, but also by the
abnormal volume of related studies which have appeared in the
last decade. There have been published six new volumes of
sources, and another has been read in galleys and another yet in
manuscript. In addition to a new *Mennonite Encyclopedia* (two
of four volumes being used in this revision) and a complete new
translation and edition of *The Complete Writings of Menno
Simons,* more than two dozen new monographs have been published treating some phase of Anabaptist thought and history.
The historical collections and studies of Professors Harold S.
Bender at Goshen College (Indiana) and Cornelius Krahn at
Bethel College (Kansas) attract a growing number of young
non-Mennonite scholars. *The Mennonite Quarterly Review*
has continued unabated its extensive efforts to make early Free
Church history meaningful to Mennonites and non-Mennonites
alike; *Church History, Theologische Zeitschrift,* and *Archiv
für Reformationsgeschichte* have given increasing space to studies
of early Anabaptist problems and personalities. It was originally
planned to reprint the first edition. Representatives of the Beacon
Press, particularly Mr. Melvin Arnold (now with Harper &
Brothers) and Miss Janet Finnie, have been helpful and encouraging. We were soon clear, however, that in the midst of a
surge of Anabaptist studies no mere reprint would suffice. The
present publication is both an extensive revision and an en-
largement.

As things have developed, the propositions originally put
forward have stood up under criticism, further research, and
the publication of large quantities of new primary sources. There
are three new sections: on the tolerance of Philipp of Hesse
(Chapter I, third section), on the opposition of the Reformers

to a literal obedience to the Great Commission (Chapter IV, second section), and on the Anabaptists and natural law (Chapter IV, last part of fourth section). For the sake of reader interest, the original Chapter I, "Former Treatments of Anabaptism," has become the last chapter: Chapter V of the present work, "The Changing Reputation of the Anabaptists."

In the former first chapter the charge was made that historians had generally judged the Anabaptists on the basis of secondary polemical sources, and that primary sources were available to those who sought them. "The Anabaptists have commonly been judged on the basis of insufficient evidence. It is time for a re-trial" (p. 18). As this is written it is not too much to say that, while the process of re-trial is not yet complete, the "prisoner at the bar" has a much different countenance from what he had before scholars began to take the evidence of the *Täuferakten* and related reports seriously.

Bad Godesberg/Rhein   F. H. L.
Easter, 1957

INTRODUCTION
A Working Definition of "Anabaptist"

Several serious impediments have customarily blocked the path of those who turned to a discussion of "Anabaptist" church life and thought. These impediments proved fatal to most previous studies. Calling them to the attention of the reader is one of the first tasks of the present study.

Inadequate Information on Anabaptism

First, it is impossible to assume that the average reader has any adequate concept of the "Anabaptists." Information on the groups so termed has been notoriously scarce and has rested in the main upon hostile polemics. Usually those who were cordially inclined have also relied upon secondary sources and attempted to present a friendly or tendentious judgment through selective citation. The conclusions thus reached have not seldom been as unjust to the true Anabaptists as those of their enemies, even if otherwise intended.

In the final chapter we shall discuss the way in which present evidence calls into question four centuries of partisan interpretation by defenders of state-church Protestantism. In addition to Martin Luther and Ulrich Zwingli, the traditional authorities cited have been Justus Menius and Heinrich Bullinger; all of these men were very hostile to the radical groups, and made no attempt to deal fairly with them in the flesh or in writing. We shall see that the typical history of the Reformation in English still rests upon the attacks which these stalwarts made upon those they called "Anabaptists," although a few of the more recent general surveys are cast in a new mold. The reputation of the Anabaptists is in fact changing. Newly published documentary materials and certain German monographs have made imperative a thorough revision of still prevailing judgments regarding those called

"Anabaptist." A reassessment of the entire movement is timely and feasible. Contemporary students who approach the radicals comment quite vigorously upon the paucity of reliable interpretative writing[1] — a paucity the more remarkable because the newer sources obviously make possible a thorough reworking of the field. The linguistic impediment is serious, however, for even a reader fluent in modern German can be defeated by the various dialects used in the middle European area before the modern languages took form. The polemics against the Anabaptists have long been available in English or in modern tongue; the testimonies of the Anabaptists themselves are still primarily the preserve of philologists and historical specialists.

Not only were the students of Anabaptism long plagued by restriction to descriptions of doubtful value, but the complexity of the movement itself provided further difficulties. As we shall see, the groups that broke away from state-church Protestantism on the Continent were marred initially by many confusions and incoherences. It is not easy to extract a central concept or classifying principle. Later interpreters, hostile or friendly, have read into the movement as it finally took shape their own stereotypes: "revolutionaries," "individualists," "liberals," "Biblicists," "enthusiasts" *(Schwärmer)*, "Bolsheviki," "Bible Christians." Various attempts at classification will be discussed in this study, and the author will make a recommendation of his own.

The term "Anabaptist" itself gives no assistance to our problem. No word in Christian history has been used more loosely. To attempt to group in a single category all those to whom the term has been applied is as hopeless as the dove's pursuit of a landing place while the waters still covered the earth. Very evidently a study of "the Anabaptist view" will come to grief in an early paragraph unless some more precise use of the word is adopted than has been usual. The word "Anabaptist" wants a definition, as will be plain from review of its history. The precise problem of defining and classifying is discussed in Chapter One. At this point the use of the word must be checked and limited; it has been one of the stumbling blocks for every generation of historians.

What Does "Anabaptist" Mean?

The word "Anabaptist" is a Latin derivative of the Greek original, *anabaptismos* (re-baptism). The German form, *Wiedertäufer,* means "one who re-baptizes." Lutherans and Zwinglians applied it in the beginning to those who separated themselves from the main body of the state churches. As for the radicals themselves: "They repudiated the name, insisting that infant baptism did not constitute true baptism and that they were not in reality re-baptizers. Their argument was of no avail. The name was so conveniently elastic that it came to be applied to all those who stood out against authoritative state religion."[2] We shall see later that even baptism itself was not the primary matter in the testimony of the radical movement.[3] The radicals wanted to be known only as "Brüder"(Brethren) or by some other nonsectarian name, and were far indeed from the later insistence of some Baptists on a formal precision in ritual. In the first period of the movement in Switzerland even the Zwinglians called them "Tauffbrüder." Baptism became important only because it was the most obvious dividing line between two patterns of church organization. "Anabaptist" was a popular term with the authorities because it afforded them an excuse for forcefully suppressing the radicals. The enemies of the movement were insistent on use of the term "Wiedertäufer" or "Anabaptistici" because the radical groups thereby became subject to the death penalty. Under the ancient Roman law against the re-baptizers (Donatists), those called "Anabaptist" could be suppressed by the sword,[4] even though the extension of the law in this fashion was at best of doubtful legality. The campaign of propaganda and suppression succeeded. At Speyer in 1529 the emperor ruled against the "Anabaptists" in final fashion, and persecution by imprisonment and exile and death spread throughout the length and breadth of the Empire.[5] But the radicals themselves did not admit the truth of the charge. And the movement itself cannot be classified properly in terms of the baptismal rite.

Historically, the term "Anabaptist" became a slippery word, an epithet flung contemptuously, in much the same way the word "Bolshevik" recently has been hurled at those of unpopular views.[6] In fact, the term has very limited value, and is used in this study only because it has found a traditional place in historical studies. The terms "Swiss Brethren," "Hutterite Brethren," "Mennonites" are far more precise. "South German Brethren" has also come to carry some meaning since the publication of recent volumes of sources edited by Krebs, Schornbaum, and Franz. In general, however, the Swiss and the South Germans were one party, and they are not always distinguished from each other, even by specialists in Anabaptist affairs. The important point is that the reader should mistrust the use of the term "Anabaptist" unless there is conclusive evidence that the typology derives from a proper use of primary sources.

A Working Hypothesis

When we review the various sixteenth-century groups which broke from the pattern of established religion, we are struck by the degree to which all shared an attitude to history which is technically known as "primitivism." This attitude was expressed in many ways. When we consider the views of those to be termed "Anabaptist," the central significance of the church view stands out. The function of Chapter I is to show how this happened, and the line of argument is developed from a critical review of the history of the movement. The view of the church came to dominate the Anabaptist movement, therefore, although initially there were several grounds for group protest against the state churches. The concern for restitution of the "True Church" was a center about which some groups coalesced. From this center other protesting groups broke away, and these are not properly termed "Anabaptists." They shared with the main-line Anabaptists the vision of a restitution of a lost virtue, but for them the nature of the True Church was subsidiary to other concerns, theological or political.

As the principle of voluntary religious association, accompanied by reactivation of the role of the laity, has come to the center of contemporary Christian discussion, the incidents surrounding the origin and validation of religious voluntaryism become vital to both theology and religious sociology. In this perspective a study of the Anabaptist Church view is a study in the origins of "sectarian Protestantism." "Sectarian" is here used in the context of the sociology of religion and not in the popular or polemical sense of a normative judgment!

There has been a marked change in writing about the Anabaptists in recent years. Many scholars are no longer content with sweeping generalizations about the movement based on polemical Lutheran and Reformed writings. In the newer writings various schemes of classification have been attempted, to define various groupings among the radicals.[7] After studied review of the materials at hand, assayed with attention to evidence yet largely unavailable to the American scholar, the writer has come to the point where an arbitrary definition seems both logical and inevitable. Such a definition can reflect, however, the verdict of history in favor of those radical groups, among many, which were able to resolve certain incoherences and approximate their ideal. For working purposes, *the Anabaptists proper were those in the radical Reformation who gathered and disciplined a "true church" (rechte Kirche) upon the apostolic pattern as they understood it.* In a treatment of the Anabaptists, the doctrine of the church affords the classifying principle of first importance.

Fritz Heyer, in his detailed coverage of the field, came to a similar but less precise proposition about the centrality of the church view. Presuming that the Reformers' judgment must have been correct, he nevertheless attempted to tie the several wings of the radical movement together: "The ultimate significance of the Anabaptism [*Schwärmertum*] of the sixteenth century is grounded in the concept of the church."[8] His treatment is a rather traditional state-church apologetic, whereas we shall concern ourselves primarily with concrete group experience.

R. J. Smithson, author of one of the few reasonably adequate books on the movement, says: "The real issue between the Anabaptists and the other reformers was on the question of the type of Church which should take the place of the old Church."

He goes on to quote the great church historian Philip Schaff to the effect that "the reformers aimed to reform the old Church by the Bible; the radicals attempted to build a new Church from the Bible."[9] According to Cornelius Krahn, an American Mennonite scholar, the central theological concern of the Anabaptists was in the church, and he goes so far as to term their style of thinking "ecclesio-centric."[10]

In a broadly theological context we might use "Anabaptist" (in quotation marks) as Heyer uses the term; but the term is applied most appropriately to those groups who effected a vigorous church life upon what they thought to be the pattern of the primitive church. Chapters II, III and IV will show what they thought that pattern was; Chapter I will discuss the Anabaptist congregations (churches) and the way they developed in the midst of vigorous and various protests against the Catholic and Protestant establishments.

The Anabaptist View of the Church

CHAPTER I

The Quest for the Essence of Anabaptism

The first step toward a better understanding of Anabaptism is a descriptive treatment of the development of the movement. This description will rely primarily upon the newer documentary sources. In the review, much of the ground of Left Wing Protestantism will be covered in the attempt to place Anabaptism in its proper place in the vast complex of radical dissent. The radical groupings developed not on the margins of the sixteenth-century Christendom, but rather in the very centers of the Reformation. This fact once lent credence to the charge of Roman Catholic polemicists that religious revolution, enthusiasm (*Schwärmerei*), Anti-Trinitarianism, and the spiritualizing thrust (religious individualism) were all the legitimate offspring of the Reformers' protest. Today we are inclined to interpret Anabaptism, at least, as a third type quite distinct from both Roman Catholic and Protestant territorial churches. Fritz Blanke has concluded a recent study with the words:

The rise of the Anabaptist group in Zollikon was the birth of a brotherhood of a purely religious character.

The young plant was soon violently suppressed, but that does not decrease its significance. In Zollikon a new type of Church had begun to differentiate itself, the Free Church type. Zollikon is the cradle of this idea, which from here entered upon its triumphal march through four centuries and through the whole world.[7]

The appearance of the radical protest in the same centers as the Reformation itself affords opportunity to compare and contrast not only the various groupings in the Left Wing, but also the state church and Free Church types of Protestantism in their formative stages.

1

RADICALISM IN THE CENTERS OF REFORM

Among the students who flocked to Wittenberg and Zürich and Strassburg were numbers who lamented the fallen estate of the church, and judged her weaknesses and apostasies by the light of the church before Constantine. As time was to prove, the great Reformers were cautious and responsible men. They hesitated to abandon the parish pattern of the medieval church. At this point the radicals passed beyond, demanding a purging of errors accumulated during the period of "wandering in the wilderness." While the Reformers waited on the decision of the magistrate *(Obrigkeit)*, certain small groups embraced the New Testament pattern with eagerness and pressed forward to restore the undefiled spirit and customs of the church of the first centuries. Such men were impatient with compromise. They believed that the Bible gave a clear instruction as to the organizational pattern of the True Church, just as it provided certain ground for her creeds and confessions.

As Walter Rauschenbusch wrote in his only essay on the sixteenth century, the Anabaptists were the "root and branch party" of the Reformation.[2] They said of Luther that he "tore down the old house, but built no new one in its place,"[3] and of Zwingli that he "threw down all infirmities as with thunder strokes, but erected nothing better in place."[4] Discontent with the slow-moving leaders grew steadily, and rifts appeared between the party of the Reformation and the party of the Restitution. With bitter disappointment the radical party turned against the "half-way men,"[5] their former leaders, and against their former brethren who rested in large part in the unseparated condition of the medieval church in the world. The Christians, particularly those who had been informed by the rebirth of Biblical truth, were worse than the pagans who knew no better: "there is no people under the sun who disgrace God's name, suffering, martyrdom and death [more] than the so-called Christians."[6]

In the beginning years this discontent was not clearly defined. Radical Biblical faith was there, but it was mixed with other elements of group protest. Indeed, sometimes the same person drew from different reserves of intellectual opposition to the medieval pattern. The attitude of the Reformers also underwent some significant changes. When the Anabaptists separated from the dominant party, and from other protest groupings, there were occasional flare-ups of dramatic moment. Nevertheless, in the main the separation came slowly and painfully. As we review the experiences at the three great centers of early Protestantism, we shall see that it took time to clarify the issues and define the distinctions between the Reformers and the Anabaptists. But it will be plainly seen that the lines became clear in time to both parties. What was truly at stake was the concept of the church, and with it the pattern of church life involved in a genuine reformation.

The radicals did not have in the beginning a clearly conceived and proclaimed doctrine of the church. In the radical protest at the first were enrolled prophets and Biblicists, anti-Trinitarians and orthodox, revolutionaries and nonresistants, independents and covenanters.[7] With the passing of months and years of persecution, the Anabaptists withdrew from loose fellowship with other styles of protest; and they acquired, in contest with other radicals and with the Reformers, a pattern of discipline and integrity. For convenience we speak today of "an Anabaptist movement," but we must avoid reading back into the Reformers and radicals a logical coherence and clarity of thought which neither party possessed until after a series of hard-fought controversies. The Anabaptists had both to distinguish themselves from the dominant party and also to achieve unity within their own ranks.

In North Germany

In North Germany the first radical upsurge of importance came at Wittenberg in late 1521, while Luther was in refuge at the Wartburg. MARTIN LUTHER (1483-1546)[8] was adored as a champion by many different groups and classes and for as many different reasons. He seemed to voice German national needs against those who bled the Germans for a trans-alpine master.

The lesser knights hoped to find in him an advocate against imperial pressures. He called for religious reform against a system of outward display and inward sterility. Among those who rallied to his banner were many to whom he appeared as a social reformer as well as religious. Such groups looked with excited eye upon the heightening of economic and religious tensions, and awaited with eager heart the revolutionary day which should usher in a New Age of history.

The point of separation was Luther's policy of reformation. However much the Anabaptists may resemble medieval sects in certain respects, they did not spring from pre-Reformation movements directly. They did not think of themselves as a correction to, or lay monastic witness against, the compromises of an intact Christendom: they demanded a change of the whole pattern. In their records they refer to Luther half in praise and half in sorrow, as a leader whom they first followed but who did not carry them through to as thorough a reformation as they had anticipated.

The "Wittenberg Puritan reformation" was not, strictly speaking, an Anabaptist movement. Its appearance and suppression are, however, of vital importance in the effect they had on later Lutheran understanding of Anabaptism. In the first explosion of radical discontent, certain men from Zwickau (the "Zwickau prophets") came forward to proclaim a thoroughgoing change with such insistence that some of Luther's own colleagues were won to their cause. Even Melanchthon was temporarily carried away, and Andreas Bodenstein von Karlstadt permanently defected. Experienced in meetings where anyone possessed of the spirit could proclaim with authority the truths of the inner life, the men of Zwickau grounded their mission to the world on the Great Commission (Mark 16:16). They strongly demanded a return to the usage of the Apostolic Age, as they understood it, and condemned the temporizing attitude in which the great Reformer still allowed some practices introduced by the Pope.[9] Marcus Thome (Stübner) claimed a special revelation from the Angel Gabriel (*sonderliche offenbarung und erleuchtung*). "Finally it was declared that the Holy Scripture was undependable for the instruction of men. For men must be taught only by the Spirit. If God had wanted to teach men from scripture, he would have sent forth a Bible from heaven."[10] There was a great impatience in their words as well as harshness of feeling toward the slow leaders, for soon the Turk would break forth into the land; the end of the world in a mighty battle, with the elevation of the righteous and the slaying of the godless, was close at hand.[11] Such enthusiastic teaching revealed dependence upon Taborite teaching. (Both Stübner and his colleague, Thomas Müntzer, had made the pilgrimage to Bohemia).[12] The prophets preferred the living word to the written. Tauler's Sermons were cited by them frequently. They also used the "Commentary on Jeremiah" attributed to Joachim of Fiore.[13] From chiliastic, mystical, and prophetic sources they drew proof that true religion depends on the inward authority and is free from external compulsion or evaluation. They went further than this. Not only the spiritual life but also the social order was to be conformed to their vision of the New Age. "This knotty spirit taught that the secular magistrate and rule must be reformed."[14]

With insistent demand for an ethical renewal and thorough-going institutional reform, the Zwickau group pressed through the town council certain measures of "Puritanical" reform in church and in town. In six blunt articles they terminated the Roman rites in the churches, eliminated bawdy houses and taverns. In the name of the Spirit they proposed to supervise the religious and moral life of the people.[15] The people responded to their message, and popular feeling was aroused in support of harsh measures: images were smashed, infant baptism suspended, the Mass celebrated in both kinds.

When Luther heard what was occurring, he returned in haste from his "Patmos." His eight vigorous sermons against the radicals stopped the new departures in mid-flight. With a strong plea for moderation he condemned those who brought about innovations by unbrotherly violence. "As a mother gives milk to the child we should also serve our brother, carry with him for a time and bear and help carry his weakness, even nurse him along — as it happened to us, until he becomes strong; and not go heavenward alone, but bring along our brother who is

not now our companion. . . ."[16] For Luther, the goal is to bring
over the whole people of the parishes. The issues are less important than unity of the people, and laws and general rules which
give offense to some should not be made about nonessentials. For
example, take images. An emperor and a Pope once warred
about this matter, and both were wrong; the isssue is not important.[17] So also with fasting: we should carry our freedom in
Christ so as not to give offense to bound brethren.[18] Luther later
accused Karlstadt of violating Christian freedom as much as the
Catholics by enforcing legalisms of minor significance.[19] Above
all, force should be avoided. "For the word shaped heaven and
earth and all things; it [the Word] must bring things to pass and
not we poor sinners. In sum, I will preach, I will speak, I will
write. But I will drive and compel no one with force, for faith
is to be voluntary, taken on without compulsion."[20] Yet the
approval and even assistance of the temporal power was invited
in the interests of order.

   With like energy, Luther wrestled against the spirit of "in-
spirationism" and "enthusiasm" *(Schwärmerei)* among the radicals. He feared the consequences of their subjectivism. When
they asserted an infallible inner authority he declared that the
hidden God is revealed only in the objective word and not by
vision.[21] The prophets were more probably inspired by the devil
than by the Angel Gabriel. Under such hammer blows the
radicals were discredited and soon left the city. Luther was
confirmed in his blunt opposition to all confusion of religious
and social concerns, whether Roman Catholic or what he
termed "Anabaptist."

   At this distance no clear view of the church can be seen
to emerge from the words of the radicals who grouped so briefly
at Wittenberg, and their later individual contributions are just
as problematical. In spite of traditional Lutheran and Reformed
interpretations, which will be discussed in the final chapter,[22] we
may question whether Stübner, Cellarius, Drechsel and Zwilling,
Müntzer, and Karlstadt are properly termed "Anabaptists" at
all.[23] We review them in part for traditional reasons, and especially because of their influence upon the great Reformer himself. Furthermore, the Wittenberg radicals introduce some of the

ideas which in time became common to various Left Wing groups of the time: repudiation of infant baptism, "Puritan" reform of morals, a definite world perspective.

After the "Eight Sermons," Luther wrote frequently against those he grouped as "Schwärmer." Among the better known of his polemics are *Wider die himmlischen Propheten* (1525),[24] *Von den Schleichern und Winkelpredigern* (1532),[25] and the prefaces to Menius' tract and Rhegius' polemic of 1535.[26] Luther thought also that he was dealing with the fruit of "Anabaptist" enthusiasm when he wrote *Ermahnung zum Frieden auf die zwölf Artikel der Bauernschaft in Schwaben* (1525)[27] and *Wider die räuberischen und mörderischen Rotten der Bauern* (1525).[28] In the process of resisting those who urged "that corner masses or separate masses must be performed,"[29] and in putting down the civil revolt led by religious revolutionaries, Luther's own view of the church underwent a marked transformation. At first he had embraced a fairly free view. In the "Lectures on Romans" he had spoken of the church as a persecuted remnant, always small, hiding in the world. This view points toward Sebastian Franck's dissolution of any visible church. On the other hand, in the "Address to the German Nobility" he spoke in terms of Corpus Christianum or *Volkskirche*, even a *Landeskirche*. However, in the "Right of a Congregation" he held that believers, if in some new or heathen land, had a perfect right to set up their own organization. Here was the congregational ideal.[30] In dealing with the Peasant Revolt and the spread of corner meetings and irregular assemblies, his view changed.[31] Dissent became a very serious matter, a breach of brotherly relations. "Even if it were true that the Mass implies a good work, and Dr. Karlstadt were in good blood, he would have addressed us first and warned, before he made such a great shame of us publicly before all the world."[32]

With embittered eyes Luther watched Müntzer and Karlstadt proclaim prophetic messages which confused social and religious issues, played havoc with the political standing of the cause of the Reformers in the Empire. Upon a basis of inner inspiration they spiritualized the sacraments,[33] preached upheaval, and poured contempt upon him and his colleagues. The

Lutheran leaders then appealed more and more to the magistrate, and in their lands the "Sakramentierer" (Zwinglians, Schwenckfelders, those called "Anabaptists") were proscribed in a common condemnation. Apart from the doctrinal issue, the ethical concern of the radicals seemed to throw them into focus as revolutionaries and supporters of peasant and guild revolt. Upon Luther their effect was like that of the Donatists upon Augustine, turning him against all dissenting movements in the years to come.[34] At the last Luther would not tolerate even quiet separations.

The Peasant Revolt was the major turning point in the attitude of the dominant groups to the radicals. The spread of the Bible among the common people produced many literal-minded efforts to re-establish God's law in the affairs of men. The confused and discrepant programs of the peasants acquired a Biblical coloring. While some appealed to the Law of Nature, many invoked the Word of God and expected support from Luther.[35] Late in 1524 Swabia was in ferment, and during the early months of 1525 the revolt spread throughout southern Germany. Among the Swabian peasants appeared the famous "Twelve Articles," asserting historic rights diminished by the spread of Roman law. The peasants called for a located clergy, the preaching of a gospel from the Bible, congregational government. They offered, in conclusion, to surrender any point which could not be sustained by the Bible.[36] For long the anonymous "Twelve Articles" were attributed to Hübmaier or another "Anabaptist,"[37] and the Reformers denounced the episode as an extreme reading of Biblical truth.

The Reformers were not without justification in failing to distinguish between economic and religious protests. As the movement spread northward to Thuringia THOMAS MÜNTZER (1488-1525) came to the fore, again giving religious coloration to the day of upheaval and judgment. In God's law, *omnia sunt communia*. All oppression in the world, both secular and religious, was to be violently overthrown.[38] Although a propagandist rather than an organizer, Müntzer was in good part responsible for the fervor of peasant action. Luther, on his part, thought that the revolt was the logical outcome of the confused and ex-

cited prophetism with which he had three years earlier contend-
ed.[39] At first the Reformer condemned the princes and lords
whose injustices had precipitated the revolt: "Our sins are before
God; therefore we have to fear His wrath when even a leaf
rustles, let alone when such a multitude sets itself in motion."[40]
But the violence of the mob alienated him, and gave cause to
worry for the future of the entire Protestant cause. "Christians
fight for themselves not with sword and gun, but with the Cross
and with sufferings...."[41]

Events moved apace, and anarchy seemed to be at the door.
The peasants had to be treated as robbers, said Luther, and suppressed for perjury (having sworn to be good subjects), rebellion, and blasphemy (calling themselves "Christians").[42] The
revolt was crushed with bloody excess — except in the domains of
Philipp of Hesse, whose moderation slowed its development and
eased its disappearance. Thomas Müntzer died by the sword he
had drawn, at Mühlhausen. When, in later years, the quiet
Brethren came before Luther's eyes his imagination called up in
their shadow the figure of Müntzer with the sword of Gideon. But
the radicals with whom Luther dealt were hardly more than
peripheral to the Anabaptist movement. Müntzer, and later Bernt
Rothmann, were at least as "Lutheran" as they were "Anabaptist." Only in their initial opposition to the Mass and to infant
baptism did they have common ground with those who came to
be the main line of Anabaptism. As we shall see, the Anabaptists
proper repudiated subjectivism and condemned revolution.

Although the fascinating figure of Thomas Müntzer usually
has claimed the center of the stage in orthodox discussion of
"Anabaptism," the community which Karlstadt founded at
Orlamünde was probably of more relevance to the movement
than the coterie of prophets which rotated about Mühlhausen.[43]
Karlstadt, having lost his influence at Wittenberg after the return
to the established order in the spring of 1522, took up residence
outside the city as a layman and a peasant. Shortly thereafter he
assumed the leadership of the church at Orlamünde, and for two
years strove to accomplish there the ethical reforms which had
met short shrift in Wittenberg. If we are interested in a vigorous
lay-centered ethic, then the radical efforts at Wittenberg and

Orlamünde are worthy of some attention.[44] The line of attack is of some significance for the permanent character of Anabaptism, but particularly for the Lutheran Reformers' misunderstanding of it.

The records clearly show that the radicals at Wittenberg and Orlamünde did not make the break from the old parish system to develop a strictly congregational (internal) ethic. Karlstadt was very little concerned with baptism and the attendant voluntarism on the part of adults. He read Acts to the people and spoke warmly of the priesthood of all believers, but went no further. In his system the whole question of leadership (*Amt*) in the church was interwoven with religious subjectivism. The clear lines of voluntary but disciplined association which marked the Swiss Brethren and other true Anabaptists were impossible in this context. In September, 1524, the experiment at Orlamünde ended; Karlstadt was expelled with his family from the land, along with his associates.[45] After traveling for a time with Melchior Hofmann, he turned to vigorous literary work in South Germany and Switzerland. Like many others of his own and later generations, Karlstadt found a professorate in Basel the fitting culmination of years of active controversy.

Luther in the meantime moved through successive disillusionments to a conservative church policy. In his early days he thought in terms of voluntary cells (*ecclesiolae*) within the territorial church. He was unable to recruit the committed members. The choice then lay between the territorial churches (*Landeskirchen*) and separatist congregations. Luther made his choice for the parish (*parochia*) and denounced as "false prophets" those who "have gone out from us, but . . . are not of us" (I John 4:1).

There were many students and associates besides the better-known figures — Müntzer, Karlstadt, Hofmann, Sebastian Franck, Caspar Schwenckfeld — who broke away when the great Reformer's economic and ecclesiastical conservatism became evident. Some were lost in the swamps of speculation and chiliasm, "standing still" in frustration or dying as revolutionaries. Others contributed an idea or practice to that movement which can rightly be termed "Anabaptism." Most unfortunate is the fact that Luther's experience with the "Anabaptist" (if the *Scwärmer* may be so termed at all) was so limited, for early in his ministry he had favored that inner concern and discipline which marked the main line of Anabaptism. His attitude to Anabaptism was molded by a succession of unfortunate events, and he turned from toleration through banishment to the death penalty for sedition and for "blasphemy" (a term which in pratice was largely equated with what hitherto had been called heresy).[46] Thereby he gave a new turn to religious persecution by directing it not against error as such so much as against the sociological and ecclesiastical effects. Yet we may doubt whether he and his colleagues would have reacted differently to more responsible congregational leaders. The corner preachers and alley congregations of the *Stille* also seemed revolutionary to those who attached salvation to the preaching of the Word and the administration of the sacraments, for which the pulpit, the altar, and the font must be undisturbed.

A number of those who broke away from Wittenberg found their way southward to Switzerland at one time or another. Müntzer, Karlstadt, and Cellarius (Martin Borrhaus) were among them. In the period before the modern documentary studies and source books were available, it was customary to attribute the origin of Anabaptism in Switzerland to their influence; the point of departure in discussing Anabaptism was, therefore, Wittenberg.[47] Gottfried Arnold, with habitual liberality, stated that Anabaptism had its origins in two different groups: first, Storch, Stübner, Cellarius, Müntzer (of Wittenberg); second, "Hubmeyer," "Mantzer," "Graebel," Blaurock (of Zürich).[48] In fact, from the earliest times the Swiss Brethren and Hutterites condemned the revolutionaries and dissociated themselves from their violence.[49] Like the Dutch, they traced their origin to Zürich. The point of view of the historian has obviously for long determined the selection of the geographical point of origin.[50] For the time being, let us continue with the record. Let us be clear, however, that in the "Zwickau prophets" and allied spirits we have encountered a definite type of radical protest, a type to which we may give the name of "Maccabean" Christianity.

In Switzerland

The function of Basel as a city of refuge has been mentioned. From 1514 the great personality at the university was Erasmus. There he became the center of a vigorous humanistic circle, pressing study of the Bible in the original languages and stressing the benefits of inward religion.[51] "You may mark your houses, your vestments, and your churches, with the cross, as much as you please; but Christ will recognize no other badge than that which he himself prescribed, love of one another."[52] His concern for the simplification of dogma and the institution led his students toward Anti-Trinitarianism and Anabaptism. Although overshadowed and embittered in later years by the Reformers, he remained for many the champion of a purified visible church. As such, his teaching affords a significant link between the great church and the radicals.[53] He was a hero to many Protestants whose ethical insistence made them discontented with both Rome and Wittenberg.

Zwingli was indebted in some respects more to Erasmus than to Luther. Luther's attack on indulgences led Zwingli to resolve to adopt the principle of rejecting in doctrine and practice whatever did not conform to the Biblical pattern. He was more deeply concerned for the ancient and inner things of the faith than Luther, and his radical Biblicism moved him beyond Luther, who was bound more solidly to the traditions of the church. Zwingli was, to anticipate a later discussion,[54] far more of a "primitivist" than Luther. For Luther, the traditions and practices accumulated by the church in the post-apostolic centuries continued to carry a certain authority.

The movement in Switzerland began in lay reading groups. In 1522 and 1523 a wave of house meetings for Bible study spread through the Allied District.[55] Andreas Castelberger[56] was leading an adult reading group in Zürich in 1522, and Johannes Kessler — having been invited to function because of his training at Wittenberg — was prominent as a reader in St. Gall. The reading groups trained lay leaders to interpret the Bible and to express themselves in meeting. They were also fruitful in encouraging Biblical radicalism among the common people. In

October, 1524, Kessler stopped holding private meetings at the request of the St. Gall Town Council, but many of the lay readers throughout the Swiss cities went on to become potent figures in the emerging Anabaptist movement.

An impatience with the reforming leadership was first strongly expressed in the circle associated with Zwingli at Zürich. At first Zwingli had opposed infant baptism, as had also Vadian; because there was nothing about it in the New Testament, they were resolved to hold to the Biblical pattern.[57] But when it became evident that the gathering of a church by faith baptism and the maintenance of a state church were not compatible, Zwingli held to the latter line. Nevertheless, in his theory of spiritual communion only in the sacraments he remained in accord with the radical position and thereby permanently offended the German Reformers.[58] In the First Disputation (January 29, 1523) there was unity of Reformers and radicals against the Romanists. During the following summer Stumpf approached Zwingli on gathering a church of believers only. But Zwingli would have nothing of a "Donatist" church and answered with "he who is not against us is for us" and the Parable of the Tares.[59] By the time of the Second Disputation (October 26-28, 1523), the radicals were already committed to a program of the complete restitution of apostolic Christianity. They urgently demanded less compromise with the Town Council's slow motion.

The chief leader of the Anabaptists during this hectic period was CONRAD GREBEL (C. 1495-1526),[60] and with him were FELIX MANZ,[61] WILHELM REUBLIN,[62] Georg Blaurock.[63] Balthasar Hübmaier[64] also took a prominent part in the second Disputation, on the side of the radicals. Grebel and Stumpf urged complete abolition of the Mass without further hesitation; when the Zürich Town Council left the matter to the discretion of each priest, Stumpf resigned from the priesthood and continued as minister to several lay meetings. On November 3, 1523, the Council ordered him into exile. Zwingli picked up the theological end of the attack in writing and speaking; the radicals replied by making faith baptism normative. On January 21, 1525, four days after a Third Disputation in which Zwingli had taken the position that the initiation of children into Christianity by baptism was comparable to the initiation of infants into Judaism by circumcision, occurred the famous ceremony in which Grebel baptized Blaurock. Thereby opposition to the baptism of children (negative) shifted to promulgation of baptism of believers (a positive program). Scriptural radicalism thus moved from opposition to what was outside the Bible to a positive position with large institutional consequences. On March 16, 1525, the Town Council decreed that all who would henceforth be re-baptized should be exiled. The Anabaptists, in return, nourished the most bitter resentment toward those who had refused to go the whole way on the New Testament pattern and now purposed to persecute those who did. They called Zwingli "more false than the Old Pope,"[65] and "the Zürich popular preachers the true anti-Christs."[66] The breach between the party of the Reformers and the radical New Testament party was thus complete.

The important point to emphasize is that the real issue here was not the act of baptism,[67] but rather a bitter and irreducible struggle between two mutually exclusive concepts of the church. Zwingli was finally committed to the state church; and the continuance of the parish system and cantonal denominational division was implied. The Anabaptists, on the other hand, were out to restore apostolic Christianity. Baptism became important because it was the most obvious dividing line between the two systems, and because it afforded the authorities an excuse for suppressing the radicals by force.

After Zürich came St. Gall as an important center of Anabaptist missionary work. Lay reading groups had flourished there in the pre-Reformation period. Leaders were Lorenz Hochrütiner[68] (who had been in Castelberger's groups at Zürich) and Wolfgang Schorant, called "Uolimann" (who replaced Kessler as leader when the latter submitted to the Council's ruling against the groups). Dr. Christoph Schappeler, the probable author of the "Twelve Articles" of the peasants,[69] and Dr. Balthasar Hübmaier of Waldshut were later very active. Grebel was in St. Gall from March 25 to April 10, 1525, preaching and baptizing. On April 25, Uolimann and his associates were called before the Town Council and asked to desist, but they said that only by

Bible proof could they "stand still." On May 12, a Disputation was held with Grebel's brother-in-law, Vadian (1484-1551). VADIAN (Joachim Watt) was leader of the evangelicals.[70] Zwingli's book on baptism had appeared, dedicated to the burgomaster, councillors, and people of St. Gall. The Town Council concluded the Disputation by forbidding re-baptism and the separate "breaking of bread." On June 5, Vadian read his comprehensive book (now lost) against the *Tauffbrüder* and the persecution began.

Three years later (1528), when the Roman practices were finally ended, a synod of the state church attempted to pull together some of the lessons learned in dealing with the Anabaptists. Meeting at Rheineck and led by Dominic Zili, the synod decided to adopt church discipline as found in Matthew 18 and I Corinthians 5. This obvious attempt to match the Anabaptist organizational intensity failed, as did also Oecolampadius' similar effort at Basel.[71] Thus, while the Anabaptist meetings were suppressed and two hundred men were sworn in as special police to suppress the movement, the first of a series of notable attempts was made to adapt to the state church some of the lessons of the Free Church way. Meanwhile, the leaders of the Anabaptist movement were exiled and their followers terrorized.[72] The restitution of primitive Christianity was to be accompanied by persecution such as the Early Church had borne. The Anabaptists were not slow to point out the double parallelism.

Among other Swiss cities, Bern is especially interesting. The large majority of American Mennonites in the first immigrations were descended from Swiss Brethren families of Canton Bern. The Town Council had early ordered scriptural preaching, but the Roman rites were not abolished for several years. Various Disputations were held between the Brethren and the representatives of the state church (notably Berthold Haller[73] and Hofmeister of Schaffhausen). A famous meeting was held at Zofingen, July 1-9, 1532, in which the radicals held to their New Testament radicalism — including ordination by the local congregation, purified and disciplined. The authorities on the other hand asserted the necessity for state control of ordination.[74] The radicals disapproved of serfdom; the authorities connected them with the Peasant Revolt. In general, the Bern Council tried at first to follow the more moderate policy of Strassburg: tolerating those outside of conventicles and exiling those organized in protest. But finally oaths to obey the Council were exacted of all under suspicion, and special police were constituted to hound into exile or death all those who would not conform.[75]

Basel, through the influence of Erasmus and Amerbach, was for many a city of refuge. In due time we find there Curione,[76] Castellio (unwelcome in Geneva), Cellarius, Hans Denck (who died there), Karlstadt, and finally the "Anabaptist flamingo" David Joris.[77] Oecolampadius arrived there in November, 1522, and in the same year Erich Hugwald, a professor at the university, wrote a book against infant baptism. The first Anabaptist congregation was gathered by Anabaptist missioners in August, 1525. Their *"wincklechtige Versammlung"* included Hochrütiner and Hugwald, the latter a friend of Müntzer.[78] The First Basel Disputation was held in August, 1525, with JOHANNES OECOLAMPADIUS (1482-1531) leading the Reformers' party; the results were inconclusive.[79] On July 6, 1526, the Council forbade re-baptism and ordered infant baptism. On June 10, 1527, a Second Disputation was held, but no record survives. On March 14, 1528, a law was made that all *Täufer* not forsaking their errors should be fined five pounds; those giving them hospitality were to be similarly penalized. In February, 1529, the party of the Reformers seized control of the city by force of arms and abolished the Roman rites. From this point on the controls grew more hostile to the Anabaptists and finally all property in their name was subject to confiscation.

With persecution increasing in the various Swiss cantons,[80] the Brethren began to spill over into the Tyrol to the southeast, Moravia to the east, and north into South Germany. Missioners had travelled widely from the first,[81] and the movement continued to grow even under persecution. Family migrations became frequent. A center had already developed in Waldshut, just across the border. There delegates had gathered in 1524 in Hübmaier's home and agreed upon a statement of faith and polity.[82]   At Easter time, 1525, Wilhelm Reublin was there preaching and baptizing. Hübmaier and sixty parishioners were re-baptized, and about three hundred eventually followed suit. BALTHASER HÜBMAIER (? -1528) had taken over from the early Zwingli the belief in an *allgemeine Kirche und Einzelkirche,* both visible and resting upon a clear confession of faith — "visible community and not (just) imagined."[83] This belief was translated into definite form at Waldshut, although Hübmaier's predilection to mysticism forbade his conceding more than earthly authority to the congregation.[84] Upon accepting faith baptism as a visible sign of the restored Christian Community, Hübmaier resigned as priest and immediately was re-elected as minister by the congregation.[85] This is a most significant point in Anabaptist history, for it marked the beginning of the congregational principle of government. In the Swiss cities small congregations had been gathered; at Waldshut an evangelical congregation was won over bodily to Anabaptism. The break came so clearly in Waldshut because the town was in Roman Catholic territory and there was not the delaying factors which in Zürich and other evangelical cities prevented an early and complete break with a "Protestant" state-church pattern. Hübmaier's career in Waldshut and the life of the Anabaptist congregation were cut short by the arrival of Austrian military forces. The leader escaped on December 5, 1525, spent a short time in the Zürich jail, and the next month made his way to Nikolsburg.[86]

When Disputations and lesser compulsions failed to produce conformity, the cities resorted to harsher measures. A wave of banishments spread out from Zürich and other cities. In March, 1525, Grebel, Manz, Blaurock, and many others were imprisoned for life on bread and water; they were released only through the intervention of Jakob Grebel (father of Conrad and a town leader), and forced into exile. On the same day, drowning was proclaimed as penalty for re-baptism, without trial or hearing. On August 11, 1527, a meeting was called by the Zürich Town Council, with representatives of Ulm and Augsburg present as well as those from Bern, Basel, Schaffhausen, Chur, Appenzell, and St. Gall. The delegates agreed upon a policy for suppression of the Anabaptist movement. To enforce their commitments the cities gradually took up the policy of using special police *(Täuf-erjäger)*. By the time the Roman Catholic (imperial) policy was formulated at Speyer in 1529, many Protestant lands were already enforcing exile and death against the radical movement.

In the meantime the movement was spreading rapidly throughout South Germany and continuing underground in Switzerland. Persecution of the groups and killing of their leadership did not halt the expansion. The gathering of small congregations by believer's baptism went on apace, and Anabaptism spread in many areas closed to Protestant state churches by their acceptance of the principle of territorialism. The Anabaptists represent thereby an early Protestant vision of a world mission unrestricted by territorial limitations, and in a unique fashion foreshadow the later concept of the church as a community of missionary people. "Their presupposition is the little band of elect, which is something quite other than a conventicle. It is the first understanding which encompasses the whole world, pressing on to the true church at the end of time. This little band shall tomorrow give the whole earth a new order. The Anabaptists [*Schwärmer*] believe in the totality of their church."[87]

At this time the Roman Catholics and Reformers were still thinking in terms of the church pattern of the Middle Ages: religion was a certain phase of civilization, controlled and bounded by the agreement of princes. The Reformers held generally that the Great Commission was binding only upon the New Testament apostles, while the Anabaptists *(Täufer)* made it fundamental to their whole attack.[88]

In South Germany and Strassburg

Some of the Swiss radicals declared that the True Church was to be gathered in spirit and in truth, "and shall not be bound, as Israel, by proof texts and ceremonies."[89] From the time of the early meetings on the free spirit revealed by this passage was contending with the Biblicism which we have seen expressed in other situations. Individuals and groups were not immediately clear as to the implications of such conflicting positions: all weapons were welcomed in the first fight against the standing order. In a comparatively short time, however, the tensions were resolved in most quarters and an Anabaptist congregational life of discipline and integrity was established. The focal centers for many of the conflicting tendencies in the radical movement, the points where the tensions were resolved in a final fashion, were the Imperial Cities of South Germany and especially Strassburg.

Students of the Swiss Brethren have noted their strong expectancy of the end of the world.[90] In this atmosphere certain types of prophetism and spirit possession could easily flower. With savage persecution launched against dissent, the chiliastic tendencies in early Anabaptist thought were augmented. Revivalist symptoms showed on occasion, with dancing, acting like children and speaking with tongues.[91] In the South German cities, the preaching of Hans Hut also made itself felt, and added to the already electric atmosphere. There was a vigorous Karlstadt/Müntzer circle at Nürnberg in the fall of 1524.[92] In this city the prophet Augustin Bader gathered a little following, looking toward the coming Kingdom on earth. His short-lived effort reveals the chiliastic note which became fairly common in certain persecuted groups: With the new age "the new understanding of the Scriptures would be spiritually revealed through Christ, as he had previously done in the flesh. Then would all outer sacraments be rooted out, and there would be no baptism but affliction, no altar but Christ, no church but the community of believing men. And all that would come and be fulfilled by him, who had revealed and opened that [fact] to the prophet previous to the [written] word. And in this revolution Christ would spiritually teach what one should do or not do."[93]

For a time also Augsburg was the center of Anabaptism in South Germany, during the years when Hans Denck was the most forceful leader. On August 20, 1527, the famous Martyr Synod was held there, with most of the prominent leaders present.[94] Denck apparently presided, and is credited with turning Hut away from chiliasm, although Denck's own dependence upon the Inner Word led him back into individual radicalism in a few months.[95] The ideological incoherences among the early leaders and groups all showed themselves during this period:

nonresistance and revolution, quiet eschatology and chiliasm, Inner Word and Biblicism, Anti-Trinitarianism and orthodoxy, prophetism and synodical discipline.

In Strassburg we see the various streams converge and separate as nowhere else. Because of its generally liberal policy, Strassburg became the meeting place of the Left Wing leaders, the point where the several issues were joined between the Anabaptists and other radical groups. Not only was it a bridge between the Lutheran and Reformed teaching, but also between the several early groupings of what was ambiguously termed "Anabaptism."[96] Storch was there in 1524, leaving a little group of chiliasts. Others who met and worked in Strassburg include Gross, Marpeck, Sattler, Denck, Servetus, Hetzer, Hofmann, Joris, Franck, Schwenckfeld, Bünderlin, Widemann.[97] Jakob Kautz of Worms and Wilhelm Reublin co-operated in a Disputation with the authorities on January 15, 1529. Here Marpeck disputed with the theologians before his banishment. From Strassburg came the counsel which Philipp of Hesse sought in his encounter with Tesch and Rinck.

Of the men who made Strassburg their headquarters, none showed more clearly the centrifugal factors in early Anabaptism than MELCHIOR HOFMANN (1495-1543).[98] Hofmann was with Nikolaus von Amsdorf (1483-1565) at Wittenberg. During the debate on the Lord's Supper between Luther and Karlstadt he presented his own peculiar views and was alienated from the Lutherans. At first he became attached to Thomas Müntzer. On leaving Wittenberg, he remained at first in the north. His standing was still ambiguous enough so that he could go as Lutheran preacher to Stockholm (with Knipperdollinck, later a leader in the Münster "Kingdom"). From there he went to Kiel, where his Docetic teaching on the person of Jesus Christ, along with other doctrinal deviations, found him out. His preaching and writings led to a bitter polemical exchange with Amsdorf[99] and permanent alienation from the Wittenbergers. He disputed repeatedly the doctrine of the real presence in the bread and wine, he proclaimed strongly millenarian views of the coming Kingdom, he expounded a heretical Christology (that Jesus passed through Mary like water through a tube). For a time Hofmann worked beside Campanus and then Karlstadt; his wide travels and prophetic fervor brought together many little groups, awaiting the signal for the New Age. The time never came, although he set a date for it. When his followers in the Netherlands were persecuted, he instructed them to "stand still" for two years (Ezra 4:24), and himself turned southward to Strassburg. There he was greeted as a prophet by a little inspired circle, but in a short time was called for a Disputation (June 3-15, 1533) and imprisoned for life. By the time he deceased (1543), sick and forgotten, the Kingdom which he had forecast had come and gone and left a trail of broken dreams and tortured bodies behind it. The New Jerusalem (Münster, 1533-1535) owed much, in both ideology and personnel, to Melchior Hofmann and the "Melchiorites."[100]

Strassburg groups were acquainted, therefore, with the revolutionary accent which was found among certain leaders and groups generally called "Anabaptist." It was also in Strassburg that another centrifugal tendency in the movement was met and reduced: the authority of the Inner Word. The men of the Inner Word *(Spiritualisten)*[101] take their place with other leaders of Anabaptist thought during the inchoate period. They could appeal to Luther, who in his early days made much of the way Paul and Augustine pitted the spirit against the letter. Yet for Luther, the inner was impossible without the outer. He vigorously rejected the Zwickau prophets for their separation between inspiration and the historic revelation of the Word. The theme of the Wittenberg radicals was taken up again by later Anabaptists, with interpretations of the Inner Word ranging from identification with the *Fünklein* of the medieval mystics (Hans Denck) to dreams and visions (Hofmann). Among the more notable spiritualizers were HANS DENCK (c. 1500-1527)[102] (who was considered the leader of the South German Brethren during the first half-decade); LUDWIG HETZER (c. 1500-1529);[103] JOHANNES BÜNDERLIN (1499-1533);[104] Sebastian Franck (1499-1543);[105] CASPAR SCHWENCKFELD (1489-1561);[106] Gabriel Ascherham (? -1545).[107]

The *Spiritualisten* are one of the definite types of sixteenth-century radical Protestantism, and are a recurring phenomenon to this day. They shared with the Anabaptists the general vision of Early Church, Fall, and Restitution. But their vision of the Restitution was not the gathering anew of the Christian Community of New Testament discipline and integrity, at least not without special commission to a prophet from God. Rather, looking to the New Age of the Spirit, they condemned all sectarianism and compulsion (including the Ban).

> Only the free, nonsectarian, non-partisan Christianity . . . is from God, and its piety is not bound to sect, time, station, law, person or party. (Franck)

> The church is not another compulsion fastened on this or that territory, whether Rome, Wittenberg or somewhere else . . . yes, whether tied to Pope, Luther or Anabaptist. (Schwenckfeld) [108]

> We pray [God] also for all good-hearted men, who hunger and thirst after thy divine righteousness.[109]

They desired to be reckoned as nonsectarians *(parteilos)*, and worshiped the tolerant *(unpartheyisch)* God.

> The true inner word is one eternal and almighty power of God, identical in men and God, and accomplishes all things.[110]

> But what man preaches is only the sign or symbol of truth. The Eternal Word will not be read or preached; the solitary man will be assured of it in the abyss of the soul by God, and it will be inscribed on a human heart by the finger of God.[111]

Jacob Kautz (c. 1500-1533?) [112] said at Worms:

> The word that we verbalize/read/write is not the living/ eternal Word of God/ but only a symbol and sign of the inner by which it makes outward appearance. No outward word or sign or Sacrament/ also no outer office has this power/ for it strengthens and comforts the inner man. . . .

Therefore Gottfried Arnold, not unsympathetic, judged that Kautz was guilty — as accused — of saying that "man must hear not only God's word [the Bible]/ but also the special revelation of God [*sonderbare Offenbarung*]/ and of course man must recognize and listen to the Voice of God himself. . . ."[113] This was the doctrine which led Luther to fear and condemn "die

himmlischen Propheten"; what Luther never realized was that
the doctrine here expressed came to be feared and condemned by
responsible Anabaptist leaders also.

The testimony of the men of the Inner Word was never to
produce a coherent church life in their generation. Essentially,
they had neither doctrine of the church nor practice of its life.
Their uneasiness concerning the increment of the ages might
produce a general renunciation of institutional life, or it might
produce indifference to "forms" (as among many of their followers who never left the state church). They hung in the middle world "beyond good and evil," in which they neither made
nor had to justify the sort of choices which beset any group living
in the world. Denck is reported to have regretted at the end that
he had ever given enough importance to outward form to re-
baptize.[114] "All true 'Christians,' that is all men who are inspired
in truth by the Spirit, 'are one in God with Christ.' "[115] Although
Bünderlin was baptized and participated in the Augsburg Synod
of 1527, under Denck, he came at last to oppose Anabaptism
and all other "forms."[116] "For him even the Church is an inner,
purely spiritual collection of men who may be a thousand miles
and further from each other."[117]

Franck and Schwenckfeld both believed that the True
Church was irrevocably lost unless a prophet appeared who was
especially commissioned to gather in the faithful. Although they
both had little bands of followers, Franck and Schwenckfeld are
therefore to be strongly distinguished from those groups which
undertook the responsibility of making a new beginning in
church life and piloting it through the whirlpools of historical
existence.

The radical individualism of the spiritualizers constituted,
in fact, a fundamentally different view of the church and Christian history from that of the *Täufer*.[118] Nevertheless, the evidence does not warrant cutting them off from our discussion of
the Anabaptists. On the contrary, it appears that in every center
of the Left Wing there was an early tension between those whose
uneasiness regarding historic "forms" led them away from community in a concrete sense, and those who moved forward and
gathered a people on a New Testament basis. At the first level,

the revolutionaries ("Maccabeans") and *Spiritualisten* have the
same relevance to the emerging Anabaptist congregations. As
opposing claimants and centrifugal forces in the movement they
competed, in the name of a general world change, with those who
viewed the world with pessimism but the "True Church" with
hope. The Anabaptist view of the church was shaped not only
by external pressures (persecution), but in a mortal struggle
with those internal tendencies which would have destroyed any
organized life at all. This situation affords a marked parallel to
that in the Early Church, where also the compulsion of a fresh
spiritual experience produced in its extreme moments a type of
prophetism which had to be suppressed to save the life of the organized congregations. Or, to put it another way, the reversion
of various radical groups to the life of the Early Church was at
first a return to its eschatological atmosphere as well as to its
ethical disciplines.

The revolutionary and spiritualizing tendencies went spin-
ning ahead through the years, and to a certain extent represent
permanent challenges to effectively organized "sectarian Protestantism." What the Reformers seldom realized, and their filial
historians have across generations been slow to grasp, is that the
Anabaptists also dealt conclusively — and without persecution —
with the same threats to the integrity of the congregations. The
main-line Anabaptist groups challenged and defeated revolutionary and spiritualizing elements in the Left Wing. To a
goodly extent that joining of issues and final victory was the
contribution of PILGRIM MARPECK (? -1556), who has been
termed "the greatest of the South German and Swiss Anabaptist
leaders."[119] Marpeck was a layman, an engineer, and for a time
managed the wood supply of the city of Strassburg. Banished
after a dispute with Butzer (December, 1531), he adopted
Augsburg as his headquarters and for decades labored among
the South German Brethren congregations.

Marpeck's view of the True Church was vigorously covenantal, continuing the Biblical insistence first articulated in Michael Sattler's "Seven Articles" of Schleitheim (1527).[120] For
centuries Marpeck's work was not properly evaluated, for the
writings in which he expressed his church view were early sup-

pressed; only recently have they been rediscovered in part. With a strong sense of the meaning of history, Marpeck became involved in disputes not only with the Reformers but with Schwenckfeld. As vigorously as he criticized the Reformers' acceptance of the medieval parish system, just as vigorously he condemned the spiritualizing and individualistic thrust in Schwenckfeld. "It was against him that Pilgram Marpeck wrote his great polemic writing in 1542, this most thorough and most profound debate of Anabaptism with all those who wanted to look at Christianity only from the pleasant and friendly side." So concludes a contemporary Mennonite scholar. Marpeck wrote in his *Verantwortung:* "Schwenckfeld teaches only the inward experience and the transfigured, glorified, unsuffering Christ in Heaven, and not the suffering one on Earth, yea, he teaches only the Word of his glory and splendor, and not of his cross and affliction as he bore it before his transfiguration and ascension and as it is still today fitting for his unglorified body to bear."[121]

The polemical exchange between Marpeck and Schwenckfeld ran from letters into books over many years, and resulted in the *Vermanung* (long lost, but recently rediscovered),[122] the *Verantwortung* (three copies extant, in Zürich, Munich, and Olmütz),[123] and the *Testamentserläuterung* (lost, partially pieced together by Loserth).[124] On Schwenckfeld's part we have a number of letters and books, including *Judicium de Anabaptistis* (1529)[125] and *Über das neu Buechlin der Tauffbrueder* (called "Juditium," 1542).[126] Schwenckfeld was in the meantime banned by the Brethren for refusing to adopt believers' baptism, which — with the Ban — he termed a new captivity of the conscience.[127]

About June, 1529, Schwenckfeld wrote *Das noch heut kain Apostolische kirch seie von den Paulinischen und Apostolischen Christen,*[128] and this theme continued in his writings throughout the years. Marpeck and his associates replied that Schwenckfeld would not have been satisfied with Christ's church if he had been contemporary with Him, and maintained that believers' baptism and spiritual government were Biblical ordinances given by Christ for the maintenance of His church. The Anabaptists not only repudiated the vision of the New Age of the Spirit, but they felt that "standing still" in the face of persecution was a sign of moral cowardice. As they saw, the *Spiritualisten* were as dangerous to the existence of a vigorous voluntary association on the one side as the state-church Reformers and their civil authorities were on the other.

Not only did the dispute of Marpeck with Schwenckfeld clear the air and define the relations of Anabaptism to the spiritualizers, but the disputes with the Strassburg Reformers led to important results. Indeed, Anabaptism had its own effect upon the Strassburg Reformers and their organized church life.[129] The leaders of the Reformation in that city never represented the same hard hostility to sectarian ideas as did the men of Wittenberg and Zürich. Nor did they persecute as quickly. For a time the city leaders, especially Matthäus Zell and Jakob Sturm, stood for a broad and tolerant policy. Cellarius (1499-1564),[130] won away from Luther by Storch, had considerable influence upon his friend Wolfgang Capito (1478-1541);[131] the writings of the latter showed Anabaptist tendencies. Capito was also friendly to Marpeck, and for a time moderated Butzer's hostility to the radicals. Martin Butzer himself doubted infant baptism at first, but finally accepted the magistrate's orders. In his views of the Lord's Supper, Butzer leaned toward the Swiss, and he wanted a stronger congregational discipline. Although he was a successful agent of Philipp of Hesse in reconverting Anabaptists, Butzer never fully cleared his mind of a connection between the nonrevolutionary *Täufer* and the revolutionaries. To Marpeck, in one of his three Disputations, he said: "The reason you don't drive and harass us physically is because you don't have the power. I doubt not that if you had, then the spirit which always brings up something new in your midst would soon teach that we should all be killed. An Anabaptist said just this to Capito and me right here in our faces, that we would compel them to use the sword, that a time would yet come when they would use such against all the godless."[132] Butzer's attack led to the expulsion of Marpeck from Strassburg. He defined the city's policy toward Hofmann. His attack was generally slow and moderate, but persistent.[133] And he was not averse to learning from the Anabaptists, particularly on the matter of church discpiline.

Mass was not abolished in Strassburg until February 20, 1529, and complete reorganization of the church was postponed until 1534. Although there were mandates against giving shelter and food to Anabaptists in 1527 and 1530, banishment was not introduced as a general practice until 1538. It was the experience with Melchoir Hofmann — and after that, the Münster episode — which put iron into the situation, and gave Butzer a lever for persuading the more reluctant Capito against the various radical groups. Although the South German Brethren (like the Swiss, Hutterites, and Dutch) vigorously protested that they repudiated the violence of the revolutionaries, especially in the Peasant Revolt and at Münster, they were finally made liable to drowning if they returned a third time to the city. It should be said in conclusion, however, that the laws were more stern than the policy, for important Anabaptist synods met in Strassburg in 1555 and 1557.

REVOLUTION

In tracing the Anabaptist experience in South Germany and in Strassburg, we came naturally to speak of those centrifugal factors which threatened during the first decade (1524-1535) to break the movement into ineffectual fragments. We have seen how religious individualism constituted a real threat, in the emancipated Christianity of the *Spiritualisten*. In this connection should be mentioned also the sympathizers, those who remained in the territorial churches to avoid separation and persecution; it has been estimated that in some areas half or more of the movement "stood still" in conventicles, although only in Hesse was there a successful policy of reincorporating ex-Anabaptists as a kind of voluntary movement within the territorial church. Groups which submitted in this fashion should perhaps be regarded as "pre-Pietist."[134] The other major threat from within appeared in the form of prophetism and chiliasm, and these elements grew to tragic proportions with the increase of persecution in the latter half of the first decade.

The "Maccabean" Type of Radical

There are various ways in which the creative tension between the "church" and the "world" may be reduced. The fashion in which the Münsterites, with their foreshortened eschatology, resolved the matter is instructive in the history of the gathering of the Anabaptist congregations. This tension, which is essentially a permanent problem for the church so long as the present world endures, can be resolved by a latitudinarian relaxation of the boundary between the church and the world. This is the standing peril to the established churches. On the other hand, the tension can be reduced by a theocratic attempt of the elect to gain control of the centers of power (usually by a revolution colored by intensely apocalyptic preachment) and to govern the world as though it were the church. This latter line is evident in the religious revolutionaries of the sixteenth century.

The Münster episode has, it is true, only secondary significance in a historical survey of Anabaptism, and we refer to it in parenthetical fashion. But there were other revolutionary attempts in the North German and Dutch strongholds of Melchiorite teaching.[135] Further, the revolutionary motif is a logical outworking of certain "enthusiastic" tendencies to be noted among several significant leaders — especially HANS HUT (? -1527) and Melchior Hofmann.[136] Hofmann we have reviewed. Hut also stands as a significant bridge between revolutionaries and *Stille* in the pre-Münster period of the movement.

The chiliastic note which marked Müntzer's call to revolution did not die out with him. Hans Hut,[137] a book peddler and lay preacher, had been won to the revolutionary party at Wittenberg and became a prophet of the last times. "They also held that in a short time Christ would come again to earth and institute an historical rule and would bestow upon them the sword of righteousness (as they call it), to root out and destroy all magistrates and those who did not accept re-baptism and were not related to their Band."[138] Thus was it reported of his followers. Hut traveled widely in South Germany, baptizing thousands and proclaiming the speedy invasion of the Turks, a time of persecution and revolution, followed by Christ's reign upon earth.[139] The ideas took different phrasing among different groups, but the tone and intention remained constant. At the time of His Coming, the dead are to rise up and "establish the reign of God here on this earth; but heaven and earth will at the same time be made new."[140] Another said of the end of the world: "then would the righteous who yet remained, come together from all the ends of the earth in the twinkling of an eye, and slay all the godless who yet lived; one would slay a thousand and another ten thousand; such triumph would be given by God to his own. . . ."[141]

After the collapse of the Peasant Revolt, Hut met with other leaders in Hans Denck's house in Augsburg (1527); there he pledged to repudiate the sword,[142] but did not change from the excited eschatology and wide missionary preaching which marked his work. In May of 1527 he participated in a dispute with Hübmaier at Nikolsburg,[143] a dispute which helped initiate the split between *"Schwertler"* and *"Stäbler"* in Moravian Anabaptism. That autumn Hut was burned to death, apparently in attempting an escape from the jail in Augsburg. But in three short years he had left a permanent mark upon the thinking of the South Germans and Hutterites.[144]

The eschatology represented by Hut and Hofman took concrete expression in the stand and fall of the Davidic realm at Münster. The incident demonstrates the tremendous pull upon all highly expectant movements: to release the tension, to press ahead bitterly, and at whatever cost to realize the dream.

The Davidic Realm at Münster (1534-1535)

JOHANNES CAMPANUS (c. 1500-1575) has been termed the father of the Münster restitution. Campanus was a follower of Hofmann and the head of the group called "the Wassenburger preachers."[145] He was a friend of Georg Witzel (1501-1573),[146] whose primitivist thought structure was basic in his many writings as evangelical and Roman Catholic. Witzel put in dramatic fashion the vision of the Fall and Restitution of the church; Campanus popularized the church view involved. From Campanus these ideas were picked up in Rol's *Die Slotel van dat Secreet des*

Nachtmaels and Rothmann's *Restitution rechter und gesunder christlicher Lehre.* BERNT ROTHMANN (c. 1494-1535), who represented the Lutheran cause for Münster in the Schmalkald League, was the leading preacher at Münster during the rise and collapse of the revolution. Rothmann moved away from Lutheran doctrine to adopt a Zwinglian view of the Lord's Supper,[147] and then came to repudiate infant baptism.[148] Shortly thereafter one of Hofmann's missionaries, Jan Matthysz, arrived in the city and assumed as prophet an increasing authority in the town affairs. The split of Lutheran and radical parties rapidly widened beyond repair, and Rothmann joined the latter in determination to gather "the believers in a holy community separated from the unbelieving godless."[149] This meant that those who wouldn't join would have to be expelled from the city; here is introduced a new element not faced by a voluntary congregation as such. The logic of the position was recognized: "The Lord God would here rule the city and the godless would be thrown out."[150]

At this point we see appearing in revolutionary circles, as before at Anabaptist Waldshut, the possibility of a combination of church as voluntary association and yet coterminous with the political community. At Waldshut, however, strict voluntaryism was maintained; at Münster the revolutionaries introduced a new element of compulsion against the unbaptized. The idea spread throughout North Germany and the Lowlands that Münster was the Key City of the New Age. The communism which began *"unter Freunden"* in imitation of the Early Church assumed a larger significance in the following January (1534), when it was made controlling for all inhabitants of the city. The second prophet (Jan of Leyden) had meanwhile arrived, and the city was proclaimed the New Jerusalem.

The word spread rapidly throughout the northern cities that the time was at hand which the prophets had declared. The 144,000 were to be gathered in.[151] A book of baptisms was kept, probably the first covenant-book of believers.[152] From many Melchiorite centers — Deventer, Zwolle, Amsterdam, Leyden — groups started out by land or water.[153] Colporteurs and missioners traveled through the North German and Dutch cities.

In October the Book of Wrath *(van der Wrake)* was released to arouse all neighboring fraternal peoples to usher in the New Age, overthrow the Babylonian tyranny, slay the godless. They should let fall the mild weapons of the apostles and seize the armor of David![154] Under Jan of Leyden ("King David" as of August 31, 1534), the crest of the city displayed a globe.[155] The prophet proclaimed that after the time of suffering and revolution, the messianic age would arrive.

Only Philipp of Hesse, among the political authorities, was prepared to attempt a discussion aimed at winning the Münsterites from their errors, and his emissary was greeted with the words: "If you have been sent by the Father you may sit down among my prophets, but if you come from men then stand over there."[156] The Kingdom was beset by combined Roman Catholic and Protestant troops, betrayed from within, and destroyed with the most ferocious cruelty. The iron cages in which the bodies of "King David," Knipperdollinck, and Krechting were placed after torture still hang on the tower of St. Lambert's Church.

Two radical departures taken during the time of rapid social movement at Münster deserve special attention: communism and polygamy. As to communism, Social Democratic historians have suggested that the economic policy at Münster was occasioned by the siege and should be considered parallel to rationing in the Paris Commune.[157] This will hardly bear analysis, however, for the practice was begun six months before the siege started, during the hot glow of successful revolutionary administration. Münsterite communism was an expression of religious conviction rather than economic necessity.[158] It resulted from a combination of admiration for the Early Church and a radical interpretation of the Love Feast.[159]

In the matter of polygamy, the problem is more obscure. When we put beside the system at Münster the bigamy of Philipp of Hesse and Henry VIII, we might be led to suppose that Protestantism was remarkably indecisive on sexual ethics. Remember, however, that the Reformers had just dealt a mortal blow to a most general adjustment on sex: monasticism. Men who had made such a break might falter in shaping a new ethic . There were two noteworthy scriptural arguments for polygamy: first, the New Testament forbids divorce but is silent on polygamy; second, by special revelation God permitted polygamy to the patriarchs, and might under similar conditions approve the institution among later servants.[160] The Münster attitude is a curious combination of asceticism and laxity. Extramarital relations were strongly condemned and within wedlock sexual relations were restricted to propagation. But marriage was expanded to permit more than one partner. This solution may have been precipitated by the large plurality of women within the city, but no doubt Old Testament influence was paramount. The command to be fruitful and multiply must be obeyed.[161] The orthodox Reformers, who on occasion condoned bigamy, and the Roman Catholics, who collected taxes on concubinage, however, were scarcely in a position to cast stones.

Persecution Intensified

The unsavory series of events at Münster had permanent consequences. The orthodox felt themselves more justified than ever in identifying Anabaptism with revolution, an interpretation which has continued among Lutheran, Reformed, and Catholic filial historians down to the twentieth century. The civil authorities intensified their repression of any person who failed to submit to the rules of the establishment where he resided. Only in Moravia and Hesse were the quiet Anabaptists spared the most brutal penalties.[162]

AN UNUSUAL CASE:
THE TOLERANCE OF PHILIPP OF HESSE

PHILIPP OF HESSE (1509-1567)[163] affords one of the very few examples of a tolerating ruler in an age of almost unrelieved brutality against religious nonconformists. To appreciate the quality of his restraint, we must remind ourselves that the cruelties perpetrated in that age in the name of religion are equaled today only by the political totalitarians. When Michael Sattler, defenseless Christian and author of the first Anabaptist confession of faith, was martyred in Rottenburg am Neckar the sentence of condemnation ordered: "That Michael should be led to the marketplace, his tongue cut off, his body torn six times with glowing tongs and still living thrust into a fire and burnt to powder."[164] Although the Imperial Mandates, the practices of his fellow princes, and the warnings of most of the professional theologians all combined to compel the death penalty, Philipp would have none of it.

Refusal to Put Dissenters to Death

His sister, the Duchess Elisabeth of Saxony, wrote him (September 24, 1530) to warn him of the threat of "the common man," and said that "the rumor was rife that the Anabaptists were growing around him and would again revolt."[165] Philipp stayed with his conviction: "Up to this time we cannot find it in our conscience to judge someone with the sword for his faith, where we have no other adequate evidence of uprising. For when this interpretation were held then we could not tolerate Jews or Papists, who blaspheme against Christ most of all."[166]

The theologians of Wittenberg, Lüneburg, Tübingen wrote him briefs to justify the use of the death penalty.[167] Philipp preferred the moderate judgment of the professors in his own university. In his last will and testament, Philipp admonished his sons to uphold the Augsburg Confession, the Concord of Wittenberg, and to fight for a reunited Christendom. He went on to write: "The Anabaptists are not all alike, therefore our sons shall order the educated to see if they can't win them away from their sects. . . . To kill anybody because he's of false belief, this we have never done and wish also to warn our sons against it."[168]

The *Täufer* missioners declared that the New Testament method of preaching and letter-writing was the only proper way to spread the faith. They further declared that the True Church was disciplined by the Holy Spirit in the meeting, and by no outside power. This meant that the use of the sword as a means of evangelization or of church discipline was improper. When the "so-called Christian authorities" put innocent people to death they gave evidence of identification with the Anti-Christ.

Thus MELCHIOR RINCK (1493-1545), the leading Anabaptist of Hesse, wrote the magistrate at Wartburg, Eberhard von der Tann: "The fact that you bring against me and all who are of the same faith murder, robbery, prison, fire, water, sword and similar lying arguments, proves by your own work that your baptism is an anti-baptism and that you are indeed the Anti-Christ, of whom all prophets, Christ and the apostles have earlier spoken."[169]　In Hesse, although banishment and imprisonment were used, the Landgraf advised the churchmen that they would do better to consider the Anabaptists a challenge to purify and reform the established church and to institute in it a larger measure of New Testament discipline.

Attitude to Church Reform

Philipp was, in fact, himself strongly affected by primitivist tendencies.　In his Confession of Faith of February 6, 1550, he wrote:

What pleases me to perform, what cannot be debated, what was maintained in the Early Church by the beloved fathers and martyrs, I do because I believe that the disciples of the apostles and those who lived right after the death of Christ without doubt knew well the opinion of the apostles. We all hold to and believe one Christian church. What now those who lived right after the time of the apostles and were martyrs of Christ and fought all the evil heresies maintained, that I desire, that we may compare ourselves to them.

For there can be no other Church than that of the old fathers and martyrs, who for Christ's sake suffered and were opposed to the Arians and heretics. And no one can or will show me another Christian church.[170]

When he was compelled to make his peace with the policy of the Interim, he did it in the name of compromise and tolerance, for "there are also many things which we have to put up with in the Lutheran and other preachers in the churches." "That must have been the opinion of Zwingli, who had then put up with many things from the Lutherans which weren't pleasant, and vice versa. There were also many things at the time of the apostles, tolerated by the apostles and Paul also."[171]

The Early Church was the test of church teachings and ordinances, and Philipp's conviction on this matter stands out from the first steps toward church reform at Bad Homburg (1526) through the calling of the Ziegenhain Synod to set the terms of agreement with a group of reconverted *Täufer*. "For the Anabaptists are nowhere more useful to us, and the comman man can be watched over and encountered by us in no better way, than that we take the matter of Christian discipline seriously."[172]

Success of Philipp's Policy

Much too little attention has been given to the fact that not only was Philipp in advance of his time as a tolerator, but his policy was successful. Under his leadership, Hesse was the only area where numbers of Anabaptists were won again to loyal obedience to the church of the land. There is no evidence that the Hutterite missioners, such as Georg Zaunring and Peter Ridemann,[173] yielded ground. But their influence was weakened by the intensive mission which Philipp established with the help of MARTIN BUTZER (1491-1551) of Strassburg.[174] In the great series of consultations (Marburg, 1538) between Butzer and PETER TESCH,[175] a formula was adopted which led to strengthening of church discipline in the church of the land and made it possible for several hundred Anabaptists to return to the fold.

By 1540 Butzer was able to report to the Landgraf: "The Anabaptists have for the most part re-converted. Some, who want to maintain their faith — the rumor is 50, but as Hermann Bastian has reported it is not so many — want to emigrate to Moravia. But of these there are some who will re-convert."[176] The success of the policy is shown by the fact that the colony at Auspitz sent a letter to the Brethren in Hesse admonishing them to persevere in the faith *(ausharren)* and not yield as had so many.[177]

In 1566 Markgraf Karl of Baden sought Philipp's advice, and the latter sent him a report of the Butzer-Tesch discussions together with the proposals of his own theologians against use of the sword. Philipp was able to look back on a successful policy and write: "Now that your excellency has desired our counsel and advice, we will in friendship not withhold the fact that in our principality, land and territory this sect has been for a long time quiet and calm and (praise God) still is. Therefore we have at this time no process against the Anabaptists in action, and further there has been no evidence submitted why we should have."[178] No other prince could say as much.

Out of the experiences of the mission to the Anabaptists, the Church of Hesse adopted certain measures which to this day give it a special structure. The first of these is an active practice of church discipline.[179] Further, confirmation was introduced and within a few years was picked up by other Protestant territorial churches in Germany and Switzerland. The original suggestion seems to have come from Schwenckfeld, during the Strassburg debates of 1533: "If you won't agree to eliminate Infant Baptism, at least there should be set up a ceremony whereby the baptized children, when they have reached the right age, will be dedicated to Christianity."[180] In Hesse, confirmation was taken up in the Ziegenhain Discipline of 1538, in the Kassel Order of Confirmation of the same year; the Hessen Agende of 1574 made it a permanent institution in the church. In the meantime confirmation was adopted by the Genevan Church Order of 1537 and in the Württemberg Church Order of 1545 (signed by Luther, Bugenhagen, Cruciger, Maier, and Melanchthon). Schwenckfeld's suggestion, popularized by Butzer's *Ad Monasterienses* (1534), thus became one of the most permanent contributions of the Protestant radicals to the life of the established churches.

WHO WERE "THE EVANGELICAL TÄUFER"?

We return to our original problem, to relate the Anabaptists adequately to contemporary movements without blurring the lines between their groups and those from whom they consciously and energetically distanced themselves.

A Covenantal People

The struggle with the religious individualists on the one hand and the revolutionaries on the other left the main-line Anabaptists with a vigorous community of discipline. The persecuted groups of the first years had little opportunity to work out their complete vision of the True Church, and less opportunity yet to live according to it. Their leaders were cut off and their meetings were constantly harassed. In perpetual tension between forces without and within that would have destroyed them, they only suggest in an atmosphere of expectancy the manner of life which they might have elaborated if given the chance. In spite of persecution, their attitude and teachings were eager with anticipation of a good life to come.

The congregations of the later period, having withstood the inroads of prophetism and violence, represent a fruition of that New Testament radicalism which marked their point of departure from Luther and Zwingli. By the second decade, inspired leadership and novel interpretations had largely disappeared. Both organizational and credal conformity were strictly enforced according to the fashion of vigorous voluntary associations. Elders and synods were the effective enforcement agencies for the New Testament disciplines of the Church of the Restitution.

The growth of effective internal discipline was accompanied by an emphasis upon the idea of a covenant-people. If the genius of the great Reformers was individualism, an interpretation doubtful at best, no such charge can be laid at the door of the Anabaptists.[181] The Hutterites traced their history back to Abraham; all branches made much of the New Covenant in Christ Jesus. The people of this covenant were known, visible to themselves and to the world, governed by the Holy Spirit acting in the midst.

The attainment of an effective measure of internal discipline, which has been noted throughout this historical exposition, reached culmination in the strength of the Hutterite colonies and the Dutch Mennonite congregations. The Swiss Brethren and the South German Brethren were largely destroyed by persecution, although their descendants in America have developed a full measure of community life.

The Christian communist colonies of the Hutterites in Moravia were founded by refugee Swiss Brethren who did not find in Hübmaier's great church at Nikolsburg the discipline which they read about in the Bible . In 1529, under pressure to take the oath to the princely family which had given a place of retreat to the fleeing Swiss, a little band of two hundred followed Jakob Widemann out onto the land and adopted a new discipline. There they laid all their belongings on a cloak and resolved to live the life of sharing depicted in the second and fourth chapters of Acts. They chose seven stewards *(Diener der Notdurft)* on the authority of chapter 6, verses 3-5, of Acts.[182] It was the duty of a steward to enforce the rules of the community, seeing that all sought the common good and none betrayed it by self-interest. This was the unpropitious beginning of the communism of the Hutterite Brethren, an economy which persists to this day in the north central United States and central Canada, and in Paraguay.

Under the brief but vigorous leadership of JACOB HUTER (? -1536),[183] in the years 1533-1536, the communism of consumption thus introduced was made a coherent social system. During the early decades the Hutterites were blessed with a remarkable series of able leaders. Besides Huter, we may mention WOLFGANG BRANDHUBER (? -1529),[184] Peter Ridemann, and Peter Walpot. Brandhuber built up a strong economy, teaching those skills and crafts by which the Christian Brethren could avoid contamination by war and commerce,[185] and through which they in time became a communist economy of production as well as consumption. Ridemann perfected the emerging communism of production and gave it a confessional grounding.[186] Peter Walpot headed the greatest missionary organization of the epoch, maintaining an extensive correspondence and guiding a large and effective corps of lay missionaries.[187] The Hutterite economy, and the contributions of these remarkable leaders, will be discussed later in connection with the Anabaptist teaching on Christian Community[188] and the Great Commission.[189] As gathered churches the Hutterites are remarkable for representing a kind of "realized eschatology": they are the one continuing section of the Anabaptists which was able at an early date to resolve the tension between church and society without descending to violence or abandoning the witness. The church became a *societas economica* itself. Throughout the centuries the Hutterites have maintained this pattern by following the frontier.

In the Dutch congregations the tension was resolved in quite another way. Anabaptist eschatology included two emphases which might be supplementary to each other or might compete. In time both tendencies fulfilled themselves. In the first place, there was a compelling drive in the Anabaptists to make their community life a total authority, economic as well as religious (to be "unspotted from the world"), in a kind of "realized eschatology." The Hutterites settled in this pattern. On the other hand, there was also a missionary world view (to "go into all the world"), which from the earliest years sent Anabaptist missioners throughout the German-speaking lands and beyond. The process of cultural accommodation and compromise which established communication with "those of the world" reached its final stages among the Dutch Mennonites.

In the years following the debacle at Münster, all called "Anabaptists" were under suspicion as revolutionaries. The independence of their small meetings, the refusal to take the oath and give military service, seemed subversive to the state-church authorities. Further, the *Stille* in North Germany and in the Netherlands ("Obbenites") owe their origin, like the revolutionaries, to the energetic preaching of Hofmann[190] and his associates. OBBE PHILIPSZ (c. 1500-1568) was a disciple of Hofmann[191] and Menno's own ordination came through Obbe from Jan Mathysz. Menno's Christology continued to be the Docetism of Hofmann and, although his followers did not follow him at this point, his own people were always questioned on this matter when heard in court.[192] Prophetism persisted for decades in nonviolent form as well as chiliastic, and the more conservative leaders had to contend repeatedly against this factor in shaping up the congregational life of the faithful. In recanting, Obbe wrote: "I shall be silent about all the false commissions, prophecies, visions, dreams, revelations, and unspeakable spiritual pride which immediately from the first hour stole in among the brethren. . . ."[193]

Sebastian Franck had a large following in the Netherlands.[194] There was a party of his name, and Henrik Niclaes,
DAVID JORIS (1501-1556),[195] and ADAM PASTOR[196] show the
effect of his writings. It might appear that the northern Anabaptists would be hopelessly frustrated by inner incoherence and external pressures following the collapse of the New Jerusalem at
Münster. That this did not happen is due in part to the fact
that for some years Hofmann and his followers were the major
representatives of "Lutheranism" in the Netherlands: Anabaptism was there not a radical split off the major parties but *the*
Protestant party. But further, the survival and greatness of
Dutch Anabaptism is in large measure a tribute to the rugged
and tenacious leadership of MENNO SIMONS (c. 1496-1561).[197]

Even during the most excited days at Münster, the majority
of Dutch Protestant congregations did not go over to the revolutionary position. They remained as they had begun, voluntary
associations of baptized evangelicals in a Roman Catholic land,
determined to fulfill the New Testament ordinances in the restored apostolic church. It was Menno who brought them
together and welded them into a permanent association of Anabaptist churches. As a priest, Menno was first moved by the
reading of Luther to doubt the Mass (1528); he decided to follow the Bible. Then he was stirred by the implications of the
scriptural command for believers' baptism (1530). In March
of 1535, a little band of evangelicals (including his own brother)
died defending themselves at the Old Cloister at Bolsward. Menno realized that many of the opinions for which they had wrongly
taken up the sword were his own.[198] He pitied their tragic and
misguided condition without responsible leadership, and he was
ashamed of his own failure to make like sacrifice for the true
faith. About a year later he gave up his protection as a priest and
began to pastor among the people who represented what he had
come to regard as the New Testament life. From that time until
his death in 1561 Menno lived the life of a corner preacher,
traveling secretly from town to town with a price on his head,
binding together the shattered fragments of a great movement
and building them into a church.

The vision of the True Church was strong in Menno.
"Menno is reported to have said, while on his sickbed — which
was to become his deathbed — that nothing on earth was as
precious to him as the church."[199] The memory of apostolic
Christianity was strong in many of the Dutch cities,[200] and
Menno's leadership meant a return to old evangelical principles.[201] After the failure of the Bocholt Conference (1536)[202]
to unite spiritualizers, revolutionaries, and *Stille,* no further effort
was made to bring together the incompatible wings of radical
Protestantism. Even more than among the South German
Brethren, the simple New Testament teachings were made central
to the Dutch movement, and paramount among them was the
inner and personal rebirth — an experience in the individual believer which parallels the break of the Church of the Restitution
from the fallen period and condition of the Great Church. For
both individual believer and the Christian Community, Christ
alone is the true foundation.[203] The dark passages of the Scripture, in which the chiliasts searched eagerly for the hidden prom-
ises, are to be shunned: the Sermon on the Mount is plain enough.

As Luther defined his position against the "enthusiasts"
[*Schwärmer*], so Menno took his stand against a like aspect of
"Anabaptism" [*Täufertum*]. Indeed his very first writing waged
this battle, in which he placed himself directly against the kingdom of Münster — which was a product of the allegorizing of
Scripture and chiliastic prophetism. He comes forward boldly
not for truth through a "revelation or heavenly inspiration" but
rather through the "expressed, written word of the Lord." He
wants to know nothing of "his own opinions, dreams, and visions."
He angrily cried out in a defensive writing that he was neither an
Elias nor an Enoch nor a "third David" nor yet a seer or
prophet.[204]

The ethical emphasis (Synoptic) was first, and the evangelical/
missionary emphasis second.[205] When the End comes it will be
sudden and by God's own act. The faithful are not preparing the
way in any programmatic sense. They are to be ready for the
Lord's own time.

In Menno's first book to John á Lasco he wrote: "as before

God who knows our hearts, we are clear of all their abominable doctrine, power, uproar, mutiny, bloodshed, plurality of wives and the like abominations. Yea we hate and from all our heart oppose them as acknowledged heresies, as snares to the conscience and deceit, as deception of souls and pestilential doctrine. . . ."[206]

Menno's weight was thrown on the side of authority in the church as well as against revolution in society. The fight against the Great Church tended to obscure the difference between laity and clergy, for some spoke with more authority than others and thus gained a hearing. But in reaction against Münster, and to control the enthusiasts, a strong policy was developed in regard to ordination and commissioning of elders.[207] Menno also adopted a more conservative attitude to the magistrate than had some Anabaptist leaders: his office is ordained of God, and he may even be a Christian. For our purposes, Menno's leadership may mark the final elaboration of a mature Anabaptist church view. His colleague and contemporary, Dirck Philipsz, in "The Seven Ordinances of the True Church" (c. 1560), listed the institutions in terms familiar even today:

1. true teaching, correct ministry
2. proper use of the two sacraments, baptism and the Lord's Supper
3. foot-washing
4. evangelical separation
5. brotherly love (including mutual admonition and communal sharing)
6. keeping all His commandments
7. accepting suffering and persecution[208]

By the time of Menno's death (1561), all necessary lines of the Anabaptist church view were drawn, and the pattern of Free Church life had attained a certain historical and sociological maturity.

During the period when the Dutch Anabaptists were missionary minded and persecuted, their discipline was strong and the tension with the "world" was maintained. By the time the Netherlands became a center of toleration, however, the Mennonites were a powerful commercial class. All restraint toward government and the sword broke down eventually, and other special ethical disciplines disappeared. Today the lineal descendants of the Dutch Anabaptists are alert in matters of profit and investment, vigorous in politics and war. Long ago the government of the Netherlands, in permitting voluntary religious association, removed the main area of conflict between the Mennonite congregations and the society surrounding them. Since they were closely tied to commercial society, and did not fasten upon any particular cultural behavior pattern like their Hutterite cousins, the Dutch Mennonites today are rather more like other representative Protestant connections than like the American Mennonites and the remaining Hutterite colonies.[209]

The Problem of Classification

The preceding survey is based on the latest source materials. In so far as previous treatments have been deficient because of inadequate use of primary sources, their lack here stands corrected. But the problem of classification, the quest for the essence of Anabaptism, still remains. The difficulty is that there were certain serious incoherences in the movement itself in the earliest years, and that most of the interpretations since then have made little attempt to understand and portray the Anabaptist effort at self-clarification and self-realization.

With the first hand evidence before us from the leaders and groups of the Left Wing of the Reformation, we are impressed by the wide diversity of teaching and practice. This was especially true in the first years of the Reformation, when the radical impulse was also fresh and uncritical. Both doctrinal and institutional problems were treated very freely and with great originality by some of the early Anabaptist leaders. The persecution which drove them underground also added to the wide variety of life in the congregations. The basic problem of the radicals, we may safely conclude, was to gather and discipline a movement, to effect a reasonable balance between the strong individualism of a fresh spiritual experience and the hard necessities of a community living in the world and in history.

Anabaptism, as it became a definite church type, was defined not only by its own loyalty to the New Testament but by its encounter with other radical types. Of these the most important were the various personalities and groups identified with revolution in the name of religion ("Maccabean" Christians) and the individualistic spiritualizers. Anti-Trinitarians and "evangelical rationalists" have a lesser significance in the emergence of the Anabaptist testimony, but share with it a considerable common ground of historical interpretation. To a certain extent, the challenges of the revolutionaries and spiritualizers are constant throughout Free Church history, down to the present day.[210]

Many of these early incoherences have been observed in our descriptive study. The problem lies not only with these factors, but in the very diversity of views regarding organized Christian life on the part of the leaders. Robert Friedmann has shown in a stimulating article that if different schemes of classification are used, various points of origin for the ideas must be admitted and different groupings appear.[211] Various classifying principles which might be used are the attitude to tolerance, the use of different books of the Bible, the view of state-church relations, the attitude to individual religion or Christian Community. The early movement was very diverse, and by taking different approaches we find some groups which may be called "Anabaptist" and others which may not; but the lines shift with the issues at hand. The Italian scholars have usually mentioned the doctrinal issues, and the orthodox Protestant historians associated the radicals with social revolution. To Rufus Jones the Anabaptists were a movement of inspired faith which broke through the encrusted patterns and rituals of centuries,[212] while to John Horsch they were Bible Christians who pursued to logical conclusion the teachings of the Reformers. Actually, Friedmann concludes, they were *sui generis* and must be treated as such: they took their departure from Luther and Zwingli upon no single idea or practice, but upon a general discontent with the compromises of the "half-way men."

All of this indicates that the movement is not susceptible to a facile interpretation; but our survey brings us again to the conviction that the view of the True Church was dominant. It must be noted, however, that it may be possible to term Anabaptism a consistent "movement" in the earliest period *only* by reading back into the decade (1524-35) certain resolutions of conflict which later authenticated themselves. Although certain teachings concerning the church appear from the beginning, it took a decade to winnow out competing concepts and make the main teachings concrete in the life of disciplined congregations. For general purposes, we have preferred the term "the Left Wing of the Reformation" to cover the miscellaneous groups traditionally called "Anabaptist."[213] "Anabaptists" has precise meaning only by limiting its use to those numbered among the Swiss Brethren, Hutterites, South German Brethren, and Dutch Mennonites. The "Left Wing" counts all the varicolored individuals and groupings associated with the movement at the first and later hanging on its periphery: the groups following Franck, Campanus, Denck, Bünderlin, Schwenckfeld, Joris, and Pastor — as well as the more centrally significant leaders and congregations.

The radical protest of the Left Wing asserted itself in a wide fashion, and coherent congregational life eventually emerged in some quarters only by throwing off certain centrifugal tendencies. At first it was not clear what might eventuate in the Anabaptist movement as a whole, although particular centers of discipline like the Swiss and Hutterites have a fairly consistent record throughout. The initial stress upon individual conscience and congregational autonomy ran its course before this disciplined life was established in all Anabaptist circles and Synods, even after the revolutionary and spiritualizing tendencies were purged. This mixed picture, which we see through the conflicts between various leaders and groups, is itself a large part of the problem of giving meaning to the term "Anabaptism." Does it mean (assuming that we cast off the traditional tendency to use the term with complete abandon) those congregations which eventually emerged, or may it be used to cover all of those diverse protesting thrusts which characterized the early years (1524-35)? In brief, we may state that the problem of later historians to define and classify "Anabaptism" is not far from that one-time problem of the radicals themselves.

CHAPTER II

The Fall of the Church

Our descriptive survey has revealed the concept of the church as the essence of main-line Anabaptism (Anabaptism used now without quotation marks). The centrality of the church view must be grasped in the "concrete" and historical sense as well as in terms of the teaching of the Anabaptist leaders. That is to say, in contrast to many groups in history and in contemporary Christianity the Anabaptists actually meant what they said. The separation between verbalization and action which has been so marked in contemporary church groups can mislead us in our approach to the Anabaptist movement: the Anabaptists meant just what they said, and their teaching is unimportant apart from the direct attempt to give it embodiment in actual groups living in history.

In the Anabaptist church view two notes stand out from the rest:

1. The church must be a voluntary association, taking its spirit and discipline from those who intentionally belong to its fellowship.

2. The church must follow the guide lines of the New Testament as to confession of faith and organizational pattern.

In the history of Christianity there have been some who said that the Bible was ambiguous as to doctrine and organization. The traditional orthodox view has been that it gives clear indications on doctrine but is ambiguous as to organizational pattern. The Anabaptists maintained that the New Testament was clear both as to the content of the Christian faith and the organizational procedures in the true Christian Community.

Anabaptism: A Form of Christian Primitivism

With the exception of Münster and the Hutterite colonies, the Church of the Restitution did not become coterminous with

46

the political community. The Anabaptist congregations were gathered as minorities within a tolerating or persecuting society. However, in terms of theory and typology the point needs to be made; for under toleration, a voluntary church may differ very little from a state church in its social outlook.[1] Continental Mennonitism has remained a voluntary association but has lost the "primitivist" marks of the New Testament community. The ethic, the attitude to the world on the part of Anabaptists, has often been called a new monasticism. A major aspect of its formulation has been nonconformity to dominant social practices. Frequently we are confronted in Anabaptism with a radical attempt to realize in the concrete the ethic of the Sermon on the Mount. But the Anabaptists went further than this: they repudiated not only accepted social standards, but a whole history of accommodation by established Christianity. The whole membership of the "True Church" was pledged to relive in studied fashion the life of the New Testament community (*Urgemeinde*) in all of its phases. *The Anabaptists proper were those in the "Left Wing" who gathered and disciplined a "True Church" (rechte Kirche) upon the apostolic pattern.*[2] We return to the definition proposed in the Introduction.

There is something deeper than mere Biblicism in this social program. It is part of an outlook on life which can best be described under the concept of primitivism. If we inquire as to the goal of these Anabaptist groups we are driven first not forwards but backwards. Their objective was not to introduce something new but to restore something old. "Restitution" was their slogan, a Restitution grounded in the New Testament. And surrounding their groups was a certain atmosphere, an atmosphere whose precipitation point was a certain vision of the Early Church. In the early period of the movement, before institutional and theological discipline had given ideological coherence to certain groups, and especially before persecution and the necessary defensive organization had weeded out the "centrifugal" tendencies, the single thread running through the Left Wing was this dream of the Early Church. This is the thread which ties together the *Spiritualisten* and *Täufer,* Swiss Brethren and Polish Brethren, Schwenckfelders and Hutterites, Mennonites and the followers of Sebastian Franck and Adam Pastor. The final pattern was to be the Restitution of the Early Church, and following on that Restitution the triumph of the Kingdom on earth.

RELIGIOUS PRIMITIVISM
AS A PATTERN OF THOUGHT

The mood of these groups was essentially determined by an attitude of religious primitivism, and as such is but a special manifestation of a widespread and recurrent aspect of "civilized man's misgivings about his performances, about his prospects — and about himself."[3] The concept is both cultural and chronological. It is Christian and it is classical. For the Anabaptists and other Left Wingers it involves a philosophy of history: an Eden in the past, a partial Restitution in the present (wiping out the scandal of the fallen period), a divine restoration in the future. Various ingredients of this attitude are discernible in previous movements.

In classical antiquity the Cynics and Stoics believed in a Golden Age without war, slavery, and property. Jews and Christians looked back to Eden as a garden devoid of strife and exploitation between both men and animals. The theory of a "Fall" runs throughout them all. In the early Fathers classical and Christian themes are sometimes fused. The classical-Christian ideal of the communism of the Golden Age was picked up again by Sebastian Franck and through him transmitted to various leaders in the Left Wing.[4]

This might seem at first to be a purely speculative discussion about the past, until we recall that the use of the primitive as a norm involves not only myths but manifestoes. Primitivism is a fertile source of ethical concern, as well as a familiar device in historiography. The projection of Eden into the future was the work of apocalyptic Judaism, from which the concept passed into Christian eschatology. In the time of the Reformation and pre-Reformation groups there were variant forms of primitivism; frequently this centered in a type of Adam-mysticism which glorified the simple, unlettered, and unspoiled man. In argument, the appeal is made to the plain man's judgement, unspoiled by institutions and less corroded by speculation than the scholar's. Those who work with their hands (craftsmen) or close to the soil (peasants) are presumed to be more receptive in spirit; their minds have not been addled by the folly of the wise and learned.[5] The type of the primitive hero is sought in some contemporary primitive situation.

The exaltation of "primitive" cultures is another form which flourished in the sixteenth century, in connection with discovery of primitive people in the New World. Various Humanistic circles spread the tales of simple living and savage nobility. On the one hand there was a high idealization of the simple life and the man of nature; and on the other there was "what is even more significant . . . . not the discovery that savages can be noble, but that civilized people can become good savages and can be regenerated by a natural life."[6] Secular and religious primitivism sometimes fused, in that the primitive man was regarded as fertile soil for the primitive gospel. Bartholome de las Casas gave wide currency to this theme in his "History of the Indies," and established a Utopian colony to implement it.[7] A group of Anabaptists at Zürich announced that they were going "to the red Indians over the sea" when their evangel was greeted with hostility and persecution at the hands of civilized men.[8] Such an attitude is a mixture of admiration for virtue in the primitive age, repudiation of "civilized" religion and religious practices, naivete as to the possibilities for the primitive gospel among primitive people.

The man of the Reformation epoch was thus profoundly uneasy about the manner of his social life and the pattern of his own formal thinking and worship. He thought that his own age was "decadent;" a threefold Fall (*triplex discessio*) had occurred — in national affairs, in the church, in the age.[9] The historians of the Renaissance and Reformation frequently rejected the historiography of Orosius, which had been dominant and which projected a pattern of progressive Christian development. The thinking man of the period was conscious of a renewal to come, a new birth of spiritual vigor following the long decline. A new periodization was introduced, with a Fall both political and religious in imperial Rome, with a Restitution of old virtue in the present.

This became the framework of much of the historical thinking of the Renaissance and Reformation.[10]

Sources of Sixteenth-Century Primitivism

Among the radical thinkers there was a frame of mind remarkably parallel to classical primitivism, and reflecting in good part the melancholy of the age. When we consider the detailed structure of Anabaptist life we find many evidences: their normative view of the Early Church, the historical expectancy implied in use of "Fall" and "Restitution." With independents like Franck and Schwenckfeld it is not so difficult to trace the effect of certain pre-Reformation ideas. But with the more Biblically centered groups, who rarely cited any non-Biblical authority, it is a speculative if not futile effort. We may, however, mark certain centers of ideology which affected their intellectual climate and, largely in indirect fashion, their ideas.

Before persecution destroyed the educated leadership of the Anabaptists, the men at the head of the movement were university trained. Among the South Germans and Hutterites there were several converted priests and pastors, highly educated. Other leaders — notably Hans Denck and Leonhard Bouwens — were trained in the literary circles which everywhere marked the spread of Humanistic learning. In Westphalia and the Valley of the Yssel, the schools of the Brethren of the Common Life supplied a number of the most able leaders.[11] To point up the discussion we may take two great leaders: Erasmus and Zwingli.

DESIDERIUS ERASMUS (1466-1536)[12] was educated by the Brethren at Gouda, Deventer, and s'Hertogenbosch. He was permanently influenced by their regard for simple living and simple Biblical truth. From Wessel Gansfort, Alexander Hegius, and Rudolph Agricola he learned concern for apostolic Christianity and its manner of life. Pacifism and tolerance were articles of faith. He knew the English Humanists (Colet, More, Warham), worked in Venice with Aldus Manutius (the friend and fellow student of Pico), and corresponded with all the leaders of thought of his day. The Anabaptists admired him greatly for his ethical insight and accent upon sincere and uncompromising New Testament truth. In his writings the return to Gospel simplicity was the way to rejuvenate the faith and the church. But Erasmus, who also influenced the Reformers more than any other single author, was the despair of both Roman Catholic and Protestant parties. If he would not accept Roman Catholic preferment by denouncing the Reformation, he would not declare for the Reformers either. He did not believe in the rancorous partisanship which characterized both sides. He believed change should be reasonable and enlightened. His last days were embittered by von Hutten's attacks and the accompanying break with Zwingli, and he died with one faithful disciple by his side: his executor, Bonifacius Amerbach.[13]

ULRICH ZWINGLI (1484-1531)[14] was educated in the Latin School, then at Bern under Lupulus. Following two years at Vienna under Conrad Celtes and Cuspinian, he returned to Basel where Wytenbach taught him the Bible. He also became acquainted with Pico's work and corresponded with Erasmus. At Einsiedeln, as a young priest, he read the Church Fathers — Jerome, Origen, Ambrose — and also Stapulensis and "Dionysius." He copied out the Pauline letters from Erasmus' New Testament, and was moved to the attitude which permanently marked his churchmanship: "Back to Christ!" He never broke, however, with the cultural and political life of the Swiss city-states; but the radicals (Grebel, Manz, Blaurock, Reublin) who left him and went beyond him were following the logic of his message.

The direction of Humanism[15] was away from speculation and dogma to pious ignorance (*pia ignorantia*), away from ecclesiasticism to the simple ethic of the Synoptics (*Nachfolge Christi*), away from the hierarchy to the elemental lay brotherhood of the disciples' democratic band. There was, furthermore, a certain attitude to the origins which is most significant: just as return to classical forms was the purifying principle for their beloved Latin, so a return to the life of the Early Church would revitalize the corrupted faith.

Because primitivism is not essentially a theory of origins but really a device for passing judgment on contemporary society, it is closely linked with views of the future. Eden is also Utopia. The imagery of the lost Paradise reverberates through the apocalyptic visions of the book of Revelation. In the Left Wing, primitivism leads straight into eschatology. The man who above all represented this combination in the age preceding the Reformation, whose thought has influenced the underground of Christian dissent ever since, was JOACHIM OF FIORE (c. 1145-1202).

The Abbot Joachim has been significant in one way or another for the radicals of pre-Reformation and Reformation thought from the time when the Fraticelli appropriated the Eternal Gospel in their fight against papacy.[16] Joachim's periodization of history was especially relevant, with seven ages culminating in the *Restitutio ecclesiae*. His followers were far more radical than he, and marked the turning point in history by his own person or that of Saint Francis. Joachim taught that through the prophet of the last times justice and peace were to be re-established in all of the Roman provinces. The prophet was to be a spiritual Constantine, freeing the church from the trammels with which the imperial Constantine had bound her. For with Constantine all heathen had streamed into the church, polluting and compromising her. The Fall of the church which followed the time of the apostles would soon be ended, however; the recovery of the church in the present would precede the last things. Whereas in the middle period salvation was linked to the institutions and sacraments, in the Age of the Spirit these lost their meaning. As Simeon took in his arms the child Jesus, so should the Curia act to fulfill the *ordo spiritualis* (the "withering away" of the Church).[17] The Great Church was near to death (following the Fall) and would be renewed by a reappropriation of the relationships in an earlier and more vigorous period *(institutio fidei Christianae* — "the people of faith were of one heart and soul," as in Acts).[18] At the end of time there is a secret unfolding, a revelation of that which was hidden in the historical process: that the oppressed, the humble, the anonymous are those who carry history.[19] At the end of time the absurd, dark, obscure passages of Scripture will be revealed as the greatest mysteries.[20] As the Living Word is encased in human and literal forms, so hidden within the outward church is the inner church, slowly revealing itself.

The history of this church leads from the apostles through the martyrs, the hermits and monks of the Greek Church to the Benedictine monasticism of the Western Church; to the Canons Regular and their effort to make the poor life of humility and submission binding upon all clergy; to the Cistercian reform; to the Cluniac monasticism; and expresses itself conclusively in the Franciscan reform movement.[21]

When the old institutional forms opposed and hindered the coming of the New Age, then the old church was recognized as cast in the image of the Anti-Christ: its efforts to hinder the revival of apostolic Christianity were the proof of its diabolical character.[22] The moving power toward the New Age was to be martyrdom, the willingness to suffer without stint for the Gospel without glosses.[23] Binding this whole structure of thought and historical interpretation together, and illuminating it vividly, was the sense of world mission, of ultimate triumph at hand.[24]

In the radical groups of the Reformation these ideas constantly occur. One of several types, Anabaptism was primitivist and eschatological. The norm is the past, the hope for the future is the Restitution of the Early Church. There is on the one hand an attitude which is conservative, even reactionary; on the other there is a revolutionary spirit which can burst the most secure of ecclesiastical or social forms. The idea of Restitution represents a studied effort to reverse the verdict of history, to shed the accumulated power and intellectual sophistication which seem to corrode and obscure the pure and inspired faith of the founders of the church. In the Anabaptist "Restitution" there was the same agitated historical mood of expectancy which we find in Joachimitism and in the Early Church itself: a keen sense that the end and final reckoning are close at hand, and conjoined with this a vigorous missionary outlook which embraced the whole world in its sweep. Above all, the True Church was a suffering church whose changing patterns were ever cast in the shadow of the Man Upon the Cross.

These were the main elements which went into the intellectual atmosphere of the radical Reformation; they form the backdrop for the emergence of a new type of religious primitivism. This primitivism, in its Anabaptist type, involves a view of the church and its place in history which explosively combines both reactionary and radical features. In its determined Restitution of the type and style of the Early Church, Anabaptism in fact introduced quite new elements in Christian history. Although the heroic period of the faith is taken as normative, the forerunners of the Free Church way departed radically from patterns of "magisterial Protestantism" which had obtained for more than a millennium.

As we move on to consider the relation of primitivism to Anabaptism, and to study the various factors which make Anabaptism a clear type of church life, we do well to introduce certain distinctions to avoid serious error. The attitudes we were just now considering formed an intellectual climate for the various groups of the time, bound together the Left Wing especially, and are to be considered along with records of their actual group experience. It is not enough to review only what was taught, what ideas circulated among individuals and groups, although this is common practice. Our discussion must deal with "concrete" groups which found a certain place in Christian history. The view of the church which the Anabaptists championed will be tested repeatedly by the actual experience of the groups, and by their encounter both with establishments and with other types of radical protest.

In total perspective, the evidence from classical primitivism and from Humanism and Joachimitism has only relative value. In spite of suggestive eddies to mark the crosscurrents, and a few instances of streaming together, the evidence as a whole is circumstantial. It gives us a good deal of help in understanding the general climate in which Anabaptism emerged, but we shall find few quotations or other evidence of direct influence. This is the case also with the Florentine rediscovery of antiquity, which contributed so much to the shaping of Reformation as well as Renaissance. The attitude to sources and origins, which has been noted, finds expression in the attitude to the Early Church and the Bible as well as to classical texts. An argument from analogy can even be entered that Anabaptism, with its emphasis upon the hidden truth behind objective evidences, is indebted to the revival of Neo-Platonic thought. But conclusive evidence is lacking. While doubtless the Zürich Anabaptists such as Grebel were familiar with the classical ideal, the prevalence of religious primitivism in Anabaptism is due more to the fact that Christianity is a historical religion with a sacred book in which all reforms seek their inspiration and confirmation. Since the norm provided by the book was itself diverse, it was in turn selectively applied in the light of the real problems of the age.

We may return to our original concerns: to discover what it was certain groups hoped to be, and to what extent they were successful. We shall draw mainly upon their own testimony — now generally available in usable form — in elaborating their church view. In judging to what extent the Anabaptists succeeded, we shall consider the problems they faced both from without (persecution) and from within (centrifugal factors, both doctrinal and organizational). And we shall speak from a footing in Free Church life, which is the eternal memorial to those who championed voluntary religious association and vigorous congregational life at a time when Christianity was for most simply the religious aspect of a civilization, indeed frequently little more than the tool of government. It is only from such vantage that Anabaptism can be truly understood and its importance properly assessed.

The Fall of the Church

The idea of a general Fall of man has been adapted by Christian reforming groups to the history of the church. There are two falls: man fell and the church fell. The whole idea of the recovery of New Testament Christianity is tied up with the thought that at some point in Christian history the pattern was lost.

A very prevalent contemporary opinion is revealed in the approach taken by Hobhouse in the 1909 Bampton Lectures:

Long ago I came to believe that the great change in the relation between the Church and the World which began with the conversion of Constantine is not only the decisive turning-point in Church History, but is also the key to many of the practical difficulties of the present day; and the Church of the future is destined more and more to return to a condition of things somewhat like that which prevailed in the Ante-Nicene Church; that is to say, that instead of pretending to be co-extensive with the world, it will accept a position involving a more conscious antagonism with the world, and will, in return, regain in some measure its former coherence.[25]

We see here the familiar teaching of a "Fall," coupled with the hope of an eventual Restitution.

It is not surprising to find that in recent years a book on *The Fall of Christianity* written by the head of the Dutch pacifist organization is being distributed in quantity by the American office of the Fellowship of Reconciliation.[26] The Constantine myth is an essential part of the discussion: "When he was converted to Christianity (in 312), and when he exalted this faith into the State religion (in 324), Christianity began to turn toward the State for support, and became reconciled to war and the soldier's calling."[27] For Heering this is the turning point of Christian history, and the pivot of every discussion of its organization, ethics, and morals.

The idea of the fall of the church with Constantine is far-flung among the Free Churches, however, and is not limited to nonresistant or pacifist elements. A recent book on *The Claims of the Free Churches* states boldly: "When the Church was persecuted by the Empire she was pure in motive and morals: but under the patronage of Constantine it became the fashion for the Roman nobility and obsequious pagans to enter the Church: and pagans they remained within her membership."[28] Nor is the idea limited to Free Churches. In his address at the Extraordinary Synod of the Evangelical Church in Germany, June 27, 1956, in Berlin, General Superintendent Günter Jacob of Cottbus proclaimed:

Aware spirits characterize the situation of Christianity in contemporary Europe by the fact that the end of the Constantinian epoch has arrived.

The Constantinian fusion marked the departure from this genuine way of the Church of Jesus Christ, a way in the world which according to the view of the New Testament will be a way of suffering before the hostility and opposition of the world.

With the end of illusions about the Constantinian epoch and a return to the early Christian witness we no longer have the right to claim privileges and a monopoly for support of the Gospel from the State.[29]

Whether it appears in its traditional setting in "sectarian Protestantism," or on occasion within the assembly halls of declining establishments, the pattern of thinking involved is well known. What is not familiar is the fact that this is Anabaptist thinking. The Anabaptists were among the first to ground the church in a total and systematic application of primitivist historiography.

ELEMENTS IN THE IDEA OF THE FALL

When we break down the various ideational associations into their constituent parts we find several different themes customarily linked together: glorification of the first three centuries (the "Golden Age" of the faith), a lamentation for the decline in association with the Empire (the "Fall" of the church), a vigorous sense of new beginnings (the "Restitution"). The latter theme will be treated in the next chapter, in a discussion of the constitutive elements in the church view. We shall consider now the attitude to the Early Church and its subsequent decline.

In true primitivist fashion, the Anabaptists considered the earliest times the "Age of Heroes." True, there had been before the sixteenth century a conscious glorification of the life of the Master and His Disciples, buoyed up by a general feeling that the men of the first centuries were spiritual giants after a fashion not equaled by later generations. The imitation of Christ (*Nachfolge Christi*) was a familiar medieval theme, of special importance to the Brethren of the Common Life — whose house at Deventer instituted the practice of community in deliberate imitation of the church at Jerusalem.[30] There were other anticipations, notably among the radical Franciscans and the Hussites. But a well-defined primitivist periodization of Christian history — with the "True Church" beginning to relive in careful fashion the life of the early heroes — was a major Anabaptist contribution.

Glorification of the Heroic Age

When we review the cardinal points in Anabaptist thinking about New Testament times and the primitive church, the parallels with the classical "Golden Age" immediately become apparent. There were certain personal virtues and social practices which characterized the good society in both schemes of thought, and we may consider them briefly.

Pacifism was a cardinal principle in the classical Golden Age.[31] In the Anabaptist vision of the Early Church, the witness to peace was accented. For them, pacifism was narrowed to the testimony of the nonresistant martyrs; the atmosphere was eschatological rather than Utopian, the pattern of behavior one of discipleship rather than social strategy. As the early Christians had won the Roman Empire by suffering, so should the martyrdom of the followers of Christ in the later age lead on to the final triumph.

The Anabaptist repudiation of violence was especially related to the integrity of life and witness of the believing community. Above all it was wrong to compel religious submission and use force in matters of conscience, for in the years of first faith and strength the Gospel had been spread only by means approved in the New Testament. Just as David, the man of war, was not permitted to build the temple, and even as Solomon built it without either hammer or axe, so the church of Christ was first created in the principle and spirit of voluntary association and without force or compulsion.[32] The law goes out from Zion and the Word of God from Jerusalem, and a people is gathered without force and without weapons.

Communism also characterized the classical Golden Age, and one of the marks of the Fall was dehumanization through the advent of private property.[33] Viewing the Early Church, Leonhard Schiemer wrote that the "Communion of Saints" was most clearly seen in the second, fourth and fifth chapters of Acts, and the true disciples should live as Christians did in that glorious time of the faith.[34] "One Christian should buy nothing from the other, but give freely (read Acts 2.3.4., whether the Christians at Jerusalem didn't have all things common!)."[35]
They were real Christians then, and the people of God most plain-

ly seen! The Hutterites wrote to the Moravian Lords (c. 1546) that their communism was modeled on that of the Early Church.[36] The Holy Spirit visited the Jerusalem community, and they were a people of power of soul. The actual Anabaptist practice differed in various congregations according to the time and place; but the insistence upon community (whether communism of consumption only, or of production also) remained constant.

Sometimes a more general historical understanding entered the picture. Thus Peter Ridemann taught in his "Rechenschaft" that everything was created common in the beginning (I Moses 1:26-29), and private property entered by sin;[37] presumably the Early Church was returning to the life of Eden by practicing communism, and the Church of the Restitution should do likewise. On the other hand, Ulrich Stadler showed a strong historical sense in his treatment of the subject, pointing out that only the church at Jerusalem had communism whereas at the other centers Christians were left alone in their own houses. In his opinion, communism was the only way for the Hutterite Brethren because they were driven together with no other place to go and no other life to lead.[38] Over against these historical observations and interpretations, however, we may place dozens of normative statements concerning the first age of the church: communism was generally considered authoritative simply because it was the style of life of the heroes of the faith in the normative period. Give all to the poor (Matt. 19:21)! Consider the widow, who gave *all she had!* As in other matters, there is an apocalyptic quality in the teaching: as time is telescoped between their congregations and the "Age of Heroes," so it is shortened between them and the end of history. Some felt the end was already begun in themselves; their community was not only a recapitulation of past virtue but a foretaste of the Kingdom of God. When asked their trade and location and station in life in court actions many replied, "No master!" (*kein vorsteer*), for in the New Age only Christ was Master. We have here an attitude as radical in social consequences as it was primitivist in religious type. The Anabaptists counted themselves members of an economy in which all were equal and all were to share according to need.

A vigorous simplicity was the mark of the man whom the

world could not victimize: his wants were well controlled, his tastes directed to the truly essential.[39] Like the classical hero, the man of spiritual power in the Early Church was also cut loose from personal display and absurd convention. This type of man appeared again in the sixteenth century. By a vigorous enforcement of spiritual discipline (including use of the Ban), unethical and immoral practices were avoided — not to mention frivolous clothes and strong language. A congregation of spiritual athletes was trained, committed to the simple life. In his testimony before the court, Julius Lober said: "Luther and the other Christian teachers do not preach nor teach baptism as it was taught at the time of the apostles . . . . Saith further, that Luther and others promote no true Christian order (in it), that they suffer and permit whoredom, avarice, usury, blasphemy and other depravity in the community, which the apostles did not bear so far, but had the ban among them."[40] The enforcement of heroic virtue by the group raised up a man of superior type and enabled him to perform wonderful deeds: he was able to fulfill the testimony of suffering and on occasion to perform miracles.

A certain attitude to art (technology) might be linked to this vigorously cultivated simplicity.[41] The agriculturalist, close to Mother Nature, was thought to be more wise than he whose spirit was corroded by the artifices of civilization. The man who worked with his hands and produced in co-operation with nature had keener insight than the usurer or trader. The craftsman was said to learn more by his handiwork in the spirit of humility than ever the scribe with his multitude of books. Hans Hut and his disciples preached the *euangelion aller creatur*, pointing out that Jesus made clear to the common man by his trade the great wisdom to which the theologians were blind.[42] The radicals never tired of pointing out that the men who knew Jesus were simple, unlettered, anonymous. They asserted that the poor and depressed and naively literal were those who carried the Gospel.[43] The unsophisticated were said to believe that Jesus meant just what He had said, without any glosses. Only those schooled in the wisdom of this world could write the commentaries and marginal notes which corrupted and rendered null and void the simple Gospel truth. In the great time of the faith, so the radicals claimed, neither doctrine nor church life were bound and corrupted by "forms," by dangerous inflections, by subtle compromises.

When we speculate on how such marked parallels could exist between classical primitivism and Anabaptist thought, since it is difficult to prove direct classical influence upon the radicals (who rarely cited any book but the Bible), we may remember their debt to Erasmus, Zwingli, Occolampadius, and especially Sebastian Franck. And, although the best-educated leadership was martyred during the first years, the early leaders — Grebel, Hübmaier, Denck, Hetzer — were men of marked accomplishment in the university world, a world inspired by the new Humanistic studies. The devotion which the Renaissance directed toward the origins and the eager quest of the religious for the origins of the faith were related phenomena. It was not a detailed program or body of specific content which carried over, but a certain attitude and method in reference to antiquity.[44] This attitude and method, when related to distinctly Christian concerns, became the hallmarks of Anabaptist thought.

After the Golden Age, a Fall

In Anabaptist portrayal of history, after the "Age of Heroes" life declines and a definite "Fall" occurs. This is an old theme, but it was given special content by the radicals. In secular primitivism the Fall marks a turning point in society and social relationships. The Fall has a cultural aspect. There is also a chronological aspect, revealed in a definite periodization of history and the hope of an eventual restoration. There is almost always a detailed theory of "Fall" in primitivist thought.[45]

It is incumbent upon the servants of the Lord to teach, to instruct and to warn to that end [*i.e., spiritual pilgrimage, martyrdom*] with all patience and neither spoil nor condemn, as we have a model in Paul. Decay had scarcely any power to hold those [who were] free, unencumbered, resigned. In the beginning they were living in the Lord. But now, because prosperity is sought, they nestle comfortably back into the world. And consequently they don't see themselves leaving the world; yes, they would far rather live than die.[46]

Lydia Müller has noted the fascination which the Eusebian history of the power and triumph of the Early Church had for the Anabaptists.[47] Here they saw the record of earth-shaking power in apparent weakness, dynamic expansion under martyrdom, triumph out of persecution. Here was the way of the church from Christ to Constantine "in a certain sense . . . . a peerless Passion-way. The Eusebian church-history is the history of the Church under the Cross. The Imperial-church and later the papal-church were no longer martyr-churches. So after Constantine [it was] above all the communities of heretics who took over and further-ed the traditions of the true and precisely for that reason per-secuted community of Christ."[48]

The growth and victory of the Early Church against incredi-ble odds was a mysterious thing, a sign of the secret workings of God. *But more mysterious still was the fact that in the very hour of her apparent triumph and well-being, the church fell into dis-grace*. The Anabaptists were led to conclude that only a little remnant *(ein klaines heuflen)* has gone the right way since crea-tion.[49] The "True Church" and a territorial church or state church were two different things.

USES OF THE IDEA OF THE FALL

The idea of a Heroic Age from which later generations have fallen away is a useful concept for polemicizing the existing scene in its many phases. The attack of the radicals was comprehensive, embracing many social issues in terms of the Christian way. The Anabaptists, which were those groups of radicals most concerned for the nature of the church, employed the idea of the Fall in both chronological and cultural aspects. They adopted the historical framework, and upon it hung a vigorous critique of the Christen-dom in which they found themselves.

Chronological Aspects

The dating of the "Fall" is a significant clue to an under-standing of what was meant by the term. Among the Polish Brethren[50] we find a reference to Eusebius, dating the "Fall" with the death of Simeon, the last of the grand old men who had known Jesus and the Twelve, said to have died as Bishop of Jerusalem in 111 A.D. at the ripe age of 120 years: "up to this time the church remained a virgin pure and incorrupt."[51] Related to this is a feeling that those who had personally known the Master could not miss the meaning of his simple and straightforward words. Those who came later, having neither the impress of his personality nor the inner inspiration of the Spirit of Truth, corrupted and compromised the purity and simplicity of the Gospel. Thus the Anti-Trinitarians commonly maintained that early Christianity was nondogmatic and inspired. In the best times there had been no scholastic disputing about the Trinity nor defining of "heresy" on dogmatic grounds. Nor was force used to compel intellectual conformity, for the concern of true religion was then ethical and moral. The "Fall" is then dated with the Council of Nicea, 325 A.D., when the crystallization of the Trinitarian formula put an end to charismatic leadership and inspired congregational life.[52]

Among the Anabaptists another aspect of the Fall was emphasized. Menno believed that the decline began early, was accentuated by Constantine, and culminated in an Edict of Innocent I, 407 A.D., which made infant baptism compulsory.[53] Generally speaking the Anabaptists dated the Fall with the reign of Constantine the Great. The Christian emperor seemed to them the very culmination of worldliness and power consciousness. For them the special mark of the Fall was the union of church and state, and the subsequent use of the civil arm in matters of faith.[54] True religion is inward, and may not be compelled by any.

But later, when Sylvester the 34th Pope paid tribute and prevailed upon Constantine the Great, who was the 43rd Emperor, with many flattering, sanctimonious words, [having] accepted him as a Christian in baptism, the Emperor provided throughout his whole realm great peace, with good intention to do thereby a service to God, to the Pope as Roman bishop, and to all who called themselves Christian. Thereby is the disease of craftiness, which creeps about in darkness, and the corruption which perverted at high noon, introduced by violence. The Cross was conquered and forged to the sword. All that happened through the slyness of the Old Serpent.[55]

With Constantine the voluntary association of true believers was corrupted and became the church of the land, with authority resting upon outward compulsion rather than upon the Sword of the Spirit which is the Word of God (Eph. 6:17).

It is notable that the radicals, both Anti-Trinitarian and Anabaptist, largely agreed in dating the Fall with the powerful administration of Constantine the Great. This is but another evidence that the ground of initial dissent was not a single issue but rather a general discontent with the formalizing and crystallizing "outwardness" of the Great Church. At first there were many leaders and groups free in both doctrine and ethical emphasis.[56] But after a decade and more of persecution and internal discipline, some groups shaped a congregational life concerned chiefly with ethical issues, whereas others went on to maintain their continuing opposition at the level of doctrine.

The Reformers were less anti-historical than the radicals, but they still found the concept of the Fall useful. Luther dated the Fall with Sabianus and Boniface III, who immediately followed Gregory the Great in asserting the temporal claims of the papacy.[57] For Luther, however, the church was never totally corrupted and the reign of Constantine was the summer-time of the faith.[58] For Zwingli, the Fall was dated with Hildebrand and the assertion of hierarchical power.[59] It is interesting to find Luther and Zwingli agreeing on their timing. For Calvin, it was the Bible rather than any evidence from history which gave authoritative ground for opposition to the old church. Nevertheless, he stated different dates of the Fall on different issues, emphasizing especially the papal arrogation of authority under Gregory the Great.[60]

Cultural Aspects: The Marks of the Fallen Church

The church in her fallen estate seemed to the Anabaptists far different from the community of true believers, the brotherhood of spiritual athletes. We must remember that they counted the fallen condition of the church *from the days of Constantine until the beginning of their own movement.*[61] *The Reformers also belonged to the period of the Fall.* The Anabaptists said that the revival began with Luther and Zwingli, but when the Reformers clung to the old idea of Christendom the radicals counted them out. The criticisms directed against the imperial Roman religion are the criticisms directed against the Reformers: church and state were amalgamated, empty formalism and spiritual slackness prevailed, infants were baptized into Christianity before their understanding could give the membership any content. The Anabaptists wanted a thoroughgoing Restitution of the church as she had been before the Fall, and they criticized the nominal Christianity of the middle period in suggestive terms.

What did the Anabaptists consider the marks of the fallen church? What did they list as the compromises and corruptions which set the fallen church off against the True Church as it had been in the Heroic Age?

The Anabaptists felt most strongly of all about the union of church and state.[62] It was here that their vision of voluntary religious association conflicted irreducibly with the amalgamation of wordly and ecclesiastical power dated from the reign of Constantine the Great. The Hutterites said that the final proof that the authorities of the so-called Christians (*vermainten Christen*) were not truly Christian was in their use of compulsion in religion.[63] In the youth of Jakob Huter the "religion" of the Tyrol changed five times according to political change of fortune. This seemed to him the most crass denial of that faith which is engraven upon the heart of the true believer, which is a secret thing and not conformed to the pattern of the masses.[64] When the so-called Christian magistrates attempted to enforce conformity, they resorted to various compulsions and in the end to persecution. Thereby the Spirit passed from them and was given to brotherhood movements which were persecuted, to "heretics" who walked the way of suffering and humility (*die geistlich Armen*). The authorities became "Turks after the Spirit," against whom the Anabaptist nonresistant would rather fight than against the real Turk.[65]

The Anabaptists were in fact among the first consistently to champion religious liberty in the modern sense. They believed that no individual might rightly be compelled by the magistrate in the matter of faith,[66] and *they distinguished between political sovereignty and those controls of the church which belong to its internal discipline and integrity.* According to a great American historian, to Hans Denck (Nürnberg, 1524) goes the honor of the first modern enunciation of the principle of a man's right to private religious interpretation.[67] The Anabaptists as a whole were more concerned about the freedom of the congregation than they were about the right of private interpretation, and their testimony is clear. The Lordship of Christ in the congregation prevents secular interference.

All outward power may not command, be used nor yet rule in the kingdom of Christ.

When outward power is allowed to rule in the kingdom of Christ it brings an offense to the Holy Spirit, the true Lord and Ruler without human assistance. . . .[68]

Such a security will exist, also in outward things, with practice of the true Gospel that each will let the other move and dwell in peace — be he Turk or heathen believing what he will — through and in his land, not submitting to a magistrate [in matters of faith]. Is there anything more to be desired? I stand fast on what the prophet says here. Everyone among all peoples may move around in the name of his God. That is to say, no one shall deprive another — whether heathen or Jew or Christian, but rather allow everyone to move in all territories in the name of his God. So may we benefit in the peace which God gives.

No one shall discriminate against the other because of faith.[69]

The Anabaptists asserted that political compulsion in religion was the denial of spiritual government and an affront to the spiritual power in the church. The *potestas ecclesiae* of the Christian congregation could not be maintained in a union of church and state.[70] Therefore the true covenantal community could not exist in such a system. Luther and Zwingli were no less tyrants than Constantine, because they also enforced religious conformity by the civil power.[71] An Anabaptist testified before the court that he did not attend communion in the church of the land for two reasons: (1) the church was not worthy, for good and evil were together (lack of spiritual government,

Ban); (2) the magistrates coerced with prison, and properly they have no true authority in matters of faith.[72] "The right, the true community compels no one, but rather is itself always suffering under another. And they seek to kill no one."[73] The free congregation is not dependent upon the magistrate's violence. It may exist anywhere a little band of faithful meet and covenant together to walk in His ways. The Ban is their only "sword."[74]

The separation of church and state which the Anabaptists represented thus involved at least two positive affirmations of vital religious significance: (1) the civic right of a free man to private religious interpretation, and (2) the Christian duty of the voluntary association to enforce a strong internal discipline. How often these two points have been confused! Far from being contradictory, these are two closely linked aspects of healthy congregational life.

Another mark of the Fall of the church was the widespread warring in Christendom. In the military politics of the day, religious controversy played a decisive role. Holding office and taking the oath were condemned by Anabaptists not only on the Biblical injunctions but also as part of a program involving total separation of the religious from the political authorities. Carrying and using the sword, taking the oath of allegiance, and serving to enforce political and economic and religious controls were all part of the feudal system. The constitutive aspect of the nonresistant position will be discussed later,[75] but here it is important to note that conscientious objection to war and killing was closely related to the Anabaptist interpretation of history and the historical hope of the movement. That "Christians" should kill other "Christians" was thought to be one of the sure signs of the fallen church. This and other sins of violence belonged to the middle period which the Anabaptists believed they were leaving behind.

When the church was no longer the free association of those who had been inwardly moved and were met together for mutual improvement, religion declined into dead formalism. In both dogma and ecclesiastical organization an empty "outwardness" obtained, a mere sham of religion which the Anabaptists scorned.

They made no distinction between the Roman Catholics and the Reformers in their condemnation: perhaps dominant Protestantism gave a greater freedom in "forms," but it still exaggerated the significance of the outward expression.[76] Anabaptism was in its rise a conscious reassertion of inspired religion, and this gave issue to certain problems as much as it produced a vivid attack upon the dead wood of old ways of doing things. The Restitution party said that strength lay in true inwardness, in the perfect simplicity of the common man. Sectarianism was itself a mark of concern for outward matters, since true believers are to be drawn together by inner power and magnetism rather than observance.[77] Beginning with the imperial pomp and display of Constantine, a type of personal ambition entered the church which was the precise opposite to the submissive humility (*Gelassenheit*) characterizing the saints of the Lord. "With all your energy read through the old patristic history how after the death of the pupils of the apostles the unspotted virgin church became a whore through the fornication of the ecclesiasts. . . ."[78]

The lust of the ecclesiastics for power and position had replaced the old democracy of the simple believers' band. Some writers have claimed that the Anabaptists, who emphasized this point, depended upon the medieval ethical criticism of the hierarchy and were therefore in fact a return to monasticism. The Anabaptists did not, however, consider themselves an "order" or marginal movement within the church: rather their congregations were the True Church. The priesthood of all believers was taken to mean the application of the *consilia perfectionis* to all Christians instead of only a special class. They pitted these counsels of perfection against the type of ambitious individual personality produced by formalism, and looked for another type of leader who would relive the virtue of the Early Church men.

Of special significance was the Anabaptists' denial of the Mass, and it must be comprehended in terms of their general reaction to display and formalism. The radicals refuted the objective merit upon which the Roman Church rested, and denied the real presence which Luther and Calvin retained. For them the Supper was a memorial and symbol of their corporate union with each other in the Risen Lord.[79] ANDREAS KARLSTADT

(c. 1480-1541)[80] played a large part in the sacramental discussion, beginning with the moment when he swung from Luther to the Zwickau prophets at Wittenberg. During the short-lived revolt there, in 1521-1522, he celebrated the Supper in both kinds, without motions or ceremonies and in civilian clothes.[81] His writings influenced Hübmaier and were known to the group in Zürich,[82] but the Swiss Brethren seem to have taken their figurative understanding of the Supper primarily from Zwingli and Oecolampadius.[83] Karlstadt's own teaching on the meaning of Jesus' words, "This is my body . . .," was not widely accepted, but his criticism of the Roman and Lutheran emphasis upon the "material" and "outward" circulated over a broad front. The Anabaptists said that Christ was not in the material but sat on the right hand of God the Father Almighty.[84] For them, to worship the physical bread and wine was the most awful idolatry and materialization of the spiritual truth of the presence of Christ in the midst of believers assembled. The doctrine of the real presence was blasphemy, wherein Christ was martyred again.[85]

Following Luther, the Anabaptists said that with the rise of Rome to power and imperial government, the heart of organized Christianity became rotten with the pomp and display of worldly power. In its prime Christianity had been a lay religion; under the imperial authority there arose a swarm of professionals, who did not comprehend the democratic simplicity of Christian brethren. The rise of the hierarchy was itself a sign of the "Fall."[86] But the faithful know that it is far better to count upon Christ and His simple Gospel than upon the pope and all the councils. Not only did the organization show the corrosive effects of power consciousness, but the very buildings indicated the concern for outward show. Great stone structures were piled up where once two or three had gathered together in His Spirit,[87] and now no sincere and simple spirit could feel at home there.

Instead of the Church of Christ that is the community and congregation of believers they have built and erected stone Temples, called them churches to deceive men thereby. Instead of the

Saints and pious men who are sanctified by God they have placed in their churches pictures — wooden, stone, silver likenesses and dumb saints. And to show honor and service to them they have robbed living Saints called for the service of God.[88]

According to Anabaptist historiography, during the dispersion of the middle period the True Church met in the woods, forests, fields, and private dwellings. They testified that they did not enter the great buildings, but gathered informally in two's and three's.[89] In every case they opposed the externalization of the faith, the compromise with worldly standards of "success" and well-being.

On the matter of infant baptism the state church rose or fell, [90] and the Anabaptists were incisive in repudiation of the rite. They maintained that there was no indication of such practice in the Bible or the Early Church.[91] The baptism of children came not from the Master, but was "established after the Age of the Apostles by the popes through their cunning in their Christian Churches."[92] Neither were sleeping adults baptized, as they pointed out when Luther said the faith of the congregation justified baptism of unwitting infants.[93] The promiscuous use of the rite to bring into the Great Church all kinds of pagans without inner reformation indicated the "Fall." When this happened the moral life of the community blended with that of the world. There came to be no difference between Christian and non-Christian; indeed, the non-Christian might walk closer to the path He walked than the professing man. The corruption of the church was precisely this: that she took in masses of people who had no understanding of what the Gospel meant in "conquering" the Roman Empire and the German tribes — and then completed the compromise in later centuries by taking in generation after generation of children who had not reached the age of understanding. "For a Christian life is no child's play,"[94] but a matter calling for stern discipline and vigorous ethical living.

When the radicals at Zürich began to condemn infant baptism, Zwingli saw that it meant a church separated from the state and he clarified his own thinking against them. At first the

Anabaptists only refrained from baptizing infants; the Swiss Reformers had themselves raised the question. But on January 17, 1525, a Disputation was held and the leaders of the "root and branch" movement were expelled from the city. Shortly thereafter adult baptism was introduced, at Zollikon, and believers' baptism became a spiritual sword aimed right at the heart of the cantonal church system.[95] As persecution increased in the following years the issue of baptism grew in importance,[96] but from the very first it implied a significantly different view of the nature of the church which the Reformers could hardly miss.

With the addition of large numbers of nominal Christians at the time of the "Fall," and successive centuries of admission of all the people of the land through infant baptism, the church was no longer the congregation of the elect. In general a slipshod practice of spiritual laxity resulted: this the Anabaptists energetically condemned. They told in contrast how the spiritual athletes of the Heroic Age conducted themselves, and warned and admonished the men and women of the latter days whose lives conformed to the world rather than to the Kingdom. Not only were New Testament truths not emphasized in the fallen church, but there seemed to be no consciousness that mere observance of ritual and professional procedure could not substitute for true inwardness. The nominal Christians met in great crowds and maintained confession and fast days, but no admonition of brother for brother prevailed. The Anabaptists were convinced that there could be no true spiritual government in an established church.[97]

In a territorial system the alternative to laxity was persecution; the hollowness of the outward religion was further exposed by the violence with which formal rectitude was maintained. Actually what was involved in the main was persecution of the few by the few, while the great masses remained untouched and indifferent. Some persecutors, to be sure, cut a wide swathe. One of the most famous hangmen of the period, Berthold Aichele of Bavaria, boasted that he had hanged over forty Protestant pastors and twelve hundred "revolutionaries" in his time.[98] The only alternatives for the faithful in most areas were apostasy, martyrdom, or fleeing into exile if a place of refuge could be found.

For the great masses of nominal Christians, the relation between Christian brethren meant no more than the general social relationship required. The Anabaptists were especially offended by this, and taught that in right living the Christians were *accountable for each other*. Christ had given the commands for true believers who lived together in the bonds of brotherhood. Cupidity and self-interest were not only blemishes on the clergy, but also scandalous among the laity. According to the Brethren, Christ threw the thieves out of the temple, showing that he didn't want traders and exploiters in His church.[99] The man who lived by rents and tithes upon the toil of another was no true Christian brother, whether clergy or lay. Andreas Castelberger of the Swiss Brethren said such a man was no better than a thief or murderer.[100] It is impossible to be friend of both God and the world![101] Perfect Christian fraternity demanded submission of selfish interests to the needs of the community. Personal display and aggrandizement were to be condemned strongly wherever they appeared, and all such tendencies among Christians were to be vigorously curbed by spiritual government.

During the centuries of her fallen estate the church was so thoroughly corrupted and compromised that a thoroughgoing revolution in her life was necessary. The Anabaptists demanded that she return to the Age of Heroes. Similarly, the nominal Christians must go through a spiritual revolution, like a new Noah's Ark setting sail from all earthly things.[102] Having submitted to empty observations and half-hearted ritual for so long, the church must be purged by the Spirit and baptized into a new life of Christian discipline. The inflections and shadings were to be sloughed off, and the new law of Christ to be enforced without any glosses.

ANALYSIS OF THE IDEA OF THE FALL

In the primitivism of the radicals we find a definite mixture of chronological and cultural elements. The glorification of the

Early Church, the "Fall," the restoration of lost virtue — all represented a heavy weight of ethical judgment as well as a historical framework. It must be understood that these elements cannot be disentangled and that different themes are interwoven with varying degrees of emphasis in various groups and leaders. What was involved, of course, was not so much a naivete concerning certain historical events and their interpretation as it was the promulgation of a myth. This myth may or may not be "true," but the "truth" or "falsehood" of the myth depends upon much more fundamental issues than the question of literal fact: i.e., whether in point of technical fact an early congregation at Corinth was superior in spiritual power and morals to a congregation at Rome in 314 or 326 A.D. The historical framework is not explicit in all recorded Anabaptist teachings, and it would appear that even the most common ethical understandings (e.g., nonresistance, spiritual government, sharing) were not present in like mass among all leaders and groups. However, during the time of clarification the main outline of Anabaptist thought became evident, and it has persisted in various ways in radical Protestant groups to this day. Our study is, therefore, a summary analysis of the basic ideas of "sectarian Protestantism," a type of Protestantism which is quite different in thought structure from either Catholicism or magisterial Protestantism.

We may well ask in what way this framework of Christian history, which we encounter in vivid form in Anabaptism, is related to more general cultural concerns and even to a special way of interpreting secular history. On occasion there may be associated with the "Fall" of the church the theme of recurring falls in history. Thus a religious revolutionary fifty years before the Reformation epoch expressed the interweaving of religious themes with social expectancy: in the coming restoration the church and the world would both be set right by the Prophet King. The worldly power of the papacy is the foremost evil, and Kaiser Frederick was the prophet's heroic type for politico-religious reform. The revolutionary writer taught that communism was the true order, and that the introduction of Roman law marked the "Fall" in both church and society.

All evil is established by the Latins; they set forth *jus Quiritum militare,* this is mine, that is yours. Thereby they broke all friendliness and the love of God, because that [Roman] law is against the natural Godly law. Thereby inferiority and enmity were established. . . .[103]

The coming politico-religious Messiah whom this revolutionary proclaimed was the King of the Black Forest, who would become the Lord of all Christendom.

The King of the Black Forest . . . will make a reformation with pious Christians, kill the blasphemous, wipe out the drunken, root out the lecherers, cut off the lustful, take power away from the frivolous, banish the clergy from the land, who needlessly distort the work of the Lord, put all the orders to work, who seek more their own [interest] than the common need, and also imprison the prelates who buy them with friendship.[104]

Many more examples could be given of plans for combined religious and social reform which circulated in the popular mind in the period before the Reformation.

Among various radicals of the sixteenth century, certain of the old themes recur. The attitude of Sebastian Franck already has been noted.[105] At Münster the revolutionaries destroyed the old historical records in the cathedral to clear the air for a fresh beginning in both church and world. Occasionally the religious primitivism is mixed in this way with general cultural primitivism among the more significant Anabaptist teachers and groups, and the expectation of a purification of church life may lead on to a broad social reform at the end.[106] Generally speaking, however, the Anabaptists proper avoided general social issues and devoted their attention to the reform within the church. The marvel is not that social ideas and cultural primitivism crept into their thought on occasion, but rather that in such a short time they were able to define a coherent pattern of lay Christian religion.

The experience of persecution was so vivid in the first years of Anabaptism that the groups looked for little in the world and had small hope for its renewal. Only in the final age would the fulfillment of the church restoration lead on to a general social renewal; they remained somewhat vague as to how this was to occur.[107] One thing was fixed in their minds: it would not occur by violence or revolution. Eventually, however, the primitivist strain expressed itself in cultural patterns also. Today, the most direct descendants of militant Anabaptism reside in cultural enclaves in America. Like the Continental Mennonites, they have "gone over to the world," but in another way: they have "gone over to the world" of a past generation. The Hutterite Brethren and some American Mennonites today represent an archaic social pattern strangely out of place in the twentieth century. The original heightened tension between the "church" and the "world" has in many sections of Mennonitism deteriorated into a tension between the eighteenth century and the twentieth century. Plain clothes have become peculiar clothes. In fairness it must be said, however, that this breaking of the dialectic is not so disgraceful as the failure of great legal and social establishments to realize that a tension exists between Christian norms and popular folkways. Moreover, there is a very live movement within American Mennonitism which is seeking to lift again the classical questions to the church, and put aside the old easy adjustments. But our theoretical review of primitivism would not be complete without note of the fact that a structure of religious primitivism tends to slip over into a pattern of cultural primitivism.

Periodization of History

The idea of the "Fall" is only part of a general periodization of history, and various styles of periodization reflect the view of the thinker involved.[108] In a prophet like David Joris, who saw three ages — each introduced by a "David" — the scheme is fairly obvious![109] In Bernt Rothmann's *Restitutio* there were a number of successive falls and restitutions, as also in Sebastian Franck's writings. We find in them the thought of a last age, a millennial reign shortly to be introduced or already begun in the congregations of the Restitution. There have been various "falls" in the past, but this is to be the final Restitution — to be followed by the eternal restitution of all things (Acts 3:21).[110] In the Anabaptists proper, the periodization seems to have been

limited mainly to Christian history, although there is the suggestion that the Restitution of the True Church will lead on to
the millennial reign.

What happened to the True Church during the fallen period
of the Great Church? There had been a gathering of God's folk
in the beginning of history, and they were being gathered up
and established again on sure foundations. But the Anabaptists
said that in the middle period the faithful were in dispersion,
like the Israelites in the wilderness. They were accustomed to
trace their succession back to the Early Church, usually identifying the faithful during the dispersion with the "heretics" condemned by the Great Church: John Scotus, Waldo, the Fraticelli,
Wyclif, John Hus.[111] There were also those radicals who said
that the succession was totally broken off with the "Fall." In
the marginal "Anabaptist" movement at Münster they said that
there had been no True Church for fourteen hundred years.[112]
Sebastian Franck, Caspar Schwenckfeld, and David Joris believed the continuity was broken, and that only a prophet with
direct divine commission could gather again a community of
believers — introducing by his appearance the New Age.[113] But
the more historically minded groups elaborated their primitivist
historiography in which the small brotherhood groups were the
bridge of evangelical faith between the "Fall" and the "Restitution." Among the Anabaptists this was the familiar interpretation: *during the middle period the True Church was in dispersion, among those called "heretics."*

Eschatology

From their cultural attitudes and periodization of history,
it is clear that understanding the radicals involves a large measure
of concentration upon their eschatology.[114] Their attitude was
no pale historical interpretation, and not primarily a matter of
historical fact; rather it involved a doctrine of *the moving power
of history itself*. There is some difference of opinion as to how
closely the Reformers and the Anabaptists followed the same
historical patterns in their interpretations, but it becomes clear
that the Anabaptists conceived of themselves as the secret mean-

ing and bearers of the New Age: we find in their church view an eschatological accent not found as prominently in the dominant groups.[115] Christian history is a history of the elect, of the vanguard, and of the wonders which God performs through their capacity for discipline and suffering. In the New Age the "Fall" is reversed, and the old corruptions and compromises are left behind by the community of believers. They hold Him true who has promised that He would perform greater things through His Disciples than He worked himself.

ORIGINS OF THE IDEA IN THE LEFT WING

The contributions of Humanism and Joachimitism to the primitivist church view previously have been suggested.[116] The paired ideas of normative Early Church and "Fall" have seen the light in various group records since Joachim and the Fraticelli, quite apart from the writings of the scholars. The Waldensians, in point of fact the first of the Free Churches, had such an interpretation of history. The Unitas Fratrum has maintained such a church view to the present day, although the adaptations introduced by Zinzendorf and the Pietist period radically affected the practice and view of the church, and modified the break from magisterial Protestantism. We may fairly conclude, however, that the total and systematic application of primitivist historiography to the life of the church was a major work of the Anabaptists.

Which is the true [Church]? The ancient, apostolic. My wish, my yearning is that the world may go back to a true apostolic church. The *Acts* and the writings of the Great [Church] Fathers and ancient Bishops show the way on which we must go back to it. The apostolic church flourished to the time of Constantine. From then on it was perverted, because the Bishops went over to the world. . . .[117]

In these words GEORG WITZEL (1501-1573) stated the feeling about the Golden Age of the faith which came to be distinctive of Anabaptism. Witzel wanted to see an ethical Reformation;

he had a great and vivid vision of the purity of the primitive community at Jerusalem.[118] When Lutheranism failed to produce the desired fruits, he broke with it. Eventually he reconverted to Rome, but not before he had greatly influenced early Anabaptism. Johannes Campanus was for a time his friend and associate and took the historical framework from him, and through Campanus' lost masterpiece — *Contra totum post-Apostolos-mundum* — the primitivist motif found wide circulation among the radicals. Campanus greatly influenced the Wassenburger preachers, whose advent in Münster was of such fatal consequence for that city. In Bernt Rothmann's *Bekenntnisse van beyden Sacramenten* (1533)[119] we find the influence of Campanus' book, to which Henrik Rol in 1529 had called Rothmann's attention.[120] Sebastian Franck was also among those who liked Campanus' denial of all authoritative teachers since the apostles, and he is accredited with being the first to promote the theme of *restitutio* among the historians of the period.[121] Thus Witzel, whose later period was devoted to the effort to reintroduce primitive liturgical practices within tthe Roman Catholic Church,[122] contributed a most influential note to Protestant radicalism.

The praise of life in the Heroic Age leads readily to the concept of restoring the lost virtue. Primitivism and the idea of perfectability are frequently confused and entertained in the same material, according to a student of primitivism, and such proves to be the case in the Left Wing.[123] Christian life in the old Jerusalem leads to the New Jerusalem. Not far from the idea of the "Fall" is the hope of an eventual Restitution. And not far from the hope is the determination to practice a new life fit for the New Age. The Anabaptists pressed forward to these positive disciplines which gave permanent form to their congregational life, moving on from the fallen church to the new ingathering.

CHAPTER III

The Restitution of the True Church

The dominant theme in the thinking of the main-line Anabaptists was the recovery of the life and virtue of the Early Church.[1] The ordinances which had characterized the True Church (*die rechte Kirche*) in that Heroic Age were to be made a program for thoroughgoing reformation. The Reformers were not willing to make so radical a break from the past, but those whose key concept was *restitutio* rather than *reformatio* were determined to erase what they considered the shame of centuries and to recapitulate the purified church life of the Golden Age of the faith. In reviewing the records, the reader is struck with the Anabaptists' acute consciousness of separation from the "fallen" church — in which they included the Reformers as well as the Roman institution. Some writers have therefore concluded that Anabaptism is not merely a variant form of Protestantism, but rather an ideology and practice quite different in kind from those of both Rome and the Reformers. If Anabaptism constitutes such a radical departure, a "Third Type" as distinct from Catholicism and magisterial Protestantism, the importance of this idea for the interpretation of subsequent Christian history is self-evident. The rise of the Free Churches, the development of the type of church life characteristic of America and the younger churches of Asia and Africa, the emergence of a new understanding of the vocation of the laity even within the old-style Continental Protestantism — all of these movements are set in a new context.[2] The present writer is moved to suggest that the Anabaptist revolution within Christian history was so thoroughgoing as to be *sui generis,* and that in distinguishing the church types of magisterial Protestantism from the sixteenth-century beginnings of the Free Churches we may properly speak of the "Church of the Reformers" on the one hand and the "Church of the Restitution" on the other.

79

THE PROBLEM OF CONTINUITY

The churches of the Reformers did not turn against the past centuries of Christian history with such abandon. Although there was a primitivist note in the thinking of Luther and Zwingli and Calvin and Butzer, they did not finally break so radically from the medieval pattern. Within the major political units the churches remained established, and at local church level the parish pattern was maintained. The Anabaptists, however, had a much different view of the periods of Christian history and of "apostolicity" itself. For them the question was loyalty not so much to a tradition of developed rites and orders, to "apostolic succession,"[3] as it was to "apostolicity" measured in terms of identification with New Testament ordinances. They believed that the devoted Christian could find guide lines in the Bible for the organization of his church life just as plainly as he could find the basic theological content of his faith.

Where Did the Restitution Begin?

For some in the Left Wing, especially the revolutionaries and independents (*Spiritualisten*), the separation from the "fallen" church was conceived in most specific terms of date and place. The point where the truly spiritual life was restored, and the names of those found faithful, were given serious consideration. The revolutionaries believed that the End was begun in their movement. They believed in the totality of their church and dispensation and world mission. Even the more quiet groups faced a parallel problem in interpreting historical events. "The Reformation hopes for a coming heavenly revelation of victory. But the *Schwärmer* believe that there is yet only a little stride to make in order to be *ecclesia triumphans* on earth."[4]

In pinpointing the origin of their movement some looked to Nikolsburg or St. Gall. Nürnberg was favored by certain groups. Some declared "that there should be a great battle about Nürnberg and whoever was baptized should not be slain. Thereupon there would come to be a new rule and all would be alike."[5] Groups in Middle Germany looked toward Mühlhausen, others to Strassburg and then toward Münster.[6] Captured missioners and many who never joined the Hutterites at all frequently declared Moravia to be the place where true Christian order had been restored.

The *Stille,* however, generally accepted the Reformers' doctrine that the True Church might be found anywhere. Also, they apparently held merely to the quiet principle that the True Church could not have been destroyed since the founding, which is a standpoint different from the pragmatic power consciousness of the revolutionary wing. Thus the question of the precise moment or place where a true Restitution is effected seems of no fatal consequence to the main-line Anabaptists. But what seems apparent is not absolutely true. The *Stille* also treasured a social hope, and among the more vigorous groups that hope was expressed by vital internal discipline and outward evangel. Certain it is that the creative state of tension which marked the early Anabaptists off from surrounding society was far from the cultural and religious resignation of many of their descendants.

All wings of the movement were agreed in a strong attack upon the standing order, with its confusion of political and cultural and religious factors. Some called for a strict return to the New Testament pattern. "For it is better and more certain to build on Christ and His teaching than to rely on Fathers and Councils. Behold Christ the Lord will judge on the Last Day and not pope, fathers, councils."[7] Others cried aloud for the inspired leadership which might deliver them from dry formalism and deadly institutionalism.

Whoever, my dearest brethren in the Lord, would learn rightly the judgment of God and the sign of Holy Writ in truth, should not turn to the noise of the hired preachers [*geltprediger*], but look to the poor, the despised of the world, those called enthusiasts and demon-possessed according to the model of Christ and the apostles. Listen to them. For no one can reach the Truth unless he follows in the footsteps of Christ and His elect in the valley of suffering, or in part at least has decided to follow in the justification of the Cross of Christ according to the Will of God. For no one may learn the secret of divine wisdom in the dens and murderous alleys of all knavery as declared in Wittenberg or at Paris.[8]

After a short period of general protest, a strict Biblicism triumphed over prophetism and chiliasm in large sections of the Left Wing, and the restored True Church began to assume definite proportions. The pattern was defined in terms of strict adherence to certain ordinances defined in the New Testament. What Christ said, could be done.

A Different View of Tradition

It will be recognized that there is involved here a different view of apostolicity from that of the Protestant establishments.

Many other Christians consider it self-evident that such a view of the Church is far from the New Testament and its churches. It can certainly be debated how far the simple relationships of early Christianity are normative for the Christians of later periods. Either the message and example of the New Testament are taken to be a binding norm or they are considered to be historically undeveloped beginning patterns which had later to be altered. Moreover, the Protestant parish- and state-churches have generally agreed with the second point of view. On the contrary, churches and religious societies on the line of the free churches have understood that the New Testament gives the standards also for the organization [of the Church].[9]

The choice might be said to lie between "apostolic succession" and "apostolicity." In any case, we have a quite different view of Christian tradition in the Anabaptists and the later Free Churches from that which obtains in Roman Catholicism and magisterial Protestantism.

WHAT ARE THE MARKS OF THE TRUE CHURCH?

What then was the given pattern, as the Anabaptists reread it from the New Testament[10] and sought to make it concrete in the life of their congregations?

Believers' Baptism

Infant baptism was challenged by many dissenting groups on scriptural grounds, and it came early to the fore in discussions at such various points as Wittenberg, Zürich, Strassburg, Münster, and among the Hutterites and Dutch Mennonites. The radicals were convinced that the practice was introduced after apostolic times, in spite of the classic rejoinder that the baptism of households must have included children (e.g., I Corinthians 10:2).

In defining the classical Anabaptist positions, we can rely heavily on the important statement known as the Schleitheim Confession of MICHAEL SATTLER (c. 1490-1527). The first of the "Seven Articles" (Feb. 24, 1527) condemned infant baptism as non-apostolic:[11] the rite would not be used, therefore, in a congregation seriously trying to relive the life of the Early Church. "A great mass of men is without God's word and command in today's world with its infant baptism — a trickery to the simple and an insidious shame to all Christianity, a brassy pretence of all godless; for in all the Bible not a single quotation can be brought forward to justify it."[12] The Great Church said it was necessary to baptize children lest they die in sin. But if children were in mortal sin in their natural state before the age of understanding, would Christ have said, "Suffer the little children to come unto me and forbid them not, *for of such is the kingdom of heaven*" (Luke 18:16)?[13] According to the Anabaptists, the children were restored by Christ's sacrifice from the depths of original sin, and remained so until able to distinguish between good and evil.[14]

When Menno Simons questioned the practice of infant baptism and turned toward the apologists, they could not allay his doubts: Luther justified it by the child's appropriation of faith from the congregation, Butzer called it a guarantee of godly training, Bullinger (following Zwingli) said it was the Christian parallel to the Old Testament ordinance of circumcision. Menno concluded that no one spoke from the New Testament.[15]

By the very example of the Master, baptism must be an adult matter. At the age of 30 he went into the Jordan to ob-serve the approved custom at the hands of John; thereby He became a sign of the New Covenant.[16] Those who would walk in His way of submission and martyrdom might thereby know that the Christian life requires mature dedication and discipline. Such commitment requires a degree of understanding (*Vernunft*) which only mature persons can possess.[17] According to the Anabaptists, such commitment begins in a thoroughgoing repentance; repentance was the key word in the oldest baptismal liturgies.[18] The new member must be deeply aware that he has foresworn the world, sin, and the devil, and in whole heart and soul and body set out to live for God and His church.[19]

The baptism of a believer is a symbol of the sinking in the death of Christ and of being raised again ("new birth") in His resurrection.[20] No one can come into the Kingdom unless he be born again (John 3:3), and this was the spiritual event symbolized by water baptism into the community.

"Marx, you have been before now a light-hearted young fellow, and must become another man, to put the Old Adam from you and take on a newer and better self." Marx answered, he would do his best. Then Blaurock asked if he longed for the Grace of God and when he answered, "Yes," Blaurock spoke: "Come here, and I will baptize you!" Then Marx went and at that Blaurock baptized him.[21]

In Anabaptist teaching, the new birth has Christ alone as foundation and must occur radically in the history of both the individual believer and the True Church. The new beginning was as fundamental for the individual believer as it was for the Church of the Restitution. It was this constitutive element which distinguished the Anabaptists from both Roman Catholic "work righteousness" and Lutheran *sola fides*.

"The Scripture speaks of Perfection, which will be initiated through the Holy Spirit when one lives according to the command of God."[22] This is the ground of the Anabaptists' uncompromising integrity in shaping up a Christian witness.[23] Optimism as to the power of the Holy Spirit working in the midst of the faithful is contrasted with pessimism about the world and its "religion." "Therefore the baptism is a battle with sin, to kill it throughout the whole of life."[24]

The real issue was the Restitution of a vigorous congregational life, as it was thought to have been lived in apostolic times, and the argument between infant baptism and adult baptism was a vehicle of the prior issue.[25] The preaching of the Gospel, often carried on the proof text of the Great Commission,[26] was an open invitation to any man to make personal absolution and to covenant a new life with God and the community of believers. The idea of a covenantal relation to God and one's fellows became the foundation of the Anabaptist community, and through it came the use of the Ban (spiritual government).[27] The Anabaptists said repeatedly that true baptism was that submission to the divine authority described in I Peter 3:18-22, the responsibility of a good conscience toward God.[28] They saw that this couldn't be done easily in this kind of a world, but required brotherly admonition and exhortation, the practice of intentional fellowship.

By baptism the believer came under the discipline of a Biblical people — a discipline which he himself helped make and enforce. If the door of entrance were closely watched, a strong and true church could be maintained. The Anabaptists noted that the Master worked long with a small group, and then one of them betrayed Him. A long time of training was required for membership in the Early Church, and the True Church of the Restitution would not add members promiscuously.[29] The church covenant was undertaken at baptism and was thought to be the highest expression of religious voluntarism short of martyrdom itself; the balancing factor was the power of the community to forgive sins.[30] This was the Anabaptist understanding of the Keys of Peter. Related to it was the Key of David (*schlüssel Davits*),[31] which in the inchoate groups of the first years had been found in the primary religious experience of the individual. As the groups took definite form, the key which unlocked Scripture and made possible a true interpretation of Biblical teaching became a collective rather than an individual possession. The right of private interpretation, still asserted against the monopoly of the "Roman doctors" in public life, became the obligation to test one's findings with those of others within the fellowship. "The Father of mercy will establish the Key of David in our hearts so that we may open thereby the closed Book, the secret of His will."[32]

In the quest for final authority, *the Key of David* (which unlocked the meaning of Scripture) *and the Keys of Peter* (which unlocked the gates of heaven and hell) became possessions of the community of believers.[33] Group consciousness became a dominant force in baptized life. Among the rules of the Hutterite communities (1529) was this: the internal admonitions exercised under the authority of the baptismal submission were not to be revealed outside the church.[34] For all practical purposes, the power of the esoteric group was final in spiritual matters.[35] Neither the unbaptized selfishness and individualism of the Old Adam nor an outside unbaptized social control might invade the spiritual dominion thus separated out for the sovereign Holy Spirit.

Spiritual Government

Spiritual government rests, in the end, upon the threat of expulsion from the congregation of believers: the Ban. Those unwilling to be so harsh complained, "They blame us especially because we don't have the Ban. They mean to separate good from evil as was frequently done at the time of the Apostles."[36] In some cases experiencing the Ban might mean social ostracism (shunning, *Meidung*), but generally it meant the loss of privileges within the brotherhood. There is no compulsion in a voluntary association but this breaking of fellowship.

And if thy brother sin against thee, go, show him his fault between thee and him alone: and if he hear thee, thou hast gained thy brother. But if he hear thee not, take with thee two or more, that at the mouth of two witnesses or three every word may be established. And if he refuse to hear them, tell it unto the church: and if he refuse to hear the church also, let him be unto thee as the Gentile and the publican. (Matthew 18:15-17)

This New Testament ordinance was the beginning of every Anabaptist elaboration of the problem of government within the church,[37] and it is obvious that it presupposed a freely acting congregation which did not depend upon any worldly power but upon its own spirit of fellowship.[38] They said of the table of the Lord:

23. It is not to be used without the rule of Christ in Matt. 18, otherwise it is not the Lord's Supper, for without that rule every man will run after the externals; the inner matter, love, will be passed by, if brethren and false brethren approach or eat it.

Go forward with the word and establish a Christian church with the help of Christ and his rule, as we find it instituted Matthew 18 and applied in the epistles. . . .[39]

The secular government and questions of natural right were quite outside the discussion: "For the secret of God is not in outward respect of persons, even if he be king or kaiser, prince or count, noble or commoner, townsman or farmer, shepherd or poorer yet [in social status]. . . ."[40]

The most famous Anabaptist confessions of faith concerned themselves very largely with the matter of spiritual government. The second of the "Seven Articles" (1527)[41] dealt with this agreed practice of the congregations, and the fifth of the "Five Articles" of the Hutterites (c. 1547)[42] dealt with a special application of spiritual government: divorce between believers and unbelievers. In Anabaptist thinking, the majesty of the church paralleled the power of the magistrate (*Obrigkeit*) in the world, and the authority of internal government rested upon the loyalty of the membership.

After the people have received the Word of God and through water baptism in the presence of the church have put themselves under obligation to God to live according to the Word, and if they are ready to walk in newness of life and henceforth not to let sin reign in the mortal body, they still have need of medicine, because men are by nature children of wrath, evil and incapable, whereby the foul and stinking flesh together with the poisoned members may be somehow cut off, in order that the whole body may not be dishonored and corrupted.[43]

Hübmaier elaborated the theme extensively in two works: *Von der bruderlichen Strafe* and *Vom christlichen Bann*. He went into some detail to describe the process:

Leonard: What is fraternal discipline?

John: When one sees his brother sin, he should go to him in love and admonish him fraternally and privately to leave off such sin. If he does leave off, his soul is won. If he does not, then two or three witnesses should be taken, and he may be admonished before them a second time. If he yields it is well — if not, the church should hear of it. He is brought before her and admonished a third time. If he leaves off his sin the church has won his soul.

Leonard: Where does the church get its authority?

John: From Christ's command, given in Matt. xviii. 18, John xx. 23.

Leonard: By what right may one brother use his authority over another?

John: By the baptismal vow, which subjects everyone to the church and all its members, according to the word of Christ.

Leonard: Suppose the admonished sinner will not correct his course?

John: Then the church has the power and right to exclude and excommunicate him, as a perjurer and apostate.

Leonard: What is excommunication?

John: It is exclusion and separation to such an extent that no fellowship is held with such a person by Christians, whether in speaking, eating, drinking, grinding, baking, or in any other way, but he is treated as a heathen and a publican, who is bound and delivered over to Satan. He is to be avoided and shunned, lest the entire visible church be evil spoken of, disgraced and dishonoured by his company, and corrupted by his example, instead of being startled and made afraid by his punishment, so that they will mortify their sins. For as truly as God lives what the Church admits or excludes on earth is admitted or excluded above.

Leonard: On what are the grounds for exclusion?

John: Unwillingness to be reconciled with one's brother, or to abstain from sin. . . .[44]

Hübmaier was not, however, able to attain any high level of spiritual discipline in his Nikolsburg congregation. Nevertheless, there were those who carried through elsewhere and left spiritual progeny organized in disciplined congregations with an active use of the Ban. These were the Anabaptists proper.

The Ban was not, as the above quotation clearly shows, the final word. Nor was even the scriptural rule the only ruling power. Menno's difficulty with Leonhard Bouwens (1515-1582)[45] is an illustration of the need to balance off mercy and common sense against a harsh legalism in application of the ordinance. Nevertheless, in the instruction of the Master the Anabaptists beheld a certain concept of what His church should be like: a community of saints.[46] They said the Great Church was apostate, for there was no moral earnestness exercised in it by the power of the Ban.[47] The True Church was a strong band of ethical discipline and integrity: the repudiation of discipline from unbaptized authorities meant in no sense a relaxation — quite the contrary was the case. "Thus saith the Lord: I have elected you out of the world. Therefore despise the world. Thereby he could plainly recognize that there is a clear distinction between God's children and the children of the world."[48] The True Church must be separated from the evil and wicked: Israel must go out from Babylon and Egypt.[49] The doctrine of separation was pronounced throughout the movement. Thus at Schleitheim it was stated:

Fourthly, we are agreed as to separation. It shall occur between [us] and the evil and anxiety that the devil has planted in the world, in short, quite plainly we should not have community with them and run with them in the mass of their strife. . . . Now we are also clear as to the command of the Lord (II Cor. 6:17f) in which he says, be ye separate and go out from evil and he will be our God and we his sons and daughters. Further he warns us (Acts 18:4ff) to go out from Babylon and the worldly Egypt, that we partake not of their unrest and misery which the Lord will bring upon them. Out of all this we shall learn that everything which is not one with our God and Christ is nothing other than the strife which we should avoid and flee. . . .[50]

The teaching and practice of separation was resented by the Reformers, who were also prone to attribute it to spiritual pride. Thus Heinrich Bullinger wrote:

Their first article is that they maintain and demonstrate and teach the one, true, God-blessed church and community of Christ/

that they are raised up in their community through re-baptism [and] of course shall have nothing in common with either the Evangelicals or any other church. This article has two parts/ which they universally maintain. The first is that the Anabaptist churches are the only true God-pleasing churches. The other is that the Anabaptists hold to this their church alone/ and have no community at all with any churches and also not with the Evangelicals.[51]

The Hutterites criticized their Anabaptist confreres, the Swiss Brethren, because they mixed with the world and made no Christian distinctions regarding war taxes, woodwork on images, and "close practice" in commerce.[52] In similar terms the Polish Brethren later criticized the Dutch Mennonites on their ethical life: "In which respect the Mennonites err not less than the others, who will not walk proudly themselves [and] yet make for others proud clothes, paint pictures, make vases and more of such things, which the world should not have for the lust and pomp of its life."[53]

In spite of differences of degree, however, separation from the world was a dominant theme in all wings of Anabaptism. The words of Jakob Huter are representative:

Furthermore, we have sundered ourselves from worldly society and its loathsome life and have gone out from it.[54]

Thereby God makes us free and purifies us from the world and all its creatures through affliction. . . .[55]

Concern for a vigorous internal ethic was to them of paramount importance; hence disagreements were inevitable as to where the line should be drawn. But the quality of life of Christians was to do honor to God and the high calling in which they were set apart. As free associations Anabaptist groups felt themselves on solid Biblical ground in expecting all who stayed in good standing to concern themselves for the good name they bore in common. Within the pattern of authority of which the Ban was the outer limit, there was a whole fabric of common concern, mutual admonition, mutual aid.

Before the decades of savage persecution, the Anabaptists were sometimes men of some substance, but during these years they lost all rights before the law. Even under the rule of Philipp of Hesse, the only true tolerator among Protestant statesmen, the Anabaptists were treated as Jews before the law and forbidden to hold land.[56] This gave rise to special problems in property holding and within the structure of the family. Anabaptist goods were commonly confiscated if there were no orthodox heirs, and holding to a heresy was sufficient grounds for a spouse to plead for divorce in the courts. This general social situation, with its natural results, was countered by rules within the congregations and especially within the Hutterite communities: provisional approval was given for divorce from an unbelieving partner.[57] Christ brought not peace but a sword. And in all congregations counsel was given against marrying out into the "world."[58] "Thus the church of the *Schwärmer* took release from all bonds in order to separate itself from the godless. For the people of God would be spotted by relations with the godless."[59]

Unfortunately Heyer and other hostile commentators have not given enough attention to the fact that separation was not alone the fault of the Anabaptists; there is ample evidence that where left undisturbed they made good neighbors. But the brutal pattern of persecution heightened the eschatological note, atrophied the interest in the general social order, and hardened the rigor of enforcement of the special teachings. Only the Swiss Brethren attempted a more moderate policy within the family, based on St. Paul's advice for the winning of a non-Christian spouse to Christ. But what should be done in the case of a partner who refused to come into exile for the faith but rather submitted? In the Hutterite society the most strict policy was evolved, for family life was organically related to the spiritual power and authority of the congregation. In any thoroughgoing communism the family affords a problem of special difficulty, and the Hutterites were that Anabaptist wing most vexed by the conflict of sovereignties involved.

The place and function of the elders are also worthy of special attention. The Anabaptists redeemed lay religion, and did not view too favorably any professional workers — certainly not those supported by rents and tithes in the parish system.[60] In their oft-mentioned letter to Thomas Müntzer (September 5, 1524), Grebel and his group made a point for voluntaryism and asked him if he still accepted a salary. In the first years there were no paid clergy anywhere in the movement, nor were there regularly constituted governors of community life. Christ's office as High Priest (Hebrews 10:14 and I Peter 2:9) was thought to be exclusive. We have a picture of the primitive Christian democracy and the way it attained its discipline in an early testimony:

XVIII. They have no rulers, one is like the other, all equal in the service of one another.

XX. When they are together it is their custom to speak of the Word of God and to admonish one another in a brotherly fashion.[61]

As has been seen in the case of Menno Simons,[62] this informal picture was altered during the struggle against religious individualism and prophetism, and in the effort to survive persecution. Like the Early Church, the Anabaptists had their Montanists; and they were hardly more successful than the Early Church in maintaining the principle of charismatic leadership with the movement after they had suppressed individual inspiration. The conflict between Jakob Huter and Simon Schützinger was primarily this: whether "inspired" or "elected" leadership should prevail.[63] As the center of authority in the movement shifted from the protesting individual conscience to the newly gathered congregations governed by the Holy Spirit in the midst, a new principle of leadership came to the fore. Other wings of the movement besides the Hutterites had to deal with prophetic leaders from time to time, and the leadership chosen by the community came generally to prevail.

The Hutterites developed clearly defined offices. Peter Ridemann wrote back from prison, where he was writing the great *Rechenschaft,* an epistle (1540) admonishing the brethren to honor one another and especially the *"Dienner."*[64] These leaders were laymen, chosen by the congregation on the authority of the New Testament example of Acts 14:23; Acts 20:17 and 28; Titus 1:5; I Timothy 3, 5:17; I Corinthians 9:14.[65] They were chosen, on the basis of piety and dedication, to shepherd the community — to read, to warn, to teach, to punish. There were other officers. Among the Hutterites the most notable were the "shepherds" (*Hirten*), the missioners (*Diener des Wortes*),[66] the stewards (*Diener der Notdurft*).

The leaders were never supported by other than voluntary collections, and at a late date it was Menno Simons' boast that he had lived for years from brother to brother and had never gone hungry nor in want. Some of the Anabaptists claimed that a minister should support himself, by handwork as did Paul. Hofmann and Rinck and some other leaders of the early years did so, but voluntary support was most commonly practiced. Despite the presence of variant practices, it is evident that the Anabaptists as a whole shared certain prejudices rooted in the New Testament, opposed to a salaried hierarchy. No special class of professionals was to be allowed to diminish the sovereignty of the community of believers in matters of faith and order.

Above all, in the matter of spiritual government in its various forms the presence and sovereignty of the Holy Spirit was accented. In practice the congregation was the center of authority, but it was the congregation informed and guided by the Lord Himself. Because the various defensive tactics of the churches (Ban, shunning, separation) draw our attention, it is easy to forget that a very positive and far-reaching understanding of the benefits of divine governance and the common life underlay the structure. Thus Hans Umlauft wrote in a letter coupling the Ban with the practice of reaching a consensus:

How can there be a Christian Community where no Christian order and command is [maintained], with separation, the ban, discipline, brotherly love and other [practice]; further that one after the other may speak openly, give of his gifts and insights freely before the people at the appointed time, I Co. 14:54?[67]

In Menno also we find a very simple and direct confidence in the fruits of discussion aimed at the attaining of a consensus. He wrote in the preface to his *Meditation on the Twenty-fifth Psalm* (c. 1537):

Then if I err in some things, which by the grace of God I hope is not the case, I pray everyone for the Lord's sake, lest I be put to shame, that if anyone has stronger and more convincing truth he through brotherly exhortation and instruction might assist me. I desire with my heart to accept it if he is right. Deal with me according to the intention of the Spirit and Word of Christ.[68]

And in his *Foundation of Christian Doctrine* (1539) Menno contrasted the ambition for position of the worldly religious with those whom God commissions:

Yes, it was with this mission and vocation that all the prophets, apostles, and servants of God appeared. They did not appropriate this honor to themselves as do the preachers of this world; but like Aaron they were called of God, or by the spotless church, as has been said. They were driven into this office by the Spirit of God, with pious hearts, and did ever esteem themselves unfit to serve the people of God or to execute such a high and responsible office.[69]

In Peter Ridemann we find a similar understanding as to the cohesive force in the gathering of the faithful and their governance. "The primary, begetting force which gathers the church, is and remains for Ridemann the Holy Spirit."[70]

We come then to a new level of understanding of spiritual government, and of the role which the negative provisions played in maintaining the integrity of the Anabaptist congregations. We are confronted with a primitive Christian brotherhood, in which each believer has his definite role and responsibility in reaching a statement of the community decision. The social scientist may be justified in considering this one of the first manifestations of government by consensus. The church historian finds it one of the first patterns of lay government in Christian history, a historical moment when the professional monopoly of theologians and canon lawyers was broken in favor of the priesthood of all believers. For the Anabaptists themselves the case rested with a simple assertion of the sovereignty of the Risen Lord and the Spirit of Truth in the midst of Christian believers in meeting. A contemporary student has found in this the key to the uniqueness of Anabaptism: "Anabaptism roots ultimately on perpetual spiritual re-creation which derives its authority from the work of the Spirit among men thereby united, and not from ecclesiastical structure."[71]

Community

The suggestion has been made that there was a pooling of goods at the time of the revival in Zollikon, but even if the interpretation can be sustained we may conclude that there was never a closed economy among the Swiss Brethren as a whole.[72] There was throughout the entire Anabaptist movement a pledged communism of consumption ("community" might be a better word), but the creation of a total Christian communist economy was the work of the Hutterites.

There were various Biblical injunctions which served to enforce the surrender of acquisitiveness and self-interest required by the community. The Anabaptists recalled a favorite text of the medieval mystics:

In the 5th of Matthew Christ says: "Blessed are the meek [*die geistlich Armen*], for theirs is the kingdom of heaven." They are also those who, excused from the world, given over and abandoned for the sake of Christ's will, have no more ownership; whoever is driven by the Spirit into this poverty and submission, the same shall be blessed. But whoever stands in opposition shall be wretched.[73]

The argument for practice of community sometimes revolved around Matthew 19:29, "sell all thou hast"; or James 1:17, "every good and perfect gift is from above"; or another passage of similar freedom from the things of this world. The widow gave all she had. "See: all her wealth! . . . Therefore we shall practice all Christian community which is nothing more than (did) this evangelical widow."[74] Occasionally there appeared a general argument belonging to the early years of the movement — "the animals in the wood and the birds in the air are free" — reflecting the economic sentiments of the old peasant movements[75] rather than the idea of Christian community. But above all and most frequently we are referred in the Anabaptist tracts and testimonies to the second, fourth and fifth chapters of Acts, the vision of the church at Jerusalem.[76] For the church of Acts was a "covenant toward perfection," a model for the true fellowship of saints throughout the ages.

In conclusion, *ain* and *gmain* builds the Lord's house and is *rain,* but *aigen, mein, dein, sein* rends the house of the Lord and is *unrain.*[77]

> Gottes Wort Wär Nit so Schwär
> Wan Nur Der Aigen Nutz Nit Wär.[78]

Even the nursery rhymes taught the children community along with the alphabet. Back of the practice of Biblical communism was the purpose to revitalize the church; it was primarily a "vocational" witness of Christians rather than evidence of a general social hope. "When true Christianity was permitted to wane and depart, the community life became an unbearable burden, it failed utterly. Twice in their history the community of goods was abandoned by the Hutterites through religious decline, to be taken up again through a revival of religion."[79] The practice of community in its various forms and degrees must be understood, therefore, in terms of the Anabaptist concept of discipleship. It is an error, although a frequent one, to confuse their understanding of the internal ethic of the Christian Church with the social and economic radicalism of the revolutionaries.

In point of fact, the opponents of the Anabaptists learned fairly early to distinguish between their Christian communism and the economic gospel of the revolutionaries. The Hutterites strongly dissociated themselves from the events at Münster, and political authorities knew it even if the polemicists pretended not to. The questions directed in court toward traveling missioners indicate the various governments' knowledge of the difference between communism by voluntary submission and communism by violence (Münster). The sum of Anabaptist teaching was that a Christian should not have anything apart from his brother: both were pilgrims and walked the martyr's way, and their citizenship was in another city than the city of this world. The Hutterite pattern was simply a more thorough and more rigorously organized result of a teaching shared by Swiss Brethren, South German Brethren, and Dutch Mennonites as well. If any will not share, then the Lord's Supper may be closed to him.

Item: our Christian faith says, a holy Christian church and a communion [*Gemeinschaft*] of saints; whoever now recognizes the communion [*Gemeinschaft*] of saints with the mouth but does not maintain Community [*Gemeinschaft*], he is false.[80]

It is important to recognize that there was a heavy note of restraint in the Hutterite writing about community. There was none of the joy in poverty and simplicity which we remember in connection with St. Francis. The Hutterites left their accustomed ways with pain and heavy hearts, recognizing that the way they had chosen was the path of suffering and martyrdom. But they thought that individualism was a sin against God. Union with others in economic affairs was not an act of religious romanticism; neither was it an optimistic expression of social hope. It was the result of an inescapable religious mandate.

The stress upon selfless sharing characterized all groups among the Anabaptists, although communism was unique to the Hutterites. Hans Hut said that he didn't teach men to sell all their property, but to share with the needy.[81] Balthasar Hübmaier said that he stood for sharing but not communism.[82] This was the familiar interpretation during the first decade of Swiss domination of the movement, and it continued in all groups except the Hutterites and the fringe community at Münster. Envisioned was a community of consumption, quite thoroughgoing at times, but without much system and without compulsion.[83] "But whoever eats and drinks alone, the same has fellowship with Judas, who [it is true] ate and drank with the other disciples from the bread and drink of the Lord. But he would not have community in the common brotherly love. . . ."[84]

For Peter Ridemann of the Hutterites, on the other hand, community with Christ and one's fellows meant having nothing for self and holding all things common: "Community, however, is naught else than that those who have fellowship have all things in common together, none having aught for himself, but each having all things with the others, even as the Father hath nothing for himself, but all that he hath he hath with the Son, and again, the Son hath nothing for himself, but all that he hath, he hath with the Father and all who have fellowship with him."[85]

Wolfgang Brandhuber related the Hutterite communism to a historical necessity, and said that it might not be always fitting to have community of goods[86]; for him, the command of Jesus to share was what was important, not the particular external organization of it. Yet the Hutterites became, through the years, very critical of those who were not thoroughgoing in their submission to community rules: "a true Christian, who would be a Christian in name and work, shall have nothing of his own, and to the extent that he already has wife, children and goods, he shall limit himself and conduct himself as if he had none."[87]

Jakob Widemann debated with Hübmaier's successor, Spitalmaier, and complained especially that the loosely defined congregation at Nikolsburg was neglecting its duty to the refugees of the faith.[88] Thus there were real differences between the Hutterites and their Anabaptist brethren of other style, and these differences sometimes led to controversy and rancor. But all wings of the movement started at the same point: in time of need, especially, it is the duty of Christians to follow the model of life given by the early heroes of the faith. Only historical circumstance and cultural adaptation made the difference between the Hutterites and other Brethren.

The Lord's Supper

The Lord's Supper became an especially important symbol for the Anabaptists. They took the description of the remembrance as given in Matthew 26, Mark 14, Luke 22, and I Corinthians 11, and interpreted the event in the most straightforward and simple fashion. In the third of the "Seven Articles" (Feb. 24, 1527),[89] and in the second of the "Five Articles" (c. 1547),[90] the Mass was repudiated and the Supper treated as a memorial only.

He had taught the flesh and blood of Christ not transformed in the bread, only, as Christ had demonstrated it bodily they should understand it spiritually. The bread which he had broken was the Gospel; if he had not broken it it would not have come into the whole world. If they took and appropriated the word and clasped it in their hearts, as Christ had taught, they were benefited in spirit by the body of Christ; and the cup, which Christ had given his disciples, meant his suffering, the blood in the cup was the blood of Christ in the flesh of men; and, if the man was a Christian, he had the blood of Christ, and to the degree that suffering becomes flesh the cup was in blood.[91]

"I am the bread of life" (John 6:32-35) appeared very frequently during the course of the discussions,[92] the implication being that the Master was speaking in figurative fashion at the time of the Supper as well. They saw that the materialistic interpretation was not needed to give the true meaning. There were other scriptural arguments commonly used as well to establish the figurative sense of the words used by Jesus: e.g., Christ could not be many thousand times in the bread and also on the Cross.[93] He could not be "at the right hand of God the Father" and also in the bread.[94] The simple understanding of the Supper was the proper one, and the speculative and involved interpretation which the learned favored was plainly an effort to remove the demand for the practice of the community which was the real meaning of the Supper. In a Swiss Disputation, one of the priests attempted to give proof for the Mass when he was accused of lying in saying the true flesh and blood were there in the bread and wine. His Anabaptist opponent shouted, "We won't have the argument from philosophy; you shall argue through the Gospel!"[95]

The opposition of the radicals to the Mass was, after all, in the line of the Swiss Reformation.[96] But the Anabaptists went beyond the Zwinglian objections and also denied the special office of the clergy, the office which had given the rite its meaning and authority and objective character, and tied the ceremony to their general concern for a purified and perfected community. Baptism had been the center of debate in the first days at Zürich; in Wittenberg, where the Reformers held to the doctrine of the

real presence, it was the doctrine of the Supper over which controversy raged. Throughout the entire history of the Anabaptists,
however, both symbols were linked to the drive toward a rigorous
internal ethic. As with many sectarian movements from the time
of the Donatists on,[97] the moral and ethical character of both
celebrant and partaker were strenuously probed. And many
who were called into court for abstaining from the communion
services of the church of the land said that they could not attend because they were not worthy.

The Anabaptists believed that an unworthy person might
do great hurt to himself by taking part in the remembrance,[98]
and they defined unworthiness in ethical and moral terms. Moreover, a large part of the general unworthiness was due to the
fact that the masses belonged to no True Church purified and
disciplined by use of the Ban. It was an important matter for
the brethren to admonish each other and exercise the spiritual
government which would prevent the spiritual damage coming
from unworthy participation. Not just the individual but the
whole congregation should be worthy of the Supper: no one
should take part in a "mixed" celebration, where the evil and
good were not separated. Therefore they condemned the parish
meetings of the territorial church, where no spiritual government
obtained and the people nevertheless went to the Mass. "If one
refrained from sins, made penance and led a pure, improving
life, he still should not go to our Supper, for the flesh and blood
of Christ were not literally in our Supper as we maintain. But
whoever was pure from sin might break the bread as Christ
broke it. Wine and bread are only a remembrance."[99] So one
of the orthodox reported the Anabaptist attitude.

In this doctrine, as in the others discussed, we find the
cornerstone to be the concept of the true community of believers.
In court one of the Anabaptists said that Christ was present in
the community of faithful, and not in the bread and wine. "The
Christian community is his living temple, wherein he dwells and
remains, O brethren, in that and not in stone houses. Because
Christ will dwell in this [economy] he may not be in the baked
bread."[100]

In any case, the sacraments were only symbols of a certain relationship within the community and between the True Church and her Lord. The metaphor of the Didache reappeared frequently, being related to the working of God in a suffering and martyr people. Luther's *Von dem hochwürdigen Sakrament des heiligen wahren Leichnams* (sermon, 1519) told the story of the working of the corn and grapes to become bread and wine, and was a popular writing circulated among the radicals.[101] "As the bread which I give you, brought together from many kernels, is fused and united through the water, so will we be united through the faith that Christ died for us."[102] The Anabaptists spoke of this process as the kneading and working of a martyr people by the hand of God, a people worked and formed by the Master of history according to His own plan for them. The Supper was not a material partaking, "'but he had thereby instituted the cup of the New Covenant, which is Suffering.'"[103]

The Authority of Civil Government; Passive Obedience

The relation of the Anabaptists to the magistrate (*Obrigkeit*) is the most difficult problem in any study of their ordinances, and it is an area in which there is much dispute. Most probably the controversy is still current because the refusal of some of their descendants to bear arms is a very practical problem to a government which attempts to wage total war and still tries to respect conscientious objection. Among Mennonites it is a problem because the present structure of self-government is quite different from any which the forefathers could have imagined. Thus a contemporary Mennonite scholar has written: "It is at best questionable whether a definition of the separation of church and state worked out under an autocratic system of government can be made normative for a democratic system in which, theoretically, at least, the government is the people and thus inevitably includes every Christian citizen."[104]

There is further difficulty in analyzing the evidence from the early groups because of the existence of the state-church system as an exclusive and compulsive structure at the time. Certainly a good deal of the restraint of the Anabaptists toward government was due to their denunciation of official religion and its requirements. Further, the question of co-operation in a free society was not faced by any of the early leaders and groups; for the sake of their very existence they kept as far from the persecuting authorities as possible.

In submissions it was customary to require the recanting Anabaptists to swear to carry the sword and fulfill their bounden duty to the authorities. Among such civic duties was to go to church.[105] Conscription did not then exist, but it is plain that the radicals were striking at the very heart of feudal civilization when they refused sword duty to the lord or magistrate, and attacked the union of church and state. By their negative attitude they were just as dangerous to the establishment, in a certain sense, as the most obvious revolutionaries. "Concerning the worldly magistrate, we recognize indeed that it was established and ordered to chasten the evil, but it is not given that a Christian can or may be it, for Christ commands one shall not resist evil. Item, we shall love our enemies."[106]

The compulsory nature of the magistrate's role was not denied (and here again the Anabaptists have been widely misinterpreted), but the Christian's role was another one. If, as some have claimed, the early Christians brought about the collapse of Rome by their restraint, then just as truly the Anabaptists foreshadowed the collapse of feudal Christendom. It must not be inferred, however, that this was their intention. They took their stand purely upon the Biblical ground that Jesus said, "Love your enemies and pray for them that persecute you" (Matthew 5:44). "We wish and desire well for all men and would also do evil to none, whether pope, monk or priest, whether emperor or king, yes, whether any creature."[107] God in His good time purposed to give them the Kingdom, and the *Stille* did not plan to force the issue from any strategic considerations.

The Anabaptists were not alone in feeling uneasy about the widespread violence and warring in Christendom. There was a general scepticism about waging war among all the Swiss, derived in part from their relation to the mercenary system.

The pope, the emperor, and the king of France were the chief employers of Swiss troops. The mercenary system was not morally elevating either to the soldiers themselves or to the influential citizens who were pensioned by the foreign powers in consideration of their good offices. But it undoubtedly had the effect of destroying superstitious veneration for the church whose carnal battles they were hired to wage and of fostering freedom of thought. When in 1518 the pope asked for twelve thousand Swiss troops to fight against the Turks, they somewhat reluctantly promised ten thousand, adding that if he liked he might take in addition the two thousand priests.[108]

Zwingli revolted against the mercenary system, and in the first flush of his evangelical faith appeared to be a pacifist like Erasmus.[109] Bonifacius Amerbach so strongly disapproved of taking up the sword for the Gospel, in the Second Cappel War, that he vowed open sympathy for the Roman Catholics.[110] In the revulsion of Conrad Grebel against warring, we may perhaps discern the depth of feeling of a son that his father should have engaged in a dirty business.[111] But the objection of the Anabaptists was not Humanistic, cultural, or national. They were concerned first of all with the purification of the Christian witness, separating the True Church from power and political interest. Their attitude was not "pacifism," but rather "defenselessness" or "nonresistance" or "passive obedience."

In Anabaptist teaching, the magistrate as policing authority was of historical origin, given by God as a necessary control over men's drive to sin. Hübmaier dated the origin of government right after the Fall in Eden, third chapter of Genesis, verse sixteen. Ridemann dated it right after the deluge; until that time God ruled men directly.[112] Both revolutionaries and *Stille* were agreed that the power of the magistrate did not reach within the Christian Community,[113] but the latter made the distinction on a vocational basis. They had no hope of bringing into being a society without coercion. The duty of the Christian Community, and their first vocation, was spiritual perfection. "You shall not participate in strange sins. Therefore we don't carry sword, nor lance nor guns nor any kind of arms or weapons."[114]

As Jakob Huter put it, "They must put away all outer and iron weapons . . . and arm themselves with spiritual [weapons]."[115] The attitude of restraint toward the magistrate's calling and various functions related to it was based upon the thought that there were two different worlds, and the things pertaining to life in one were not proper in the other. In a sense the Anabaptists were already practicing the disciplines of the life to come.

All warring, upheaval, concern for worldly goods, killing, and hating were now forbidden within the new dispensation.[116]

Yet further it was noted that the Christian was not permitted to be a magistrate. Wherefore? The world regime is after the flesh, but the Christian regime is according to the spirit. Their house and dwelling is physical, in this world, where the Christian's dwelling place is in heaven. The world citizenship is in this world, but the Christian's citizenship is in heaven. Their warfare and armaments are fleshly and according to the flesh, but the Christian's arms and warfare are spiritual against the sovereignty of the devil. The worldly are equipped with armor according to the flesh, but the Christian's arms are the armor of God, that is truth, righteousness, peace, faith, sanctity, and with the Word of God. . . .[117]

There is in such teaching an eschatological note which is unmistakable, as though the things of the last age are different, and a small minority is already living the last age in the midst of a society of force and violence that is already passing away. Wars in the Old Testament were permitted, "for servitude was not yet separated from childhood and the way to dominion was not yet revealed."[118] The Christian was fighting a different battle with different weapons from those of the world. The angel with the sword in mouth indicates "that for us Christians also the sword doesn't belong in hand, but in the mouth — namely, the sword of the Spirit."[119]

The authority cited for this restraint toward government and civil functions was the New Testament command and example of Christ. Andreas Castelberger, the earliest to emphasize this testimony, considered the warrior no better than a murderer.[120] The Sermon on the Mount was enough for him, and the command of Jesus against the oath (taken by vassals and soldiers): "Let thy words be 'Yea, Yea,' and 'Nay, Nay'."[121] The Master forbade all swearing (Matthew 5:34 and James 5:12). As for executing the office of judgment and wrath, "we shall love our enemies." The Anabaptists observed that the magistrate cannot forgive enemies. His was by its very nature "an office of wrath" *(ain ampt der raach)*.[122] One Anabaptist confessed his misgivings about the absolutist position: "The Magistrate shall not kill, that was against the 5th commandment, yet he had doubts therein, as in Just Wars [*in billichen kriegen*]."[123]

Thus it was not always clear at what points the line might be drawn by various Anabaptist groups. Some said that they would support only the magistrate who obeyed the Bible: to exercise his office to put down evil and to aid the good. "Also we pray for all princes and magistrates and lords, that thou wilt enlighten them with thy divine truth, that they may use the power which they have received from thee for protecting the good and punishing the evil ones; and watch, that they stain not their hands in the blood of the innocent."[124]

But the more general rule was that the magistrate was given for the sins of the world and should be obeyed in all things favorable or adverse except those of conscience. This is essentially a position of *passive obedience*. The Swiss Brethren refused to bear arms but paid war taxes, for which the Hutterites criticized them.[125] The magistrate's office was generally enough to ban a person from the congregation, but Menno permitted some such to remain members.[126] Although there were differences in application of the New Testament aversion to violence, all Anabaptists went back to the Sermon on the Mount for proof and to the Early Church for example.

Only the revolutionaries seemed to have much general social concern. The *Stille* had almost no mind for questions of public policy and natural law. A more general pacifist note seemed to enter with the saying of Grebel that Christian should not kill Christian. A case of non-co-operation occurred among the slaves in the war galleys at Trieste (1539) who refused to put their hands to the oars although beaten for their passive resistance.[127]

There is no reason for supposing, however, that they would have refused to row as slaves for a ship engaged in peaceful pursuits. But these incidents were rare departures in an otherwise Bible-centered, church-centered, vocational nonresistance.

In reducing the various emphases of the peace testimony to a logical scheme, we note *three accents in the Anabaptist view of the magistrate:* first, their opposition to compulsion in religion; second, their opposition to revolution; third, their sense of destiny as the Church of the Martyrs.

The Anabaptist opposition to compulsion in religion grew out of their sense of the incongruity between the Early Church pattern and the establishments. When they were persecuted, they grew even more rugged in condemnation of the state church. The whole matter has been reviewed in connection with the idea of the "Fall,"[128] but it is useful at this point to call attention to the way in which it tied in to the Anabaptist nonresistance. The only power recognized within the congregations was spiritual government, and they kept their distance from magistrates who compelled religious conformity for political purposes.

The Anabaptist opposition to revolution grew out of their pessimism in regard to the uses of power and the prospects of social betterment in this world. After the Münster episode, all branches of the *Stille* reacted strongly against ethical concern outside the True Church, and vigorously asserted the authority of the magistrate within its proper sphere.[129] "Our will and mind are not, however, to do away with worldly government nor not to be obedient to it in goods and sanctions. For a government shall and must be in the world among men just as the daily bread and just as the schoolmaster must have the rods among the children. For because the great house of this world will not admit and let rule the Word of God, the knaves and rascals or children of this world who pursue no Christian piety must yet have a worldly and gallows-piety. . . . Therefore the magistrate is an institution of God."[130]

But the Anabaptists would not serve in the magistrate's capacity themselves: the calling of the Christian is to other work and disciplines. They reported that the Ban was exercised within the community, and their law-abiding quality was such that their restraint at this single point of faith should not lead any to think that they were not wholeheartedly for good order and sound government. It is patently false, although polemically popular, to confuse the Anabaptists with the revolutionaries.

The Anabaptist sense of destiny as the Church of the Martyrs is of highest importance. They were a disciplined lay community with a vivid eschatology. The Bible, which tells of the Good Shepherd, frequently calls His flock the sheep. "By sheep Christians alone were meant. A sheep is a meek, weaponless, submissive beast, that has no other defence for itself than to run as long as it can and may. And it resembles the governance of the sword not at all, as little as a sheep resembles a wolf or lion."[131] The Anabaptists taught, as indeed they experienced, that the Christians must expect persecution and exile, for this was the inevitable lot of those who submitted to Christ and would not wrestle for political control. It was also the martyrs' testimony which validated the authority of their Christian Gospel through the baptism of blood.[132]

In many quarters of the Mennonite movement today, the peace testimony has lost all eschatological content. In some cases it has been confused with Utopian pacifism, a product of post-French Revolution politics and post-Enlightenment philosophy. On the Continent the peace testimony has been generally abandoned, but in America it is associated with an agrarian economy and has survived. Dutch and German writers have attempted to show that the early Anabaptists were not really nonresistant in the complete sense, but rather opposed to revolution and restrained toward government because persecuted.[133] This interpretation has been combatted by the Americans,[134] who nevertheless sometimes combine the traditional testimony and cultural primitivism in a strictly "vocational" and certainly also non-evangelical way. It is hard to deny on the face of the records that the early New Testament literalism of the Anabaptists cuts through most of these differences, and a review of the Anabaptist vision of the nonresistant church as it was in the age of heroic witnessing makes such later disputes seem quite pragmatic and historical.

When we survey, both historically and doctrinally, the ways of "nestling back into the world," we are forced to the conclusion that cultural enclaves which have lost their missionary passion and their hope of a new world to come are hardly more true to original Anabaptism than those who have acclimated themselves to commerce and warring. For the "evangelical Täufer" linked their suffering nonresistance to the evangel of Him who commanded "Go ye into all the world" (Matthew 28:19), and they had great expectations of the time to come. They were certain that after the long centuries of the dispersion they were gathering together again the faithful people of the Lord, to be His Blessed Community and to live the life for which he gave precept and example. And in that restored community there dwelt the promise of great things to come on earth.

CHAPTER IV

The Great Commission

Myr ist geben alle gewallt ynn hymel vnd erden/ dar umb gehet hyn/ vnd leret alle volcker/ vnd teufft die ynn den namen des vaters vñ des sons vnd des heyligen geysts/ vnd leret sie halten/ alles was ich euch befolhen have/ vnd sihe/ ich byn bey euch alle tage/ bis ans ende der wellt. Matthew 28

Das Newe Testament Deutsch (Wittenberg, 1522)

Gehet hyn ynn alle wellt/ vnd predigt das Evangelion/ alle Creaturn/ wer do glaubt vnd taufft wird/ der wirt selig werden/ we aber nicht gleubt/ der wirt verdampt werden. Mark 16

Die erde ist des HERREN vnd was drinnen ist/
Der erdboden vnd was drauff wonet. Psalm 24.
Biblia/ das ist/ die gantze Heilige Schrift Deudsch (Wittenberg, 1534)

No texts appear more frequently than the above in the confessions of faith and court testimonies of the Anabaptists, and none show more clearly the degree to which Anabaptism was different in conviction and type from the intact and stable ways of magisterial Protestantism. The Anabaptists did not think of themselves as a minority witness, temporarily withdrawn until the Great Church should mend its ways. Neither did they accept the status of conventicles, little cells of piety, acting as a leaven within the great masses of baptized believers in the territorial churches. They believed that the Church of the Restitution, the True Church with its disciplined laymen, carried history. The Restitution which had occurred was full of meaning on the world map. The Anabaptists believed that they were forerunners of a time to come, in which the Lord would establish His people and His law throughout the earth.

It was the Holy Spirit who gathered and governed.

Therefore is such a people, community, assembly or Church gathered and led together by the Holy Spirit, which from henceforth ruleth, controlleth and ordereth everything in her. . . .

The children of God . . . become his children through the unifying Spirit. Thus, it is evident that the Church is gathered together by the Holy Spirit: also that she hath being and is kept in being by him, and that there is no other Church apart from that which the Holy Spirit buildeth and gathereth.[1]

The Spirit who gathered and governed was also a *sending* Spirit. "But after it had all been accomplished according to the Scriptures, and had been made new in Christ, He did not send out the scribes and Pharisees with Moses' law, but His disciples with His own doctrine, saying: Go ye into all the world. . . ."[2] Against the pattern of compulsion and territorial conformity, the radicals proposed to restore the New Testament missionary method of proclamation and letter-writing. Both revolutionaries and *Stille* had the missionary vision, although their understanding of the particulars of the approaching fulfillment differed greatly.[3]

No words of the Master were given more serious attention by His Anabaptist followers than the Great Commission. In the words of Menno Simons: "He sent out His messengers preaching this peace, His apostles who spread this grace abroad through the whole world, who shone as bright, burning torches before all men, so that they might lead me and all erring sinners into the right way. O Lord, not unto me, but unto Thee be praise and honor. Their words I love, their practices I follow."[4]

The form of the Commission seemed to sum up His whole teaching in a glorious program comprehending the whole world. The pilgrim, familiar seeker of the Middle Ages, was transformed in the fiery experience of the "evangelical Täufer"[5] into an effective evangelist and martyr. The pilgrim missioner, eschatological figure and personality type whose reappearance signified the break-through of the Age of the Spirit in Joachimitism,[6] became a characteristic type in the Anabaptist network of communities and congregations. His wandering footsteps and shedding of blood were a determined if not always systematic testimony to the influence of a lay mission which counted no cost too dear to him who would walk in the steps of the Crucified.

THE ANABAPTIST UNDERSTANDING OF THE COMMAND

Central to Their Testimony

According to Anabaptist understanding of right faith, the Great Commission was fundamental to individual witness and to the ordered community of believers as well. The proof text appeared repeatedly in Anabaptist sermons and apologetic writing. Confessions of faith and court testimonies gave it a central place, and the series of questions prepared by various authorities for use in court indicates that the governments expected it to be of prime importance in Anabaptist argument.[7] "Our faith stands on nothing other than the command of Christ (Matthew 28, Mark. 16). . . . For Christ didn't say to his disciples: go forth and celebrate the Mass, but go forth and preach the Gospel."[8] The very order of the words, conveyed His intent to His followers:

Firstly, Christ said, go forth into the whole world, preach the Gospel to every creature. Secondly, he said, whoever believes, thirdly — and is baptized, the same shall be saved. This order must be maintained if a true Christianity is to be prepared and though the whole world rage against it. Where it isn't maintained there is also no Christian community of God, but of the devil, and thereby of the whole world and all false Christians who alter it in their topsy-turvy order, and fight perversely.[9]

The evangel comes first, and then faith, and finally baptism. A failure to respect this Scriptural sequence indicated a lack of respect for the mind of Christ for His disciples: "Go forth into the whole world and preach the Gospel; whoever believes and is baptized the same shall be saved; for the preaching of God's word shall go before and not after baptism. . . ."[10] Baptism of those in whom faith was stirred by the preaching of the Gospel was the logical culmination of the mandate which begins, "Go forth!"

The article on believers' baptism in the "Five Articles" (c. 1547), confession of faith and second most important document of the Hutterites, found its cornerstone in the twenty-eighth chapter of Matthew and the sixteenth chapter of Mark.[11] The great missionary preacher Hans Hut baptized thousands, telling them to obey the commandments, preach the Gospel; he quoted the Great Commission during the simple service, and taught his followers to preach and baptize further under that mandate.[12] Other evidence is of a kind. For the Anabaptists, the freely spoken evangel was the moving force in a complete reworking of the Old Man, whose crucifixion and rebirth in the faith were sealed by the sign.[13] Only those of mature judgment passed through a crucial and transforming adult religious experience, and could rightly be let through the door to a responsible convenantal relation to God and to their fellows.[14]

Not only was the missionary mandate obeyed most seriously, but it was given sweeping application. *It applied to all Christians at all times.* By traditional exegesis the words were directed only toward Jesus' immediate audience, the disciples and apostles, whose travels to the far corners of the earth had long been a part of Christian legend.[15] After the Commission had run out, at the end of the Apostolic Age, "no one any more [had] such a general apostolic commission, but each bishop or ecclesiastical leader has his own church role or place."[16]

There had been from time to time vocational groups in the Great Church which strove to fulfill the Master's world view — notably the Franciscans.[17] *But the Anabaptists were among the first to make the Commission binding upon all church members.* In their organization, the promise to go where sent was part of the ceremony of admission to the True Church. They "went freely under the cross" where the representatives of the state churches dared not go, and for the Gospel's sake were made pilgrims and martyrs throughout the known world.[18] If, as a great historian of the missionary movement has described it,[19] the expansion of the faith has only in modern times become the concern and activity of the total membership rather than the princes, it is not too much to call the *Täufer* forerunners of the modern missionary movement.

Relevant to the Life of the Common Man

Not only was a new historical significance given to the Great Commission, but its application was made relevant to the life of the ordinary layman. The missionary mandate was no longer the prerogative of special orders or selected professionals. The layman was no longer limited to remaining obediently in his appointed place and status.[20] The Commission applied to the most simple believer and claimed him as an evangelist. Until this time the ordinary Christian had looked largely to the higher authorities, both secular and religious, to make decisions of policy and to carry the weight of Christian statesmanship. In the Church of the Restitution, the world view was no longer restricted to the powerful and educated. In Anabaptist opinion, the craftsman might make a better missioner than the cultured man. Jesus himself preached to men in terms of their trade, not with many books. "For the common man can be better informed by [lessons from] the creatures than through writing."[21] When the missioner Hanss Schmidt was asked about his studies, he told the authorities: "I study with pick and flail."[22] For the Brethren that was honorable and sufficient, and it better equipped him to go forth into all lands "in order to gather the sheep of the Lord" and "to fish for men" than would participation in the wranglings of the philosophers.[23]

There lies a deeper meaning here, as well: from the peasant who plows his field for the planting, the faithful were to learn how God works His people in fulfilling His purpose.[24] In suffering and travail, His faithful are plowed for the Kingdom's sake. And the ordinary layman, the common man, can best proclaim the Gospel to common men. The domination of the outward, the material, the powerful, will give way before the calm speaking of the simple Christian whose only authority is the Gospel. And it will be the babes, the naive, who will come through where those wise and understanding "after the flesh" will fail.

THE OPPOSITION OF THE REFORMERS
TO LITERAL OBEDIENCE

James Thayer Addison once summed up the attitude of the Reformers as follows: "For nearly two centuries the Churches of the Reformation were almost destitute of any sense of missionary vocation. The foremost leaders — men like Luther, Melanchthon, Bucer, Zwingli, and Calvin — displayed neither missionary vision nor missionary spirit. While conceding in theory the universality of Christianity, they never recognized it as a call to the Church of their day. Indeed some of them even interpreted 'Go ye into all the world' as a command already executed in the past and no longer operative. And the very few thinkers who rejected this deadening view remained without influence."[25]

Command Exhausted in Apostolic Age

Justus Menius, the famous Lutheran polemicist against the Anabaptists, acknowledged the point of difference in reporting "that the misleaders charge we are not true servants of the Gospel because we are sinners, and don't outselves practice what we preach; because we don't wander around in the world like the Apostles, but stay put and have definite residence and also have our appointed pay. . . ."[26] Menius stated flatly that "God sent only the apostles into all the world"[27] and attributed the parish system itself to the apostles:

Therefore the Apostles made disposition not only for themselves but also left behind them — through their disciples and in their writings/teachings and examples — [instruction] as to how the Church should act in calling servants of the Gospel: namely, that the servant of the Gospel does not travel here and there about the land — in one church today, another tomorrow; preaching one time white, another time black. But one servant steadily watches over his assigned church with true industry and remains with it, leaving other churches untroubled and in peace. Each church has thereby its own constituted servant and excludes strange unappointed spiritual gypsies — as is seen in *Acts* and in Paul's *Epistle to Timothy* iij and *Titus* j.[28]

This challenged the whole Anabaptist interpretation of the Early Church and the recapitulation of its life. The Reformers knew well the mobility of the Anabaptist leadership and congregation, and they opposed it in principle as well as in practice. Their criticism serves to establish further the fact that the Anabaptists conceived of the church as a voluntary association of committed pilgrims, who regarded the Great Commission as a clear ordinance of Christ.

Maintaining an Intact Christendom

Above all the Reformers resisted the "wandering" of the Anabaptists. Lutherans taught that each calling has divine blessing, and condemned the irresponsibility of those who cast loose from family and job to be missioners. They came, in their resistance to the corner preachers and radical congregations, to enforce tight authority in the parish. Orderly ordination and calling to the ministry were vigorously championed against the Anabaptists, "for they cannot establish their calling."[29] Such separatists were the devil's apostles, for "no one can have a ministry outside and without command or calling."[30] "Whoever preaches without an appointment, that one is an enthusiast [*Schwärmer*]."[31]

The Great Commission itself proved that the apostolic office had been established by the Head of the church as a definite *Amt*, and could not properly be the object of the enthusiasm of disorderly volunteers. Luther denied that Karlstadt's band of brethren at Orlamünde had the right to elect a pastor, for the power of appointment was properly vested in the prince and his office.[32] When Luther referred to a mission to the heathen world, he was almost always referring to the so-called Christian world. "We have among us all too many Turks, Jews, heathen, non-Christians, with both public false teaching and exasperating, scandalous life."[33]

At the Zofingen Disputation (1532), the Swiss Reformers

declared ordination properly rested only in the civil authorities; the Anabaptists on the other hand asserted that it was the duty of the Christian Church itself to ordain qualified ministers and maintain discipline.[84] Heinrich Bullinger based his critique of Anabaptist literal acceptance of the Great Commission on the premise that a true Christian remains in his calling and station and doesn't wander around.[35] Johannes Brenz suggested that if the Anabaptists were to erect a new system of apostolate outside the magistrate's control, like the apostles, they should also prove their authority by miracles.[36] Only one writer among the Reformers, Adrianus Saravia (1531-1613) published a book claiming the apostles could cover only a small part of the world and that the mission was still a duty of the whole church; against him Theodor Beza wrote a counterattack again asserting that the Great Commission, discharged by the apostles, was no longer operative.[37] As late at 1651 the theological faculty at Wittenberg put out a *Gutachten* against missionary work: First, the apostles preached the Gospel to the whole world in their time; secondly, the Commission was exhausted. The heathen outside Christendom were under the judgment of God. The missioner's *Amt* was a matter of personal privilege for the apostles, but is now controlled by the church order and appointment system.

This was the pattern of opposition in territorial Protestantism, although on one occasion Butzer gave the spiritualizers' answer to the Anabaptist emphasis on the Great Commission: Baptism is only an outward form anyhow, and what occurs within is alone important. "It is however certainly not to be concluded that because there's no baptism there is no faith. For it cannot be established that baptism and faith are bound together. Baptism is a sign of the saving from sins; this occurs before a man is baptized."[38]

The student of Sebastian Franck or other spiritualizers will readily note that to avoid the binding quality of the Great Commission, Butzer here took a position as destructive of the church and her mission as the arid scholasticism of those who simply denied its force for later centuries.

What the Reformers were committed to maintain was the fiction of an intact Christendom and one which at that had already slid far towards particularism. While the orders, particularly the Jesuits and other post-Reformation orders, brought a new burst of missionary energy in the Roman Catholicism of the sixteenth and seventeenth centuries, the dominant Protestantism was stagnant until the rise of Pietism nearly two centuries later brought a missionary energy and world mindedness into magisterial Protestantism.

The Anabaptists, on the other hand, believed that the Early Church was the time when the missionary command was obeyed most faithfully, and that here too the Church of the Restitution would recover a lost virtue. Indeed, those called by Jesus were known as "missioners" (*Evangelisten*); Matthew 28 was the first order, and Luke 24 the second.[39] Christ did not conceive of winning by iron or prison, but by the glorious and contagious forthgoing of the inspired community.[40] The Anabaptists contrasted the winning of the world by free evangel with the compulsion which had controlled the Great Church's fallen estate. The community organized about an evangelical purpose, like the True Church of the first centuries, was to be a standing testimony to religious liberty.

THE RECAPTURE OF EARLY CHRISTIAN MISSIONARY ZEAL

The Method:

Religious liberty, which is frequently considered to be the major contribution of the Free Churches, consists of at least three factors:

1. Affirmation of the New Testament method of the expansion of the faith;
2. Affirmation of the Holy Spirit as the sending and disciplining authority in the church;
3. Rejection of the sword as a means of evangelization and as an instrument of church government.

We are dealing here with the way in which the first factor became part of the Anabaptist recapitulation of the Early Church ideal.

It is notable that the Schwenckfelders and Anabaptists were frequently thrown together in proscriptions. Their meetings faced many of the same problems vis-à-vis the persecutors. Both of these evangelical groups were threats to the establishments, and in some respects they had a common strategy. When Luther held fast to the medieval parish system, Schwenckfeld defended the Pauline missions method of letter-writing and visitations.[41] A definite pattern of charismatic organization had emerged in the early years of free evangel, in the Early Church, and the same development would characterize the church in the New Age.[42] Schwenckfeld's quarrel with the *Täufer* was because they established Biblical rule, notably government by elders and practice of the Ban (Matthew 18); to his mind this coercion of the free movement of the Spirit was as wrong as any compulsion exercised by secular government.[43] His conception of the Restitution was limited to the free preaching of the Gospel; the Anabaptists also affirmed the evangel but built upon it a disciplined New Testament community. Both Anabaptists and Schwenckfelders dreamed of the Early Church, and both strove to reestablish the free proclamation of the faith and to free it from corruption and compulsion.

The gathering of voluntary religious associations[44] by a freely and comprehensively conceived evangel, sealed by believers' baptism, constituted in early times a challenge to the imperial power — and in the sixteenth century was a threat to magisterial Protestantism. The establishments sought to offset the winning power of the broadly conceived and energetically pursued mission by infant baptism. This bulwark of the standing order was introduced in the Roman Empire, according to Jakob Huter, as a blunt reaction of tyranny to the power of the Great Commission.[45]

The maintenance of infant baptism and compulsion in religion by the state churches of the Reformation placed them in the period before the Restitution, in the fallen time of the Great Church. The words of the New Testament were clear enough, and the example of the Early Church could hardly be misinterpreted. The Anabaptists looked out upon the known world as a great missionary territory, and they sought to evangelize on the comprehensive scale of the great heroes of the past.

The Heroic Prototype

In the life of the Anabaptist congregations the man of the Early Church reappeared. He was a hero with one supreme loyalty, to Christ his Master. He performed miracles. His persecutors sometimes died terrible deaths.[46] He strove to obey literally the counsels of perfection which were now binding upon every believer, and he lived "loose from the world" as a pilgrim, missioner, and martyr.

From prison a pilgrim of the faith wrote of his condition: "I am cut loose from all the world, from wife, from father, and mother and sister according to the flesh, and from all men; but that is right; Christ was also cut loose from all men and from his disciples; it is enough that I be as He was. . . ."[47] This ascetic emphasis led to a glory in pilgrimage and a triumph in martyrdom. Scores of missioners traveled from Waldshut throughout Switzerland, from Zürich through the Tyrol and southern Germany, and finally, from Moravia as far as Venice, Amsterdam, and Krakow. Lay evangelists moved among the corner congregations, threading all Europe, and a chain of synods and free gatherings tied the movement together. Occasionally we find rather startling evidence of the wide holding of Anabaptist opinion. A Hutterite missioner was martyred at Aachen, October 19, 1558. When Hans Beck was in prison at Passau, delegates from a Christian brotherhood (Anabaptists?) came from Salonica in Greece and held fellowship with him.[48]

Missioners were bound by Scripture to travel and carry the word, and they were bound by church discipline to be pilgrims for the faith wherever sent. "Blessed is the man whom the Lord finds watching when he comes. First he speaks of cutting loose — in this, we have to understand to wander, that we shall lift up our countenance and thoughts to heavenly things so that the world will not spot us."[49] The missioner was also instructed to maintain his vigorous ethical testimony against the corruptions and compromises of the world: "Furthermore we shall light our light; that is the light whereby they see our good works and glorify our father who is in heaven. . . ."[50] (Matthew 5:14!) The Anabaptists felt that God Himself showed them where to go and bring their testimony of word and deed, and the land should not be forbidden them: for the earth is all the Lord's (Psalm 24:1).[51] When Matthias Binder was held for questioning and warning, this proof text came out with peculiar pathos in his pilgrim's testimony: "The question if he would leave the principality he answered with a clear 'No', for the earth was the Lord's. He didn't know yet where the Lord was leading him, or in what land his death was fixed."[52]

The deliberate strategy which marked the later period of missionary endeavor was hardly a part of the early picture. The faith spread by persecution, exile, the journeying of craftsmen, the haphazard wandering of lay preachers.[53] Anabaptist leaders at first wandered as pilgrims, seeking relief from persecution, and shepherding from time to time the little groups of the faithful. As persecution grew more savage, hundreds of families took to the road, moving slowly eastward toward the Moravian settlements. A whole people thus became pilgrims, exiles for Christ. Hutterite missioners such as Brandhuber and Ridemann and Walpot and Glock worked among them and helped many to make the trip. Others applied to the Brethren directly for aid in migrating, and a "Servant of the Word"[54] was sent to investigate and make a recommendation.[55] That their judgment was not infallible is evidenced by the watering down of vigorous internal discipline due to the advent of economic refugees,[56] as well as by the number who later went home and made submission.[57] Nevertheless, the Moravian colonies became through the devotion of the great leaders and the discipline of their people perhaps the greatest missionary center of the sixteenth century. The pilgrim people became a great intentional power for spreading of the Gospel to every creature, and their internal community structure was organized to sustain the enterprise.[58]

There was a definite transition from the Anabaptist pilgrim, who evangelized and taught wherever he found temporary refuge from the hounds of the established order, to the missioner whose trips were assigned as part of a grand strategy of spiritual conquest. By and large the establishment of the Hutterite economy in Moravia may be used to mark the line between one type and the other.

For an example of the early itinerant evangelist, committed to spiritual independence from the things of this world and destined to early martyrdom, we may consider the Swiss leader, GEORG BLAUROCK (c. 1492-1529).[59] Blaurock was outstanding for his wide travels and noteworthy because he linked the circle at Zürich with the congregations in the Tyrol and the colonies in Moravia. Blaurock and Stumpf were those who pressed Zwingli most insistently to gather a purified "community of all things as also the apostles [had it] in Acts 2."[60] Blaurock led the little band on to the first adult baptism when Zwingli refused to move in the desired direction, and the simplicity of Blaurock's life and witness won many common people to the movement. A powerful preacher, utterly fearless in commanding a hearing for the Word, he was popularly called "the second Paul," "sturdy George." At Zollikon a crowd of a hundred and fifty persons was swept into mass baptism by his preaching, and at Hynwyl he entered the chapel and preached to two hundred people before the regular minister arrived.[61] When imprisoned, Blaurock said Christians should go out as missionaries as Paul indicated, and the magistrate was not necessary in matters of faith. "The earth is the Lord's." He was driven into exile and wandering, and in May of 1529 began his great work in the Tyrol, laying the foundations there for an Anabaptist movement which later supplied large numbers of members of the Christian colonies in Moravia.[62] Among those who watched his heroic death at the stake was a boy, Peter Walpot, who later became the greatest missionary executive of the Hutterite Brethren.[63]

The "evangelical Täufer" carried on extensive missionary cultivation rotating around several centers of the new life. Even before the Moravian settlements grew powerful, there was occasional central planning. The original circle at Zürich scattered widely and apparently on a spontaneous basis: Blaurock, after working with Manz in the Grisons, went on to the Tyrol; Reublin and Sattler went to Alsace and Swabia, Hetzer to Nürnberg and Augsburg, Gross to Strassburg and Augsburg. Waldshut, center of a great reformation under Hubmaier, was the center of concentric circles of influence: Ulrich Teck and Jakob Gross were especially active in trips from this base of operations.[64]

Recorded planning began with the famous Martyr Synod of Augsburg, August 20, 1527, which could as well be termed a Missionary Synod.[65] This synod not only effected co-operation between the parties led by Hans Hut and Hans Denck, but divided the land on a grand map of evangelical enterprise. Brethren were sent out from it to centers in South Germany, Switzerland, and Moravia. Those attending included outstanding leaders and missioners — Denck, Hut, Jörg von Passau,[66] Hetzer, Jakob Gross, [67] Jakob Dachser[68] Sigmund Salminger, Eitelhans Langenmantel,[69] Leonhard Dorfbrunner,[70] Gall Fischer[71] — most of whom died as missionary martyrs within a few years. The fate of an Anabaptist missioner ("agitator" in Christendom) usually was sealed without adequate trial or hearing. But the answer of the heroes of the Restitution was the gallant testimony of the cup of blood. Persecution only changed them from wandering pilgrims to missionary strategists, ready when the time came to be martyrs also.

The cost in trained leaders was tremendous in the early years, before semi-permanent bases of operation had been established and the means of support and communication worked out. Only two or three of the Martyr Synod lived to see the fifth year of the movement. (A long list of those martyred, 1527-1531, is still extant.[72]) In Switzerland and South Germany, the leadership and supervision of the congregations fell into the hands of laymen, supported by the occasional supervision afforded by visiting missioners.

The unarmed knight of the faith, whose chief virtue was long-sufferingness (*Gelassenheit, leijdzaamheid*),[73] became the character type of the movement. The knightly symbol was revived to describe the weaponless defender of truth, God's champion against the powers of this world's darkness. "In place of the athlete the knight is at the point of conflict . . . in place of the arena, the tourney or field of battle is entered. In this sense the Anabaptists speak of the battle of the Cross which must be fought. For martyrdom is no case of laziness, but of strength . . . only the Hero can go the martyr's way."[74] This spiritual warfare has run all through history, from the dualism of Cain and Abel through Judas and Jesus to the persecutors and the Anabaptists.

All Biblical writing speaks entirely of the suffering of the elect from Abel up to the apostles. Therein is the lamb slain from the foundation of the world.[75]

I pray to God . . . that in carnal souls Christ will create and illuminate the eternal fire of his love, the soul courtrobe of all Christians. Even if today there is no Abel without a Cain; no Jacob without an Esau; no Peter without a Herod; no Paul without a Nero; God loves us just the same: yes, the old God of Israel — the ruler of the earth — will not let us be overcome. He gives to all of us a free, constant spirit and an unflinching heart in all trouble. May this remain true.[76]

In a certain sense, then, Christ's example was made a type of all suffering in the world, and the fact of suffering itself achieved divine significance. "Even as you contend in knightly fashion for the truth, so will the Lord God contend for you."[77]

Economic Factors of Importance

No set of ideas can survive, nor can it even come to birth, except "in the fullness of time." In particular, the theoretical pattern must be related to large historic forces that create the atmosphere in which the intellectual movement can live and give concrete form to its internal drive. ⌈At the time of the Restitution there were certain given factors including important economic developments, which favored the emergence of a new solidarity and joined forces with the Anabaptist vision of religious reform to make a new style of Christian Community workable. ⌋

The sixteenth century was a time of social unrest and economic upheaval, of revolutionary dreams and attempted reforms. In an economy made fluid by commerce with Asia and wealth from America, craftsmen and peasants found themselves displaced. These were the chief classes to produce programs and centers of revolt, to respond most readily to the intense eschatology of the Melchiorites, and to go in goodly numbers to the Christian communist villages in Moravia. Though court records show that many who joined the colonies had had some substance, the Hutterite mission found ready response from the hungry and depressed as well as from the religiously dissatisfied.[78] Journeymen without fixed place of residence or master were a common sight in this age as they wandered from city to city. If they were also Anabaptist in sympathies, they added to their testimony that Christ alone was "Master" (*vorsteer*). The Anabaptist craftsmen transformed social misfortune into a religious vehicle, and glorified in "living loose from the world."

Groups disjointed by a changing economy became wanderers in the land, their economic status and style of life throwing them into constant contact with the large numbers of religious expellees and persecutees. On the social side they were torn loose and dispossessed; on the religious side they were generally seekers if not adherents of some Left Wing movement. Women imprisoned at Erlangen in 1527 reported that their husbands left, seeking the word of the Gospel where it might be found and consigning the children to their care. One journeyman said, "I will go and will search out the old and new faiths [to see] which is the true and best."[79]

The savage persecution loosed on the Anabaptist congregations threw hundreds more into the general currents of economic and religious unrest. Poor relief records show the travel of families toward Moravia. Most of them were, like Veit Frick, "a poor, unpromising people, that have to do their daily work and have many children."[80] Standard processes for confiscation of property and goods were worked out in the courts, and affected the most able craftsmen and farmers as well as those cast adrift by economic circumstances.[81] Whole families were uprooted, and many men traveled from city to city leaving families to fend for themselves.

Those able agriculturalists or handworkers, who were expelled from their former stations by religious persecution rather than by unrest, constitute a somewhat different phenomenon from the individual wanderers. But displacement for religious causes became increasingly important with the years. Such dissolution of social bonds was a permanent and inevitable function of religious territorial agreements like that of Augsburg, 1555. In the years of preparation and early ingathering, the individual wanderer was important. Later, under the impact of community life and discipline, the collective responsibility for the mission loomed large. The more responsible groups were concerned to maintain a sound and integrated economy within the fellowship of believers, and within the Hutterite communities real honor was tendered craftsmen in terms of their work.

But in the larger society there was a looseness of relationships toward job and family which the Reformers considered thoroughly irresponsible,[82] without realizing that it was at least as much a product of economic change and political repression as it was of radical religious separatism. They could not understand the apparent instability of one who "had a wife and four children, no home place and was the citizen of no city."[83] They hoped to carry over from medieval civilization those relationships which made for a stable society, and did not comprehend the fact that economic and religious change, coupled with the pluralism of religious persecutions which they themselves justified, made such stability impossible. To the religious radical, driven by persecution and the Lord's Commission, all such considerations were "worldly." We can almost hear the Anabaptist say to the authorities of the Great Church and the magistrates who tried to hold him fast in his "natural" responsibilities: "I no longer live, but Christ in me and the world crucified in me!"[84]

Just as economic displacement joined forces with the religious drive to make wandering and pilgrimage common, so the establishment of a planned economy in Moravia became the cornerstone and the surety for a consistent and planned missionary effort. The practice of Christian Community established in Moravia was intimately tied to Anabaptist evangelical operations in the German-speaking lands. The Great Commission itself seemed to argue for the kind of selflessness best expressed by a strong discipline of community or communism.[85] In all Anabaptist groups a communism of consumption functioned for the state of the evangel, and the Hutterite communities maintained their strongest internal discipline during the years of ardent missionary passion.[86] A base of operations was built which served the entire movement, and the most missionary minded were the congregations fraternally related to that economy.

Congregational communism was introduced when the non-resistants under Jakob Widemann separated from the followers of Hübmaier after the Nikolsburg Disputation,[87] establishing themselves on the apostolic disciplines. They were joined in 1529 by Jakob Huter, who had been working with Georg Zaunring in the congregations founded in the Tyrol by Blaurock. Huter saw in the new religious economy of Widemann's followers "the communion of saints" of his ideals. Huter worked as a missioner until 1533, when he brought the last group from the Tyrol,[88] and took responsibility as leader[89] in the Auspitz community which Reublin and Zaunring had established (1530) in secession from Widemann's autocratic leadership.[90] In three years the extremely able leadership of Huter left an indelible mark on the communities which came to bear his name.[91] These groups concentrated on the practices of community (*Gemeinschaft*) and separation (including *Ehescheidung,* a special phase of spiritual government),[92] and laid the groundwork in the discipline of a missionary people who reached out from Venice to Aachen to win men to "community" in Christ.

The strength of the Hutterite missionary economy was evidenced by acquisitions not only from the "world," but from the more loosely organized Swiss Brethren[93] and the Gabrielites and Philippites, whose leaders had originally resisted Huter's energetic program.[94] Through the years the finest Hutterite leaders approached the erring Brethren for union,[95] and the last group came in about 1565. When a man such as Ulrich Stadler, leader of the "Austerlitzers," was gained (1545), the vision of "the pilgrim of the Lord" was accented among the Brethren.[96] In Stadler's mind pilgrimage for the faith required a strong discipline: there are some who say all should be by free will, but the Biblical requirement of communism and rule by elders was plain.[97]

In PETER RIDEMANN (1506-1556), who came to Moravia in 1531[98] after succeeding Brandhuber as leader in the groups in the land of the Ens, the Brethren found a most powerful leader. He was author of the 1540 *Rechenschaft,* which became the basic document of the movement.[99] He was the Hutterites' outstanding hymn-writer. He served for years as minister to Gabrielites in Franconia and Nürnberg, and to the loosely knit *Täufer* groups in South Germany.[100] After decades of service in bringing groups in ten's and twelve's to Moravia,[101] and in other positions of community leadership, Ridemann died a natural death on December 1, 1556. His most notable contribution was in organization and discipline, but his importance as missionary teacher and executive must be underscored. As with other leaders, the tight community life was a function of Ridemann's world view.

The Hutterite Brethren developed one of the most perfect missionary organizations of the sixteenth century, and strongly supported the work in the Tyrol, South Germany, Hesse, and even in the Netherlands, with personnel and place of refuge. The original Anabaptist impulse to restore the life and disciplines of the Early Church survived most impressively in those congregations which were most missionary minded.

QUIET ESCHATOLOGY

However be comforted in your pious Christian hearts, realizing and accepting indeed that it has been so for all the prophets, Christ the Lord, his apostles, and in fact all saints from the beginning of the world, yea all them whom the Lord God has loved. Such is plainly and frequently demonstrated for you without gloss, namely, that all lovers of divine truth will be elect saints and all will be driven and hounded until the Judgment, as the Bible gives us sufficient evidence and shows in all places.[102]

Eschatology a Common Ground for Revolutionaries and Nonresistants

At the core of the formal organization of both revolutionaries and nonresistants there was a missionary mind. Even the radicals at Wittenberg sent out twelve missioners to proclaim the day of wrath and judgment, quoting the Great Commission and calling for moral reform.[103] A dozen years later, when the New Jerusalem was established at Münster, missioners were sent forth to gather the people of the New Age, and all northwest Germany contributed supporters.[104] March 24, 1534, was set as the day of mass migration, and although the authorities stopped most large groups, Münster continued to be even during the siege a center of the most excited evangelism. As the siege intensified, evangelism gave place to prophecy and the New Zion looked forward to a world revolution, the slaying of the godless, the restitution of all things.[105] They proclaimed that in that very generation Christ would come again, His Kingdom would come on earth, and all the ends of the earth would bow before Him.[106] "God's people, who remain eternal . . . must inherit the earth and establish Christ the king to rule over the whole world."[107]

The Restitution of the true apostolic church and the gathering of the Church of the Dispersion were to lead on directly to the restitution of God's law in the world. Unbelievers marveled at the calm assurance with which the faithful faced their unlikely prospects, as for instance when Jan Matthysz led a futile sortie of two hundred hymn-singers to disperse the besieging forces. Even after the revolutionaries "let drop the apostolic weapons to the earth and seized the armor of David,"[108] their spirit of certainty was a wonder to the sceptical. Through "special revelation" and not through lack of expectancy they took up the sword.[109] The missionary passion and eager world view of the revolutionaries never flagged, and in both significant social explosions (in the Peasant Revolt and at Münster) constituted an essential part of their eschatology.

We recognize Hans Hut as the bridge in the early period between the revolutionary section of the Left Wing of the Reformation and the evangelical Anabaptists. [110] When he agreed during the Missionary Synod (1527) to give up appeals to violence, he did not cease to travel and preach: a large percentage of those called up by the authorities in central Germany attributed their conversions and baptisms to Hut.[111] No missioner traveled more widely and constantly; he won so numerous and enthusiastic a following that he was accused of drugging the multitudes with a potion.[112] When held by the authorities before his death he testified in significant words:

> The word which stands on Mark 16 had moved him to preach, namely, that preaching was first, afterwards faith, and thirdly baptism. And one must let the word of the Lord stand. [He is] not to do anything apart from it, [and] also shall depart neither to the right nor the left, according to the last of Matthew that one shall first teach and afterwards baptize. Item, also in Acts 19 it is written that John called some to repentance and baptized those whom the Apostle Paul himself later permitted to be re-baptized.[113]

Hut was first a book peddlar associated with Thomas Müntzer, and in Jörg Haug's church at Bibra he called upon the peasants to take the sword against the magistrate.[114] In the summer of 1526 Hans Denck won him to the nonresistant position, and he confirmed it in a later meeting of the Anabaptist leaders; the following year he debated with Hübmaier in several meetings at Nikolsburg which led to the split-off of the *Stäbler* and the establishment of nonresistant/communist communities. In preaching and winning thousands[115] he would begin by citing the Great Commission, and pass on to a fiery proclamation of the coming again of Christ.[116] The structure of his message did not change when he repudiated a violent ushering in of the Kingdom. In fact, the chiliastic mood stayed with many of the *Stille* after revolution was repudiated. Some said that Armageddon occurred whenever a Christian bore persecution.[117]

We have already seen that among the nonresistant Anabaptists, the missionary personality and congregation were of primary importance. They interpreted the very meaning of history in terms of the world mission of the True Church. The

True Church of the Restitution, like the individual heroic prototype, was *a pilgrim church, a missionary church, a martyr church.* Throughout history the True Church had been both forbidden and persecuted. "It is solidly packed in God's word and the three words: the first, many are called but few are chosen; the second, the way of God is narrow and straight and few there be who find it; the third, not all who cry unto me, Lord, Lord, shall enter the Kingdom, but those who do the will of my heavenly father, they shall enter the Kingdom."[118]

Although the authorities were perfectly capable of making the necessary distinction between those who actively opposed the magistrate and those who only refused to obey on matters affecting their faith, they generally regarded all corner meetings as hostile to ecclesiastical and political order. The radicals in turn justified their small, secluded meetings: "The gospel is not to be preached openly in churches, but only in secret byways and privately in houses."[119]

The True Church is where two or three are gathered together in the Lord's name and not in the "idol-temples."[120] Indeed, since creation, only a little remnant has gone the right way, and this band of elect has been anonymous and persecuted. For the radicals, the forbidden church was the True Church.[121] "For the Babylonian harlot who sits on the seven hills, I mean the Roman Church, a synagogue of the living devil, only spits out all the children of God and drives them into wastelands, into their byways."[122] They believed that it was God's plan that His people should be strangers and pilgrims in the world and, as citizens of a better city, persecuted and hounded in this one. "For power is given to the beast to fight against the saints and triumph over them — not in spirit but in the flesh. For the suffering of Christ must also be fulfilled and made concrete in their limbs."[123]

The martyr church was to be able to establish its place in history in terms of its suffering. In the special logic of Anabaptist eschatology Menno wrote:

O Lord, with that unjust hatred they hate me; whom have I wronged in a single word? Whom have I shortchanged a penny's worth? Whose gold, silver, cow or cattle, ox or ass have I desired? I have loved them with a pure love, even unto death; Thy Word and will have I taught them, and with earnest diligence I have shown them by Thy grace the way of salvation. Therefore my enemies are so many, and hate me with cruel hatred.[124]

It is the wolf which drives others; the sheep is a poor, defenseless beast. The Anabaptists made much of the struggle and suffering in Hebrews 11:33-38, and of the analogy between baptism and death ("blood-baptism"), in restoring the martyr theology of the Early Church. Martyrdom was the carrying power of the movement, the triumph beyond obvious defeat, the final long pilgrimage free from the world and its controls.

The Anabaptists saw themselves living again the painful persecution of the apostolic church, hounded by cruel political and religious lords who had no mercy for the defenseless, the sick and helpless.[125] The author of the first confession of faith (Schleitheim, 1527) was sentenced to death on particularly barbarous terms,[126] and his martyrdom left a deep impression upon contemporaries and later generations. The Anabaptists knew what it was to invite new members to "take up their cross." In this trial by fire and water and the sword, where their faith was tested as gold in the furnace, they were fortified by the memory of Christ's suffering and by the hymns and records of other brethren of the cross.[127] The first hymns were from prison,[128] and the finest records were stories of the martyrs who "have sealed in knightly fashion the truth of God with their blood."[129]

The full believers' baptism, of which water was the first order, was according to I John 5:8: "And there are three that bear witness in earth, the spirit, and the water, and the blood: and these three agree in one."[130] The true follower of Jesus will not hesitate to drink the cup he drank (John 18:11); indeed he will expect it.[131] ("For whoever will not suffer with Christ also will not rule with Him, and whoever doesn't have this holy spirit is no Christian."[132])

A Theology of Suffering

Thus the Anabaptists developed a theology of suffering, transforming the persecuted remnant into a triumphant church, rich in historical significance and bringing the means of present salvation.[133] The idea of suffering became their moving power and hope in the Third Age, a refined and nonviolent parallel to the revolutionary conquest conceived by the radicals at Münster. "Suffering is the way, the door, and the means to God, the door into the sheep-stall."[134]

In baptism the believer learned that he was to leave all selfish concern — including private ownership — behind, and through the cross and suffering come to salvation. The internal significance of suffering is revealed in Anabaptist records of the uses of communism and the Ban. When threatened by the authorities, Hanss Schmidt said, Let the Lord's will be done: he had suffered all his life as a pilgrim loose from the world, and his brethren would take care of his wife and children.[135] (Here again communism's utility as a base of operations for the missionary work is clear.) Even the community's acceptance of responsibility for the education of children, in which the Hutterites made remarkable pedagogical contributions,[136] became a part of the realistic measures that made the sustaining of the mission possible. The cross of Christ (*Creutz christy*) and the communion of saints (*gemeinschaft der heilligen*) are the key ideas in Anabaptist thought at this level. Good and evil must be separated by a vigorous use of the Ban, so that the individual hero and the heroic community will be able to stand in time of trial. "For a Christian without suffering is like an untrained doctor, and like a house whose beam has not been hewn."[137] The internal organization of the community was a function of their capacity as pilgrims, missioners, and martyrs.

There is no doubt that the *Stille* consciously repudiated the revolutionaries' shift from weaponless warfare to the taking of the sword, but it is questionable whether all chiliastic thinking was purged.[138] And certainly there was a great surcharge of eschatological thinking, in which the missions method came to play a dominant part in the vision of the coming Kingdom on earth. The teleological necessity of suffering remained, and with it the *Täufer* sense of participating in the last scene of a world-shaking drama. When the last cup of blood had been shed, they might look for the Day of Victory. The quiet eschatology which became exclusive after Münster did not change the world view nor the expectation of a Kingdom on earth; *it changed the attitude to power*.[139] The manner of the coming of the Kingdom was, for the nonresistant Anabaptists, the Pauline missions method rather than by the "slaying of the godless" and violent revolution. The willingness to suffer martyrdom[140] for the faith was their strength.[141]

The expectation of a coming Kingdom of God on earth, to which the faithful come through a welter of blood, can be seen to link the revolutionaries and the nonresistants.[142] The lack of historical concern in the secular sense, which is frequently noted in Anabaptist thinking,[143] was not truly nonhistorical, but rather it stemmed from a contempt for the traditional things upon which God had already passed judgment and which were soon to pass away. Their unconcern with present matters was rooted in a great vision of things to come. Hübmaier said that those who deny a visible church and say His Kingdom is not of this world are faced with the prayer, "Thy Kingdom come. . . ."[144]

The Hutterites expected the wrath to break out over the world, and yet their eschatology blended with the theology of suffering in such manner as to blunt its harshness. They retained confidence, however, in the "restitution of all things" (Acts 3:21) to follow upon the Restitution of the church.[145] The precise nature of this impending finale was not clear. Some said that it would bring the return of created things, and others, only those things of which the prophets speak (chapter sixty-six of Isaiah).[146] The revolutionaries expected the taking of the sword to herald His coming; the *Stille* replaced this act with the method of pilgrimage-mission-martyrdom. For the *Stille* as well as the revolutionaries the Restitution of the True Church leads into a restoration of justice and peace in the world; but suffering, rather than violence, was the co-operative act of God and man which provided the moving power of history.

This was explicit in Menno: "But the martyrdom of

Stephen, in which the situation sharpened up by the experience of Christ appeared for the first time, and as a lesson, showed not only that the disciple must undertake suffering and death according to Christ's example, but *how* he must do it. He cried out in the way and manner of his Master on the Cross, Father do not count these sins unto them! That is according to Christ's mandate the new concept with which the elect conquer their fate, their opposition."[147] The simple missioner, who went forth in obedience to the Lord's command, assumed thereby a significance as social strategist which never occurred to him in the period of our study.

The Anabaptists and Natural Law

Because of the Anabaptist concentration on Biblical issues and matters of discipleship, and because of the speed and efficiency with which their movement was buried in a bath of blood by the persecutors, it has been customary even for many latter-day friends of the movement to assume that the Anabaptists contributed nothing to social and political thought as such. The assumption is that the study of the contribution of the Free Churches to democratic development must be postponed until the Commonwealth period in England. However, some of the implications for a constitutional and just government are also there in the period of classical Anabaptism. There was a certain attitude to social justice which cannot be concealed, even though subsequent developments augmented the tendency to emphasize distance from the Peasant Revolt and other efforts at economic reform. Paragraph 18 of the Waldshut Articles (1524) was rather to the point: "Whoever doesn't earn his bread in the sweat of his brow, he is excluded [and] also isn't worthy of the food which he eats. This will get rid of all loafers, whoever they may be."[148]

The fact that many of the death penalities and other forms of persecution ignored even that measure of rudimentary due process to which common subjects were entitled did not go without comment, either. Michael Sattler, when he heard the barbarous sentence passed upon him, reaffirmed his faith and then said: "You know that you with your fellow-judges have sentenced me contrary to law; therefore take care and repent."[149] Other points might be made, indicating a fruitful area of research as to the ideas of the Anabaptists which have general social and economic and political significance.

Of course the most significant contribution was the conviction that a just state does not persecute. The political implications of this position have been beautifully summarized by the Old Catholic scholar, Professor Döllinger, in an appraisal of Cromwell:

He was the first among the mighty men of the world to set up one special religious principle, and to enforce it so far as in him lay: . . . the principle of liberty of conscience and the repudiation of religious coercion. It must be clearly understood how great the gulf is which divides the holders of this principle from those who reject it, both in faith and morals. He who is convinced that right and duty require him to coerce other people into a life of falsehood . . . belongs to an essentially different religion from one who recognizes in the inviolability of conscience a human right guaranteed by religion itself, and has different notions of God, of man's relation to God, and of man's obligations to his fellows.[150]

There is perhaps some room for difference of opinion as to how accurately this represents the views of Oliver Cromwell. There can be no doubt that it fairly states the difference between the coercive pattern of religion which the Anabaptists repudiated and the free and disciplined faith which they proposed as an alternative. Their concern was for the purity of the Church of the Restitution and the winsomeness of its Gospel. The converse is, quite naturally, the elimination of one of the most damaging abuses of governmental power in human history: that which in the name of religious unity splinters the foundations of a just society and dwarfs the perspectives of the faith intended to embrace all nations.

THE VERDICT OF HISTORY

We may find it fruitful to consider briefly at what point the spirit of renunciation ceased to be identified with a simple evangelical concern, and became instead the cultivated manner of a sectarian community. What happened in the years toward which the Anabaptists looked with such eager hearts? We are now in a position to assess the movement and its statesmen, both in terms of internal discipline and in terms of the broad impact made upon society at large. What message and Christian testimony did the Anabaptist movement carry into the ongoing stream of Christian history, and over the world?

The problem has been put before in our discussion of the Restitution,[151] and it remains with us. In Biblical living, the tension between the "church" and the "world" is progressively overcome by the missionary outreach of the Christian Community. The relaxation of the tension by any other means — usually by acceptance of the status of a "religion," established politically or socially — is a betrayal of the faith. The people of the Covenant is a special people, a royal priesthood (I Peter 2:9), with a special mission and responsibility for those who dwell in darkness. Judging from the subsequent history of the Anabaptists, based on a glance at a period later than that involved in our study of the formation of the church view, two changes may occur which are prejudicial to the Church of the Restitution. On the one hand, adaptations accepted as necessary by those determined to live responsibly, accepted at the time as new insights, become in fact a "going over to the world" which cancels out both special witness and missionary passion. This is the experience of the Dutch and Prussian Mennonite groups, who became in the course of the years opulent in economy, proud in intellect, and effective in competition and war.

On the other side of the dialectic, a strong internal discipline and agrarian economy, at first developed in flight to the frontier to escape persecution, may lead in time to the development of completely self-centered religious and economic communities, in which the inevitable egotism of a group living in history is translated into a technological and cultural as well as religious primitivism. With the decline of missionary passion, the latter is the fate that overtook those groups which followed the frontier into Moravia, Transylvania, Russia, America, and

Paraguay.[152] In these apparently opposite resolutions of the tension there is a common factor: both later expressions of the movement have lost to a large degree the creative tension, the eager expectancy, the catalytic effect upon church and society which was the original genius of Anabaptism.

But there is another and broader basis on which the significance of the Anabaptists may be judged: in terms of their early witness to certain New Testament ordinances now widely taken for granted among Free Churches. Until the comprehensive history of sectarian Protestantism is written, we can only suggest the indebtedness of large sections of twentieth-century Christianity to these early champions of disciplined discipleship and religious liberty.[153] Certainly the true importance of the Church of the Restitution, its realizations and its hopes, goes far beyond those communities which today admit lineal descent from the Anabaptist movement.

CHAPTER V

The Changing Reputation of the Anabaptists

The Critical Problem

The preceding chapters form a unity. Whereas in the previous edition of the present study it was necessary to have a chapter discussing former treatments of Anabaptism before a new thesis could be put forward, we have assumed that by this time the interpretation of Anabaptism as a type of Christian primitivism could be allowed to stand on its own feet. Nevertheless the critical problem — the discussion about primary and secondary sources, the distinction between polemics and accurate reporting, the evaluation of recently discovered documents — remains an interesting, even exciting, aspect of the study of Anabaptism.

The student of history or of church history in America has usually known very little about the Anabaptist movement. He has been able to find only a few summary statements in the familiar surveys of the Reformation, and these brief paragraphs have done little to fill in the outlines of a blurred impression. Although the situation is changing, it is safe to say that most general interpretations of Anabaptism are faulty even today: the historians rely upon the dogmas of the Social Democratic interpretation, and the church historians depend upon the polemics of magisterial Protestantism. Both groups have ignored the primary sources. The student would be surprised indeed to learn that the leaders and groups of the Restitution were early champions and martyrs for some ideas about the nature of the church which he may be taking for granted. When we review the reference works best known to him, the reason for his lack of knowledge becomes plain.

Most historians who have written about the Reformation

138

in the intervening four centuries have treated those they called "Anabaptists" in one of two ways: either dismissing them as peripheral, or basing their elaboration of the subject upon extremely hostile polemics. The Anabaptists have been the abandoned people, who passed in dim review behind the glittering personalities of the chief Reformers and their protecting princes. In the usual fashion, a *History of the Reformation* recently republished by the S. P. C. K. and Macmillan Company dismisses the Anabaptists in three rapid pages out of six hundred.[1] We are left to assume that the radical groups were totally peripheral to the main concerns of Protestantism, barely worth a passing reference. Certainly there is no suggestion that a reader might be led to fuller understanding of contemporary religious life through familiarity with the primary sources of Anabaptism. There is no footnote to indicate that such sources exist.

A treatment typical of the second type of writing, perhaps more common among the general surveys of the older school of historians, is that found in Preserved Smith's *The Age of the Reformation*. Without apology he relied upon secondary sources of negligible value: "Mary of Hungary was not far wrong when she wrote that they planned to plunder all churches, nobles, and wealthy merchants, in short, all who had property, and from the spoil to distribute to every individual according to his need."[2]

Even in 1907 (Whitney), and certainly by 1920 (Smith), there was enough source material accessible to call into question any simple reliance upon the polemical writings of men who drove those they termed "heretics" to exile or death. The Anabaptists could no longer properly be dismissed in casual fashion; neither could a fair and thorough work rely uncritically upon hostile testimony *about* the radicals without regarding the growing body of *primary* evidence. Both Whitney and Smith, however, reveal the traditional tendentious dependence upon the colored reports of Luther, Melanchthon, Zwingli, Bullinger, and the like. The sources edited by Cornelius, Keller, Beck, and Egli, although available, were not given a hearing, and the in-group writings of the Swiss and South German Brethren, Hutterites, and Dutch were apparently unknown to the authors.

The volume by Thomas M. Lindsay in the International

Theological Library,[3] still widely sold, and used in leading seminaries, presents a more adequate handling of sources. His list of references includes the best materials available before 1903; the author evidently was anxious to present a fair picture.[4] In spite of limited sources he went far to give a generous estimate of some aspects of the movement. He appreciated the passionate ethical concern of the Anabaptists, and hit upon a clue of key significance in discussing their uniform aversion to a state church.[5] In the final analysis, however, Lindsay depended upon other writers who classified the Anabaptists as the remnants of medieval brotherhoods.[6] Although his work is to be praised beyond the volumes by Whitney and Smith, the most significant primary sources now available have been exhumed from the archives since his survey was written. The large mass of newly published court testimony, the sermons and epistles, the confessions of faith and other records — although only the beginning of a full representation — go far to refute his fundamental conceptions. Yet Lindsay's writing, along with the two previously mentioned, is that commonly allowed to stand in our seminaries and universities. The three standard surveys of the Reformation in English are thus ruled inadequate simply from the point of view of sources utilized. If the Anabaptists have any significance for an informed discussion of contemporary church life,[7] the priority of these surveys becomes even more intolerable.[8]

We find a similarly inadequate use of source material in more limited studies, such as Vedder's *The Reformation in Germany* (1914) and Allen's *A History of Political Thought in the Sixteenth Century* (1928). Henry C. Vedder was far more generous in his estimate of Anabaptism than the authors previously mentioned. As his eyes swept over the scattered fragments of Anabaptism then exposed to view, he concluded:

They were the only party among those protesting against the errors of Rome who were logical and thoroughgoing. They alone accepted in absolute faith and followed to its necessary consequences the principle avowed by the leading reformers, that the Scriptures were the sole source of religious authority. . . . The Anabaptists alone had penetrated beneath the surface of traditional Christianity and comprehended the real Gospel of Jesus.

They were centuries in advance of their time in perceiving that the Good News of Salvation, as taught by Jesus, was a social gospel, and that the acceptance of it implied and necessitated a reconstruction of society until all institutions could endure the measurements of the Golden Rule. In a word, the Anabaptists were the real reformers, and the only real reformers, of the Sixteenth century.[9]

Spoken like a good American Baptist! But where is the documentation for such a sweeping opinion? And where may we find the Anabaptist writings on church reforms which make clear what they were driving at? The references will not be found in Vedder's footnotes.

In turning to Allen, we find an author who cites primary sources at length. But his basic interpretations are frequently far afield, and the chapter on those he thought to be "Anabaptists" is the poorest in the book. The evidence contradicts several of his basic assertions:

Belief in the "inner light" seems to have been the most fundamental of the beliefs that characterized the Anabaptists. [p. 39]

The Magistrate, so far from being a lieutenant of God, is simply the most persistent offender against God's law. They do not merely deny his right to coerce them into religious conformity — they deny his right to exist at all. [p. 41]

There appears [*sic*] to have been in Moravia communities of Anabaptists who actually had a common store of goods from which distribution was made by an elected official. But there is little evidence of any organized or systematic communism among the Anabaptists. [p. 42]

I do not think it can be said, even, that the Anabaptists proclaimed any principle of religious toleration, otherwise than indirectly. They denied of course the right of the Magistrate to punish heretics, but they denied his right to punish anyone. [p. 47][10]

Allen missed the most significant contribution of the radicals to political thought. His whole writing, although detailed, shows dependence upon the usual polemics — interspersed with citations from "Anabaptists" whose connection with the main line of the movement was very attenuated.

The outstanding limitation of the dominant interpretation of Anabaptism has been this: when the authors gave any detail at all they usually relied upon the traditional Lutheran and Reformed polemics against the radical groups, and not even upon the candid reports of contemporaries when they were not engaged in polemics.[11] This procedure is in part a sign of unwise dependence upon partial evidence, but it also reflects the serious problem of getting at the sources in the field. The major primary materials have only lately become generally accessible, and scholars in the English-speaking world are not yet habituated to their use. As a result, there has been little "concrete" study of the movement. Opinions expressed generally can be said to reflect the theology of the Reformers more than the economy of the Anabaptists.

The important point to register at this level of our discussion is simply this: the treatment which usually has been afforded those called "Anabaptists" in surveys and general studies is extremely faulty, and *for the most part because it is not informed by an adequate use of the primary sources now available.* There were, even at the time when the earlier surveys were written, documents which critical scholars should have used. Today there is no excuse whatever for permitting to pass unchallenged that slighting notation which dismisses the Anabaptists as peripheral and unworthy of intensive firsthand study, or that morbid dependence upon questionable sources which seems to satisfy many of those historians who do pause to assess the movement.[12]

The realization comes hard that the most significant materials upon which informed judgments might be based lay relatively untouched for four hundred years in the archives in Swiss, Austrian and Czechoslovakian, German, and Dutch cities. For more than three centuries most historians depended entirely upon the colored and partial reports of the enemies of the Anabaptists. Only within the last twenty years have materials of greatest value become generally available, making possible a thorough rewriting and reassessment of the movement. Only a beginning was made before World War II, and the hostilities interrupted production and distribution. Used along with the works of earlier editors, however, the initial volumes of the *"Wiedertäuferakten"* of the *Archiv für Reformationsgeschichte*[13] and fraternal organizations provided enough data to launch a reinterpretation. Since the war, with the help of American Mennonites, additional volumes have been published. Any discussion of the Anabaptists today must cling closely to the primary sources. A structural analysis of Anabaptism, in fact, must begin with the romance of source exhumation and rediscovery.

FORMER TREATMENTS OF ANABAPTISM AND THE SOURCE PROBLEM

Traditional Interpretations

The inadequacy of many currently used surveys of the Reformation will be more evident as we review the progress of Anabaptist historiography. And it will be clear that there is one problem which must be solved before the Anabaptists and their ideas can be definitely established: to assess the comparative reliability and value of the authorities usually cited in studies of Anabaptism. Within recent decades there has been, as we shall see, a notable shift of attention from polemics about those called "Anabaptists" to the primary sources of the movement itself. But for most of four centuries the accredited historians have been as uncritical of their sources as the official theologians have been filial in their polemics.

Some former treatments can be grouped according to schools of thought, and we may well begin with those writings of the dominant groups which for long determined all semi-official interpretations and are still definitive for many.

The views of Martin Luther already have been considered, in their proper setting at Wittenberg.[14] There were also several of his disciples who were distinguished for their polemics against those they called "Anabaptists," men whose writings helped to shape a school of thought about Anabaptism. Of these, the most noted as opponents of Anabaptism were Justus Menius, Urbanus Rhegius, Philipp Melanchthon, and Andreas Althamer.

JUSTUS MENIUS (1499-1558) wrote two very widely circulated works, which Luther prefaced: *Der Widdertauffer lere vñ Geheimnis/ aus heiliger schrift Widderlegt* (with Myconius, 1530),[15] and *Von dem Geist der Wiederteuffer* (1544).[16] When he could not move the tolerant Philipp of Hesse to more harsh measures against the Anabaptists, Menius wrote bitterly to his friend blaming Hesse for the spread of heresy — "culpa omnis in Hesso est."[17] It was said of his years as superintendent in Ansbach that Menius "put out many much needed writings against the *Stenkfeldischen* and Anabaptists."[18] Menius, an avid and bitter controversialist, is still one of the most commonly cited writers in any discussion of "Anabaptism."

URBANUS RHEGIUS (1489-1541) wrote more numerous polemics against what he called "Anabaptism" than did Menius, although his writings have not been so highly regarded by the orthodox.[19] Nevertheless, Luther looked favorably upon them and several were widely used: *Wider den newen Taufforden Notwendige Warnung an alle Christgläubigen* . . . (against Hans Hut, 1527);[20] *Widerlegung der Münsterischen newen Valentinianer vnd Donatisten* (1535);[21] *De Restitutione regni Israelitici* . . . (1536).[22]

PHILIPP MELANCHTHON (1497-1560) was a prolific writer against "Anabaptists," and for long his authority was second only to Luther's, although his treatment is not especially keen or useful. He thought in terms of Müntzer and Münster,[23] and it is not clear that he actually came to grips with Anabaptism (without quotation marks) at all.

ANDREAS ALTHAMER (1500-1539) was active against the Anabaptists at the time of the Bern Disputation; against Denck's *Wer die Wahrheit wirklich lieb hat* he wrote *Dial/lage, hoc est,/ conciliatio loco/rum scripturae qui prima facie inter se pugnare wi/dentur* (1527), which went through many editions, including a German translation by Sebastian Franck (1528).[24] As a regional leader of the Reformation, Althamer found other occasions to strike out against the ideology and practice of the radicals.

Menius' views may be considered typical of the Lutheran theological interpretation of radical dissent. The false prophets were signs of the end of the times, on a par with a Turkish invasion.

Nothing has been so dangerous in all this as the false teachings whereby he [the devil] causes many factions and sects to appear within Christendom.[25]

But when the Devil is a God he also has a Gospel, and in the nature of his gospel he also sends apostles out for it, and in the nature of his apostles they also build a church. Now our dear Lord Christ said the devil was an arch-liar and murderer; therefore his gospel is also not a gospel of grace and peace but rather directed toward murder and revolution with a lie as foundation. Therefore he sends his apostles not as Christ did — as sheep among wolves — but as raging and roaring wolves to rob and murder among the sheep. . . .

For although Müntzer is thrown down, yet his spirit is not; it lives even yet, indeed rules in many corners — especially in the Anabaptist sect which was planted by Müntzer in this part of the land — and it has been impossible up to now to root it out.[26]

Anabaptists are thereby classified as social incendiaries, and to their polemics the traditionalists added lurid descriptions of the Münster episode of revolution, communism, and polygamy. This typology has remained standard in many quarters.

In recent Lutheran writing, the learned monographs prepared by Heinrich Böhmer's seminar are useful; yet they are colored by the intention to show that Luther's view of the origin and consequences of Anabaptism was sound. We do not find even in modern Lutheran historians any great willingness to modify the old views.[27] Karl Holl, it is true, was prepared to admit the special significance of Anabaptism for the Free Churches; but this only proved the case for his theological criticism of "the sects."[28] Fritz Heyer's *Der Kirchenbegriff der Schwärmer* (1939) is a penetrating and exhaustive study, which is nevertheless committed to the traditional intention to prove

Luther right in grouping revolutionaries and nonresistants, mystics and Biblicists, Hutterites and spiritualizers together in a common condemnation.[29] The entire body of Lutheran interpretation is generally marked by an unfamiliarity with the primary sources of Anabaptism, and by a studied determination to uphold that interpretation of the radical groups which came from the Reformer himself. In the twentieth century, some Lutheran sociologists have allowed new schemes of classification,[30] but the apologetic intent remains the same for the official writings. They entertain with difficulty the thought that the church view of the Anabaptists may have had an integrity and vitality of its own, distinct from the opinions of Martin Luther.

In the Reformed churches the polemics of Zwingli, Bullinger, and Calvin were circulated on a wide front against "Anabaptism." Bullinger is still the most frequently used writer among the traditionalist historians of both Lutheran and Reformed camps, Menius alone excepted.

Ulrich Zwingli's writings were the fountain source of the Swiss Brethren and through them of the South Germans and Hutterites.[31] Yet when the radicals broke with the territorial church in 1524, public Disputations were held in several cities and Zwingli wrote bitterly against his opponents on the left.[32] On December 7, 1524, he countered their attack on the tithes and rents of the establishment with *Wer ursach gebe zu Aufruhr, wer die wahren Aufrührer seien, und wie man zu Christlicher Einigkeit und Frieden gelangen möge.*[33] In 1525 he published the well-known *Vom touf, widertouf und kindertouf,*[34] which precipitated an exchange; *Von Predigtamt und Wahrhafte und gegründete Antwort auf Dr. Balthasars Taufbüchlein* followed.[35] In July, 1527, appeared *In Catabaptistorum elenchus.*[36] Zwingli was sorely troubled by his former associates, who derived their Biblical radicalism and doctrine of the Lord's Supper from his own teachings.

Zwingli's disciple and successor in the battle of ideas was HEINRICH BULLINGER (1504-1575), who began writing against the Anabaptists after the Disputation of January 17, 1527. His polemics were widely read and translated, and are still cited with definitive accent: *Von dem vnuerschampte fräfel, erger-lichem verwyrren, vnd unwarhafften leeren, der selbsgesandten Widertöuffern, vier gespräch Bücher* (1531), and *Der wider-töuffern ursprung/ fürgang/ Secten-/wäsen/ etc.* (1560).[37]

JOHN CALVIN (1509-1564) was also among those whose writings lent misunderstanding to the study of the Anabaptists.[38] Among widely read authors, probably none understood less about them. His *Brière Instruction pour armer tous bons fidèles contre les Erreurs de la Secte Commune des Anabaptistes* was written against the "Seven Articles" of Schleitheim (1527), and when he attacked the free-thinking spirituals at Geneva he believed he was dealing with the same movement.[39] Calvin thought "Anabaptists" were individualists, descendants of the medieval mystics, and he made no distinction between the spiritualizing and the Biblicist wings of the movement — if, indeed, he was aware of the distinction.

The writings of Bullinger may be taken as authoritative for the Reformed churches.[40] Again and again he returns to attack those who spread dissension and factionalism in the church. Bullinger felt that true and humble Christians should not be so hasty to declare themselves the only True Church, nor should they sever themselves too eagerly from their fellows. Let each remain in the calling wherein he is called in the social order, and let none hasten to rend the community of the Holy Church because of some matter of secondary importance. Bullinger believed that "Anabaptism" began with Thomas Müntzer, and he divided the radicals into eleven types — a wide variety of manifestations due to the religious subjectivism which he con-demned. He especially opposed adult baptism, which meant a sundered community. His writings were definitive in Reformed circles until Emil Egli went back to the primary sources, at the beginning of this century.[41]

Along with those of the Lutheran and Reformed writers, the polemics of the Roman Catholic writers deserve mention. Among the early authors of this tradition none gained a wider hearing than CHRISTOPH ERHARD and C. A. FISCHER. Both func-tioned in opposition to the Hutterite Brethren. Erhard was associated with the Counter-Reformation under Adam von Dietrichstein at Nikolsburg (c. 1583);[42] Fischer appears to have been a Jesuit opponent of Claus Braidl (c. 1600).[43] Both were very prolific writers and enjoyed the approval and encouragement of Roman Catholic rulers.

In general, Lutheran, Reformed, and Roman Catholic writers have inclined to look upon Müntzer and Münster as representative events in the Anabaptist movement. The Catholics have also informed the reader that the revolutionaries represented Protestantism carried to its logical extreme of religious anarchy. The logic of "Protestantism" is discovered in connection with the Peasant Revolt and the New Jerusalem at Münster. In all three types of orthodox writing, the Swiss phase of the movement is credited to short visits in the cantons by Müntzer and Karlstadt, and Menno Simons' strict nonresistance is considered a kind of "tired radicalism" following the collapse of revolutionary hopes.

The secondary sources which we have considered above have generally prevailed in the subsequent writings about the Anabaptists, and we may no longer be surprised at the lack of insight which has characterized those who depended upon them. Nor is it surprising that the orthodox opinion still prevails in many quarters when the name "Anabaptist" is mentioned. Generation after generation, the Anabaptists have been called up for trial by the historians, the words of their accusers have been heard, and the persecuted forerunners of the Free Churches have been sentenced to oblivion without having an opportunity to speak in their own behalf.

In-Group Records and Writings

To a certain extent the continued misunderstanding of Anabaptism can be explained in a very brief statement: *the writings and records of the movement were successfully suppressed, whereas the polemics of their enemies circulated widely and were early translated into various languages* (including English). From the beginning this fact has played a large part in the dominance of hostile views, for even historians who wished to be fair and objective have lacked primary sources. Indeed, the churches descended from the radical groups have frequently lacked vital validating records, and, like discriminating out-group historians, have not had in hand the evidence on which to build a case.

The Anabaptist writings, as originally printed, found only limited circulation. Many never existed in other than manu-script form. The very important history attributed to Carl of Ghent, *Het beginsel en voortganck der geschillen, scheuringen en verdeeltheden onder degene die Doopsgezinden genoemt worden, in deze laetste eeuwe van hondert jaren herwaerts, tot op den jare 1615, getrouwelick beschreven door J. H. V. P. N.,* circulated for forty-three years in handwritten form before find-ing a printer.[44] Because of dangers to life and limb, the perse-cuted "heretics" frequently sought protection in anonymous publication; the printer also might well hesitate to let his re-sponsibility be known.[45] Writer and printer knew that the au-thorities of church and state were efficient and thorough, col-lecting both men and books for the flame. The religious and political powers endeavored to suppress both opinions and Anabaptist leadership; court actions and attendant judgment by the clergy frequently list the titles of writings to be confiscated. The governments were determined to destroy the ideas which the Anabaptists represented, and they were, to a marked extent, successful in preventing informed discussion both in their own time and subsequently.

A bibliography of Anabaptist works will contain a large majority of rare items. Many of the most significant books within the movement, originally published secretly and in limited num-bers, exist today only in single copies; many more are lost al-together. The story of the Greater Chronicle of the Hutterite Brethren is not atypical. Although this comprised the core of tradition, records, and rules by which a major Anabaptist party lived, Josef Beck was unable to find a copy by 1883 and assumed it to be lost.[46] Rediscovered in the American settlements in this century, the Greater Chronicle was first edited and published in 1923 and, under the auspices of the Carl Schurz Foundation, was republished in 1943. Among the most significant long-lost writings was Pilgram Marpeck's *Vermahnung* (1542), written during the dispute with Schwenckfeld. It is the basic source for the South German Brethren's concept of the True Church. In recent years a copy was found by John Horsch in the British Museum, and another was discovered by Ernst Crous in the Württembergische Bibliothek.[47] Among the lost items, none is more to be mourned than Johannes Campanus' *Contra totum post-apostolos mundum,* listed by Melanchthon as *Wider die Lutherischen und alle Welt nach den Aposteln und derselben wunderbarlicke und seltzame Irrthumb* (1531). This book is one of the fountain sources of the idea of the Fall of the church.[48]

The Bible was the only book which could not be taken from the Anabaptists and could not be kept out of circulation. And they relied upon it implicitly. For an understanding of the sources of their ethical teachings, however, it would be very useful to have more of the "commentaries." These have been kept from later generations by the conspiring forces listed above. The *Ausbund*[49] and the *Märtyrer-spiegel*[50] were the only in-group records widely circulated, and to those out-group scholars who had them in hand these must have seemed to convey only the mournful and credulous apologetic of a harried people.

Just as their enemies wrote broadly in their attacks, so the Anabaptists made sweeping claims for themselves in their apologetic. Their writings must be viewed with the same critical eye that we turn toward the polemics of their enemies. The Anabaptists picture themselves as the "True Church," a Christian gathering of eternal significance.[51] From the beginning of history only a small band went the right way, and the Anabaptists took their position in that line of the faithful. Their hymns and records of martyrdom are the self-conscious account of a people with a message, whom God has chosen to carry the meaning of history.[52] With the fresh life of those given a primary religious experience, the communities kept records like those of the Early Church: uncritical and inspired sermons, confessions of faith, epistles to the saints. This naive picture persisted in the more isolated American communities almost to the present day; even such an informed historian as the late John Horsch

(1867-1941)[53] was resistant to the comparative method and to critical research by students outside the group.

In Europe, however, the Mennonite historians imbibed earlier the spirit of German historical criticism, and were able to regard their own movement with a certain measure of detachment. This second stage of in-group writing was heralded by Samuel Müller's *Jaarboekje voor de Doopsgezinden Gemeenten* (1837-1850). In the next few years appeared Steven Blaupot ten Cate's regional histories of the Dutch Mennonites,[54] and separate studies by A. M. Cramer and S. Hoekstra. These histories will compare favorably with other studies written in the nineteenth century, both for use of sources and devotion to the historical method.

The real flowering of in-group research and writing has occurred within recent years among the American Mennonites. This renaissance of scholarly work is associated with the person of Harold S. Bender, and the magazine which he founded and has edited for over thirty years: *The Mennonite Quarterly Review*. The *MQR* began with the January issue, 1927, continuing the *Review Supplement* to the *Goshen College Record* (Indiana). It has frequently made known some of the rare materials collected in the Mennonite Historical Library through the industry of Dean Bender and the late John Horsch and Edward Yoder. More recently the Mennonite historical collections at Bethel College (North Newton, Kansas) have also become important, under the leadership of Cornelius Krahn. The volume of material made available over the years, in magazine form and in monographs, is truly astonishing when we consider that the American Mennonites number approximately 200,000 souls. The quality of scientific research is not surpassed by that of any church body in the world. The American "Mennonites" stem mainly from Swiss and South German forerunners, and their recent historians have pursued the Continental as well as the American records. The Mennonite Historical Society is today one of the most active and significant groups of American historians, with a sharp concern for bringing out the early sources. The Society has also encouraged the preparation of critical monographs by out-group as well as by Mennonite scholars.

Friendly Out-Group Writing

For a long time the only historians to treat the Anabaptists with any degree of sympathetic understanding and constructive analysis were independent thinkers like Sebastian Franck, and Pietists like Gottfried Arnold, von Mosheim, and Füsslin.

SEBASTIAN FRANCK (1499-1542/43)[55] was a great independent writer and contemporary who reported the "sect" of the Anabaptists critically but in great detail. He condemned all "sectarianism" — Roman Catholic, Lutheran, Reformed, Anabaptist — in the name of the God of true inward religion, and was most critical of all those who would not tolerate dissent in the things of the inner man. Above all he was opposed to the identification of Christianity with cultural mores and political power. He was therefore a champion of the persecuted, and published extensive excerpts from the early documents of the Anabaptist movement.

Gottfried Arnold (1666-1714)[56] was more widely read by eighteenth-century Mennonites than any other out-group author. Products of Pietism, his writings were sympathetic treatments of the "heretics" and brotherhood movements across the centuries. He accepted, indeed, a very large share of the primitivist interpretation of Christian history which the Anabaptists had defended in the previous century.

Johann Lorentz von Mosheim (1694/95-1755),[57] and Johann Konrad Füsslin (1704-1775)[58] represented in the eighteenth century a highly developed historiography with a similar ring: the "heretics" carried the True Church, which had existed only in dispersion since the time of Constantine the Great. From this theoretical base in Christian primitivism von Mosheim and Füsslin also gave sympathetic hearing to the persecuted groups of the Reformation epoch.

In the nineteenth century, several scholars contributed to a more adequate and accurate appraisal of the Anabaptist movement. The names of Max Goebel (1811-1857),[59] Alfred Hegler

(1863-1902),[60] and Karl Müller (1852-1940)[61] ought especially to be mentioned. Müller's work carried over into recent decades, and as a member of the executive committee of the *Verein für Reformationsgeschichte* he shared credit for launching the series of *Täuferakten*. In approximately the same period, two writers not alien to the primitive scheme of Christian historiography also contributed to an understanding of Anabaptism and introduced novel propositions for their classification.

Ludwig Keller (1849-1915), whose significance in the discovery of sources will be discussed shortly, endeavored to trace back a continuous succession of radicalism from the insurgents of the Reformation through the pre-Reformation brotherhood movements. He interpreted the Anabaptists in terms of medieval mysticism and ethical concern.[62] They looked for true inwardness, and were not content with faith alone: they thought that ethical concern would flow from a true repentance.

Albrecht Ritschl (1822-1889) proposed a similar scheme, relating the Anabaptists to the Franciscan tertiaries. Anabaptism stands clearly on the side of the Middle Ages and Catholicism in two important respects: claiming a visible church, and perfecting the religious life. Simplicity, nonresistance, and the return to Jesus in the whole of life, were common concerns of both the Franciscan circles and the Anabaptists.[63] As with the various attempts to trace Anabaptism back to the Waldensians,[64] the evidence is too slight to sustain the weight of the theses advanced by Keller and Ritschl. Nevertheless they represented friendly attempts to classify and define the Anabaptists in Christian history.

Another frame of mind which led to sympathetic interpretation of the Left Wing of the Reformation was that revealed by the modern "social" writers. The German Social Democrat, Karl Kautsky, and the English Guild Socialist, Belfort Bax, made a like case for Anabaptism.[65] They were unfamiliar with the best sources, and for them "Anabaptism" was the religious overtone of the revolutions of peasant and guild-worker. They placed the marginal incidents in the Peasant War and at Münster at the center of the stage. In effect, this interpretation means accepting the traditional misunderstanding, giving praise rather than blame.

CURRENT DEVELOPMENTS IN INTERPRETATION

The traditional interpretation of Anabaptism has been doctrinaire, and the apologetic of in-group writings and friendly out-group commentaries usually has been founded in a doctrine opposed to institutional church life. More recently, there has come a review of the movement which seeks to remain critically aware and at the same time understand Anabaptism as a church type in itself. This approach owes most to two forces: the impact of the religious sociologists, and the rediscovery of primary materials.

Impact of Religious Sociologists

A marked change in interpretation came in the twentieth century, when certain trained sociologists analyzed the Anabaptist church life and historical significance "concretely." The traditional historiography dealt with the leaders and groups in terms of certain fixed ideas and categories quite apart from historical evidence, but the sociologists departed from this well-worn path.

Before wide use could be made of the edited sources now available, a great religious sociologist — Ernst Troeltsch (1865-1923) — displayed his acute judgment in comprehending the Anabaptist movement as a body of phenomena of unique character, with a pattern different in kind from that of the dominant state churches.[66] He recognized that the nature of the Anabaptist congregation and the structure of Anabaptist thought grew out of an idea of Christian discipleship very distant in standpoint from the teaching and practice of the Reformers. Troeltsch also distinguished between individual radicals (*Spiritualisten*) and the radical congregations (*Täufer*).[67] Finally, he concluded that the evidence pointed to an origin of the movement in Zürich rather than Wittenberg, a finding which threw him into strong controversy with Karl Holl and other champions of the orthodox historiography.[68] Indeed, the watershed between the doctrinaire writings and the newer scholarship has come to be at this point: *whether the movement took its start with Müntzer and Karlstadt at Wittenberg, or with Grebel and Manz and Reublin and Blaurock at Zürich.*

Among those who have added to the evidence at this level we may note especially Ernst Correll. In Germany and America his research has carried on the great tradition of Ernst Troeltsch and Max Weber, with *Das Schweizerische Täufermennonitentum* (1925), and numerous articles in the *Mennonitisches Lexikon* (1913, 1937, etc.) and *The Mennonite Quarterly Review*. This "concrete" approach to the Anabaptist groups has had a profound effect upon the writing of both hostile and in-group writers. The Lutheran and Reformed scholars have come to give more time and attention to the radicals,[69] realizing that the careers of Luther and Zwingli cannot be interpreted intelligently without portraying the insurgency on the left with which they were in conflict. On the other hand, the modern Mennonite scholar takes seriously the findings of the critics outside the group. He is resolved to relate Anabaptist teaching to the actual historical situation in which the doctrine took shape, and to relate the ideological conflicts to the real issues in the life of the congregations. Cornelius Krahn's *Der Gemeindebegriff des Menno Simons im Rahmen seines Lebens und seiner Theologie* (1936) may serve as an example of this type of work.

Strange to say, Continental historians have to date been moved more by the recent analyses, and have shown more concern for proper revision of the traditional opinions, than have scholars in the English-speaking countries. Among the number of European scholars mentioned throughout this study, Johannes Kühn — for his *Toleranz und Offenbarung* (1922) — Walther Köhler, and Fritz Blanke deserve special mention. In the American scene, Albert Henry Newman and Roland H. Bainton have been foremost among out-group scholars for their research and understanding of Anabaptism. The number of specialized studies by non-Mennonites is far greater, however, on the Continent. And yet the Anabaptist view of the church is most significantly related to the Protestant "sectarianism" important in England and dominant in the United States.

The Rediscovery of Primary Sources

Along with the contributions in the field of sociology of religion, and the effects of these studies, we must mention also the publication of the new source materials. In the long run the availability of primary sources will determine the issue among historians. Although a great deal of data is yet unworked and unpublished, and the project begun by the *Verein für Reformationsgeschichte* is only in progress, significant gains have been made in recent years both in the discovery and in the publishing of primary materials.

The first outstanding contributions in the way of using and making difficult sources more generally available were made by two independent scholars of liberal tendencies: C. A. Cornelius and Ludwig Keller.

C. A. Cornelius (1819-1903) was in a position of political responsibility in 1848, and was moved by the events of that year to study the Münster episode and related concerns. He energetically sought new sources and distinguished himself from the polemical writers by the breadth of his treatment. He wrote frequently and well, and documented his reports with copious footnotes and appendices.[70] A man of large churchmanship as well as sympathies, he was among those Catholic leaders and scholars who broke with Rome at the time of the affirmation of papal infallibility (July 18, 1870).

Ludwig Keller represented a new and significant turning point in modern treatments of Anabaptism. His *Ein Apostel der Wiedertäufer* (1882) brought forward a stimulating thesis on the relation of Anabaptism to Christian history, a thesis which he furthered in a number of brilliantly written and provocative volumes.[71] In October, 1890, he established the *Comeniusgesellschaft* for furthering sympathetic research in the history of the Christian brotherhood movements, and its publications contain some valuable items too little used by historians of the Reformation. In 1879 Keller joined the Freemasons, hoping to find in their fellowship champions of free and ethical religion of the type which had attracted him to the radicals of the Reformation, a tolerant type he had not found in the established churches.

Although some interpreters, of whom Cornelius and Keller are most worthy of note, made their fellow historians aware of hitherto unknown evidence, the most conclusive work was done by editors: Beck, Egli, Cramer, and Wolkan. Through their hard work a new assessment of the radical movements became possible to those who share their diligent concern for primary sources.

First we consider Emil Egli (1848-1908), like Cornelius an Old Catholic, the editor of sources which have become invaluable to students of the Swiss Reformation dealing with the origins of the Anabaptist movement in Zürich. Especially noteworthy are the two volumes, *Actensammlung zur Geschichte der Zürcher Reformation in den Jahren 1519-1533* (1897).[72] In 1897 he founded *Zwingliana,* an organ whose pages have continued to provide first-class historical scholarship to the present day.

Next in line is Josef Beck (1815-1887), Knight of Mannagetta, who found time in the midst of a busy career to prospect many lost sources. He edited *Die Geschichts-Bücher der Wiedertäufer in Osterreich-Ungarn* (1883), and exhumed other materials which have seen the light of day in the articles of Johann Loserth, who carried on his work. Beck first opened the teachings of the Hutterite Brethren to the careful scholar.[73]

Priceless materials of the Dutch wing of the movement, including fragments sometimes extant only in one or two copies, were made available to scholars through the erudition and sacrifices of Samuel Cramer (1842-1913). Cramer participated from the beginning in the publishing of the *Doopsgezinde Bijdragen,*[74] and wrote a large number of critical essays on Dutch Mennonite history. His monumental work was the ten-volume *Bibliotheca Reformatoria Neerlandica* (1903-1914), completed after his death by F. Pijper.[75]

More recently, the available source materials of the Hutterite Brethren have been greatly enlarged. The Greater Chron-

icle, which Josef Beck had thought to be lost, was rediscovered
and edited by Rudolph Wolkan (1923) and A. J. F. Zieglschmid
(1943).[76] Some other valuable single items have recently been
published in usable form. Foremost among them is Peter Ridemann's *Rechenschaft*, published in German (1938) and English (1950) in beautiful editions sponsored by the new communities of Hutterite Brethren in England and Paraguay.[77]

The last seventy-five years of Anabaptist study have been
highlighted, then, by the digging up and editing of long-lost
and previously circumscribed records of the movement in Switzerland, Moravia, and the Netherlands. The work of these editors
is directly responsible for rescuing the Anabaptists from the
limbo to which they had been consigned by their enemies, and
from those historians who for three and four centuries have
depended uncritically on the polemics of these enemies in analyzing Anabaptist thought and practice.

We are now familiar with the way in which the Hutterite,
Swiss, and Dutch sections of the movement have come up for
review in the light of newly published sources. Within recent
years the German phase also has been presented more adequately.
Certain monographs (largely in German) had previously been
written which suggested the need for reorientation, but of greatest importance are the volumes made available in the *Täuferakten* of the *Verein für Reformationsgeschichte* and related
bodies. In 1930 was published the first of thirteen planned
volumes: sources on Anabaptism in Württenberg, edited by
Gustav Bossert, Sr. In 1934 appeared the Markgraftum Brandenburg sources, edited by Karl Schornbaum; and in 1938 part
of the South German/Hutterite sources, edited by Lydia Müller.
The war interrupted the enterprise, but it is now going forward
with supplementary sponsorship of individual volumes by the
Historische Kommission für Hessen und Waldeck and certain
Swiss historical societies, and with direct co-operation by the
Mennonite Historical Society (United States) and *Mennoni-
tischer Geschichtsverein* (Germany).[78] Sermons, confessions of
faith, court testimony, pastoral letters, and other priceless materials have for the first time become generally accessible, and their
significance for a proper assessment of the Anabaptist movement

can hardly be exaggerated. The earlier Swiss sources edited by Egli are being superseded, and Beck's work on Hutterite materials will also be replaced by far more extensive materials. Perhaps most illuminating, however, have been the insights into the German phase of the movement. We recall that both Lutheran and Reformed writers (since Menius and Bullinger) have traditionally found the point of origin of Anabaptism in the union of economic rebellion and religious enthusiasm in Thomas Müntzer, and have given a German point of origin to the whole movement. It is now clear that the South Germans, at least, did not significantly differ from the Swiss. And in lands further north, Melchior Rinck and others held to the main line; even Melchior Hofmann comes off better than had been supposed by objective historians.

This discussion would not be complete without reference to a splendid volume of sources recently edited in English by George Huntston Williams of Harvard University, supplemented by materials on Juan de Valdés edited by Angel M. Mergal of the Evangelical Seminary of Puerto Rico: *Spiritual and Anabaptist Writers* (1957). Professor Williams has made available representative excerpts from the Left Wing, many of them appearing in English for the first time, and has included a useful bibliography of other English translations.[79]

The Disputations

We may do well to note in passing the existence of another largely unexplored mine of information about the movement: the Disputations. A favorite device of the Reformers was to hold public debate with the radicals, seeking thereby to discredit "subversive" opinions. Not infrequently, however, the keen wit and Biblical orientation of the illegal preachers turned public opinion their way. More often, the hearings were held before selected circles from university and church. Sometimes the dissenters were guaranteed safe conduct to come to the Disputation. Frequently they were brought from prison cell to be faced with the mortal charges leveled against them by the authorities of state and church. The records of such Disputations were sometimes published and distributed by one or more parties to the controversy, and they afford an interesting but little used body of evidence on the opinions of the Anabaptists. Among the most famous of these meetings which dealt with Anabaptism were those at Zürich (1525), Basel (1525), Bern (1528), St. Gall (1530), Zofingen (1532), Bern (1538), Pfeddersheim (1557), Frankenthal (1571), Emden (1578). The reports from these and other such hearings need to be reworked so that historians can make ready use of the materials contained in them.[80] As it is, they are little used; they are not part of the rediscovery discussed above, and do not yet figure to any major extent in the reassessment which is now occurring.

IN CONCLUSION

The comparatively recent discovery of most vital primary sources, unknown and unused by most historians for four centuries, has required a thorough reworking of our understanding of the Left Wing of the Reformation. The previous chapters of this book attempted a re-appraisal. In subsequent writing on the sixteenth century, as it relates to Anabaptism, the modern historian will concern himself with information drawn directly from the movement, seeking to understand and define what it was that the leaders and congregations hoped to accomplish. And the Anabaptist vision will be judged not only by what their enemies feared and wrote about them, but what they were in fact able to accomplish. For the first time the sources and analytical equipment are available for such an assessment. It may not be amiss to remark that the data in hand suggest not only a new interpretation of the radical leaders and groups, but a rewriting of the current representation of the major Reformers. If the Reformers were incorrect in appraisal of such opponents, they are themselves set in a new light. We have noted this in the course of our study, although our first concern has been to understand the Anabaptists. The Anabaptist life is especially relevant to present problems in sectarian Protestantism, and in the Free Churches in general; coming to grips with the Anabaptist church view has both historical and contemporary significance.

The Anabaptists commonly have been judged on the basis of insufficient evidence. It is time for a re-trial, and the re-trial has begun.

Notes

Certain references to pages appear in the form: pp. 5-11, 8. This means that the article itself runs from pages 5-11, and the quotation used or paragraph referred to occurs on page 8.

INTRODUCTION

1. See, for instance, the comments of the religious sociologist Joachim Wach, "Caspar Schwenckfeld, a Pupil and a Teacher in the School of Christ," XXVI *Journal of Religion* (1946) 1:1-29, 3.

2. Evans, Austin P., *An Episode in the Struggle for Religious Freedom: the Sectaries of Nuremberg, 1524-1528* (New York: Columbia University Press, 1924), pp. 14-15. For the Law of Justinian, see p. 14. fn. 13. On uses of the term "Anabaptist," see *ME* (1955) I, 113-16. Further, Wiswedel, Wilhelm, "Rechtsprechung über die Täufer," *ME* (1956) 40:433-38; Loserth, J., "Reichsabschiede," *ibid.*, 450-51; Neff, Christian, "Bestrafung der Täufer," *MI* (1913) I, 201-09; Schraepler, Horst W., *Die rechtliche Behandlung der Täufer* (Tübingen: Fabian-Verlag, 1957).

3. *Infra*, pp. 14, 85.

7. *Infra*, pp. 43f, I:211.

Toleranz im 16. Jahrhundert (Leipzig: M. Heinsius Nachf., 1937), p. 11.

5. See documents printed in *WtQ1934*, pp. 1-5.

6. The term "Bolshevik" actually has been applied to the "Anabaptists" by partisan historians. See Smith, Preserved, *The Age of the Reformation* (New York: Henry Holt & Co., 1920), p. 154: "those Bolsheviki of the sixteenth century." Also, Dosker, Henry Elias, *The Dutch Anabaptists* (Philadelphia: Judson Press, 1921), p. 66.

7. *Infra*, pp. 43f, I:211.

8. *Der Kirchenbegriff der Schwärmer* (Leipzig: M. Heinsius Nachf., 1939), p. 3. Perhaps worth noting is the fact that John Baillie, writing on *What is Christian Civilization?* (New York: Charles Scribner's Sons, 1945), settled upon the church view as the essential matter — and especially cited the doctrine of baptism as the dividing point between traditional territorial and sectarian views (pp. 34-35).

9. *The Anabaptists* (London: James Clarke & Co., 1935), pp. 14-15.

10. "Prolegomena to an Anabaptist Theology," XXIV *MQR* (1950) 1: 5-11, 10-11.

CHAPTER 1

THE QUEST FOR THE ESSENCE OF ANABAPTISM

1. "The First Anabaptist Congregation: Zollikon, 1525," XXVII *MQR* (1953) 1:17-33, 33.

2. "The Zürich Anabaptists and Thomas Müntzer," IX *American Journal of Theology* (1905) 91-106, 92.

3. *Beck*, p. 12, fn. 2.

4. *Beck*, p. 13.

5. Thus the Anabaptists termed Zwingli and Luther and other Protestants of the establishments. In his *Deutsche Messe* (1526), Luther had stressed the organized fellowship of committed believers, and Free Churchmen of both sixteenth and twentieth centuries have "regretted that Luther did not have the courage to actualize his ideal." See Mueller, William A., *Church and State in Luther and Calvin* (Nashville: Broadman Press, 1954), pp. 24-25.

6. Schlaffer, Hans, "Ein Kurzer Underricht zum Anfang Eines Recht Christlichen Lebens," in *WtQ 1938*, p. 85.

7. The types of radical protest can be listed as follows: a) religious revolutionaries ("Maccabean" Christians); b) spiritualizers (*Spiritualisten*); c) evangelical *Täufer* (the Anabaptists proper); d) Anti-Trinitarians; e) evangelical rationalists. See *GHW/M*, pp. 19-38. For our present study the first three types are most important.

8. On LUTHER, see Köhler, Walther, in *ML* (1937) II, 702-08; by the same author, as supplemented by Harold S. Bender, *ME* (1956) II, 70-74; Bender, on "Germany," *ME* (1956) II, 483-501; Köstlin, Julius, on "Luther," in *Real.-3* (1902) XI, 720-56, with supplement by Ernest G. Schwiebert in Loetscher, Lefferts A., ed., *Twentieth Century Encyclopedia of Religious Knowledge* (Grand Rapids, Mich.: Baker Book House, 1955), II, 679-83; Bainton, Roland H., *Here I Stand* (New York & Nashville: Abingdon-Cokesbury Press, 1950); Gerdes, Hajo, *Luthers Streit mit den Schwärmern um das rechte Verständnis des Gesetzes Mose* (Göttingen: Göttinger Verlagsanstalt, 1955); Maurer, E., *Luther und die Schwärmer* (Berlin-Spandau: Luther Verlagshaus, 1952), *Schriften des theol. Konvents Augsb. Bek.*, Heft 6; Steck, Karl Gerhard, *Luther und die Schwärmer* (Zollikon-Zürich: Evang. Verlag A. G., 1955); Oyer, John S., "The Writings of Luther Against the Anabaptists," XXVII *MQR* (1953) 2:100-10; Köhler, Walther, *Reformation und Ketzerprozess* (Tübingen & Leipzig: J. C. B. Mohr, 1901).

9. Müller, Nikolaus, *Die Wittenberger Bewegung, 1521 und 1522* (Leipzig: M. Heinsius Nachf., 1911), 2nd ed., (#43 [1521]), p. 88.

10. *Ibid.*, p. 143.

11. *Ibid.*, p. 160.

12. See Spinka, Matthew, "Peter Chelčický, Spiritual Father of the *Unitas Fratrum*," XII *CH* (1943) 4:271-91; Kaminsky, Howard, "Chiliasm and the Hussite Revolution," XXVI *CH* (1957) 1:43-71.

13. Wiswedel, W., *Bilder und Führergestalten aus dem Täufertum* (Kassel: J. G. Oncken Verlag, 1928, 1930, 1952), I, 30.

14. *WtQ1934*, #6 (testimony of February, 1525), p. 7.

15. Barge, Hermann, *Andreas Bodenstein von Karlstadt* (Leipzig: Friedrich Brandstetter, 1905), I, 352. See II, 188ff, for other evidences of a "Puritan" movement. The sharp ethical concern is common ground for both Wittenberg and Zürich radicals, but the latter gave attention to internal church discipline and were little concerned with general social reform.

16. First Sermon (March 9, 1522), *WA* X, 3:1f, 6-7. The sermons were preached on successive days and are of mollifying effect, in contrast with

Luther's later bitterness toward those who seemed to press too far and too fast. See also Müller, Karl, *Luthers Äusserungen über das Recht des bewaffneten Widerstands gegen den Kaiser* (Munich: K. bayer. Akademie, 1915). Luther was always opposed to use of force in matters of faith, although he finally shifted to defensive war against imperial Catholicism — a problem parallel to war against the Turks. "It would be less harmful to have three devils in the army than one disobedient, apostate bishop, who had forgotten his office and assumed that of another." "On the War Against the Turk" [1529], *Works of Martin Luther* (Philadelphia: A. J. Holman Co., 1915-32), V, 77-103, 86.

17. Third Sermon (March 11, 1522), *WA* X, 26.

18. Fourth Sermon (March 12, 1522), *WA* X, 36f. The rulers were to make the necessary rules putting down the "outward" forms.

19. "Wider die himmlischen Propheten," *WA* XVIII, 37f, 111.

20. Second Sermon (March 10, 1522), *WA* X, 18.

21. Discussed in Loewenich, Walter von, *Luthers Theologia Crucis* (Munich: Chr. Kaiser Verlag, 1929), pp. 16, 39.

22. *Infra*, p. 143f.

23. See Bender, Harold S., "Die Zwickauer Propheten, Thomas Müntzer, und die Täufer," VIII *Theologische Zeitschrift* (1952) 4:262-78.

24. *WA* XVIII, 37ff.

25. *WA* XXX, 3:510ff.

26. *WA* LIV, 116ff; XXX, 2:209ff; XXVIII, 336ff.

27. *WA* XVIII, 279ff.

28. *WA* XVIII, 344ff.

29. Third Sermon (March 11, 1522), *WA* X, 21.

30. Köhler, Walther, "Zu Luthers Kirchenbegriff," XXI *Christliche Welt* (April 18, 1907) 16:371-77, 373.

31. Bainton, Roland H., "The Development and Consistency of Luther's Attitude to Religious Liberty," XXII *Harvard Theological Review* (1929) 2:107-49.

32. "Wider die himmlischen Propheten," *WA* XVIII, 103.

33. Fifth Sermon (March 13, 1522), *WA* X, 45.

34. Bainton, Roland H., *Concerning Heretics . . . An anonymous work attributed to Sebastian Castellio* (New York: Columbia University Press, 1935), pp. 43-44.

35. They based their assumption upon Luther's "Von der Freiheit eines Christen Menschen," among other writings; see *WtQ1938*, p. xiii.

36. "Zum zwelften ist vnser beschluss vnd endtlyche maynung, wann ainer oder mer artickel alss hie gesteldt (so dem wort Gotes nit gemess) weren, als wir dann nit vermainen die selbigen artickel, wo man vns mit dem wort gots für vnzimlich anzaigen, wolt wyr daruon abston, wann mans vns nit grundt der schrifft erklert. Ob man vns schon etlich artickel yetz zu lyess, vnd hernach sich befendt das vnrecht weren, sollen sy von stunden todt vnd absein. Nichts mehr gelten, der gleichen ob sich in der schrifft mit der warhait mer artickel erfunden, die wider Got vnd beschwernus der nächsten weren, wöllen wir vnns auch vor/behalten, vnnd beschlossen haben, vnnd vns in aller christlicher leer neben vnd brauchen, darumb wir gott den herren bitten wöllen, der vns das selbig geben kan vnnd sunst nyemant, Der frid Christi sey mit vns allen." Böhmer, H., "Urkunden zur

Geschichte des Bauernkrieges und der Wiedertäufer," 50/51 *Kleine Texte für Theologische und Philologische Vorlesungen und Übungen* (1910), p. 10.
37. *Ibid.*, p. 11f.
38. Franz, Günther, *Der deutsche Bauernkrieg* (Munich and Berlin: R. Oldenburg, 1933), I, 408ff. Also, Unruh, B. H., "Die Revolution 1525 und das Täufertum," in Neff, Christian, ed., *Gedenkschrift zum 400. Jährigen Jubiläum der Mennoniten oder Taufgesinnten, 1525-1925* (Ludwigshafen: Konferenz der Süd-deutschen Mennoniten E. V., 1925), pp. 35f.
39. Brandt, Otto H., *Thomas Müntzer: Sein Leben und seine Schriften* (Jena: Eugen Diedrichs Verlag, 1933), pp. 18-21. On MÜNTZER, see Lohmann, Annemarie, *Zur geistigen Entwicklung Thomas Müntzers* (Leipzig and Berlin: B. G. Teubner, 1931); Kolde, Theodor, "Münzer," in *Real.-3* (1903) XIII, 556-66; Seidemann, J. R., *Thomas Münzer* (Dresden and Leipzig: Arnoldsche Buchh., 1842); Böhmer, Heinrich, *Studien zu Thomas Müntzer* (Leipzig: Alex Edelmann, 1922); Strobel, Georg Theodor, *Lebren, Schriften und Lehren Thomae Muenzers* (Nürnberg and Altdorf: Monath & Kussler, 1795); Hege, in *ML* (1940) 34:187-91; Merx, Otto, *Thomas Münzer und Heinrich Pfeiffer, 1523-25* (Göttingen: Vandenhoeck & Ruprecht's Verlag, 1889); Schiff, Otto, "Thomas Müntzer als Prediger in Halle," XXIII *ARG: Texte und Untersuchungen* (1926) 287-93; Bloch, Ernst, *Thomas Muenzer als Theologe der Revolution* (Munich: Kurt Wolff Verlag, 1921). (Bloch is now a collaborator in the Communist section of Germany.) For more of the "new" interpretation of Müntzer, see Meusel, Alfred, *Thomas Müntzer und seine Zeit* (Berlin: Aufbau-Verlag, 1952), and Smirin, M. M., *Die Volksreformation des Thomas Münzer und der Grosse Bauernkrieg* (Berlin: Dietz Verlag, 1956). *KSch,* #15957, #15995, #16001a; *GHW/M*, pp. 47-48.
40. "Ermahnung zum Frieden auf die Zwölf Artikel der Bauernschaft in Schwaben. 1525," *WA* XVIII, 279f, 297.
41. *Ibid.*, p. 315.
42. "Wider die räuberischen und mörderischen Rotten der Bauern. 1525," *WA* XVIII, 344f, 358.
43. On Karlstadt, see *infra*, p. 68.
44. Scheel, Otto, "Individualismus und Gemeinschaftsleben in der Auseinandersetzung Luthers mit Karlstadt 1524/25," XVII *ZTK* (1907) 352-75, 358. For the study in contrasts see Müller, Karl, *Luther und Karlstadt* (Tübingen: J. C. B. Mohr, 1907), and, by the same author, *Kirche, Gemeinde und Obrigkeit nach Luther* (Tübingen: J. C. B. Mohr, 1910).
45. His brother-in-law, Gerhard Westerburg of the "Wassenburger preachers," was with him. Cornelius, C. A., *Geschichte des Münsterischen Aufruhrs* (Leipzig: T. O. Weigel, 1855), I, 39.
46. Bainton, Roland H., ". . . Luther's Attitude to Religious Liberty," *loc. cit.*, p. 119.
47. Otte, Johann Heinrich, *Annales Anabaptistici* (Basel: Jacob Werenfels, 1672), p. 8, said the Swiss movement stemmed from Müntzer and Nicolaus "Storck", and from the work of Cellarius, who went from Wittenberg to join Oecolampadius, serving as professor of theology at the University of Basel until his death in 1564 (p. 15).
48. *Kirchen- und Ketzer-Historie* (Frankfurt a/M: Thomas Fritsch, 1700), II: XVI, XXI, 262f. Arnold distinguished both of these groups strongly from Münster; 264a.

49. Letter of September 5, 1524; printed in Neff, ed., *Gedenkschrift*, pp. 89-99. "If your benefices, as with us, are supported by interest and tithes, which are both true usury, and if you do not get your support from an entire church, we beg that you give up your benefices. Ye know well how a shepherd should be supported." In a second letter: "The brother of Huiuf writes that thou hast preached against the princes, that they are to be attacked with the fist. Is it true? If thou art willing to defend war, the tablets, singing, or other things which thou doest not find in express words of Scripture, as thou doest not find the points mentioned, then I admonish thee by the common salvation of us all that thou wilt cease therefrom and from all notions of thine own now and hereafter, then wilt thou be completely pure, who in other points pleasest us better than anyone in this German and other countries. . . ." Translated by Walter Rauschenbusch, *loc. cit.*, pp. 94, 97-8. This famous letter is also printed in English in *GHW/M*, pp. 73f, and in German in *WtQ:Zürich*, pp. 13f. For other evidences of Anabaptist opposition to violence, see note 206 of this chapter.

50. *Infra*, p. 155.

51. Burrage, Henry S., *The History of the Anabaptists in Switzerland* (Philadelphia: American Baptist Publication Society, 1882). Burrage gave a paramount place to Erasmus in the coming of the Swiss Reformation. Harold S. Bender minimizes the importance of Erasmus in the development of Conrad Grebel's thought: *Conrad Grebel (c. 1498-1526)* (Goshen, Indiana: Mennonite Historical Society, 1950), pp. 66f. The Hutterites treasured the memory of Erasmus for his insight into the ethics of the New Testament; Müller, Lydia, *Der Kommunismus der mährischen Wiedertäufer* (Leipzig: M. Heinsus Nachf., 1927), p. 67. On Erasmus, see *infra*, p. 50.

52. *The Complaint of Peace* (Chicago and London: Open Court Publ. Co., 1917), pp. 25-6.

53. Lüdemann, H., *Reformation und Täufertùm in ihrem Verhältnis zum christlichen Princip* (Bern: W. Kaiser, 1896), p. 30.

54. *Infra*, p. 51.

55. Newman, Albert Henry, *A History of Anti-Pedobaptism* (Philadelphia: American Baptist Publication Society, 1897), pp. 103f. One of the best books of source material in this period is Kessler's *Sabbata*, edited by Emil Egli and Rudolph Schock (St. Gall: Fehr'sche Buchhandlung, 1902).

56. *ME* (1955) I, 523-24.

57. Usteri, J. M., "Darstellung der Tauflehre Zwinglis," and "Zwinglis Correspondenz mit den Berner Reformatoren über die Tauffrage," 55 *TSK* (1882) 205f, 616f. Hottinger said that Zwingli for years had said children shouldn't be baptized and now said they should, thereby showing himself a liar and a heretic; *WtQ:Zürich*, #43, p. 53. Leo Jud, Zwingli's asssistant, was one of those who repeatedly expressed doubts regarding the union of church and state (after the Cappel War), and in regard to infant baptism; Usteri, J. M., "Leo Judae über die heilige Taufe," 56 *TSK* (1883) 618-20. On Jud see Weiss, Leo, *Leo Jud, Ulrich Zwingli's Kampfgenosse (1482-1542)* (Zürich: Zwingli Verlag, 1942); *Real.-3* (1901) IX, 550-53.

58. It has been claimed that it was the dispute with the Anabaptists on the issue of baptism that led Zwingli to the position that all sacraments are symbols only; XXVII *Goshen College Record, Review Supplement* (1926) 4:11-12. A better-known interpretation is that which attributes the symbolic

view of the Eucharist to Hoen of the Brethren of the Common Life; Hyma, Albert, *The Christian Renaissance* (New York and London: Century Co., 1925), pp. 332f. See article on Hoen in *ME* (1956) II, 776. See also Fast, Heinold, "The Dependence of the First Anabaptists on Luther, Erasmus, and Zwingli," XXX *MQR* (1956) 2:104-19.

59. Egli, Emil, *Die Züricher Wiedertäufer zur Reformationszeit* (Zürich: Friedrich Schulthess, 1878), pp. 14-17. Also #692 (April E?, 1525) in *Egli*, I, 308-14. See also Burrage, Henry S., "The Anabaptists of the Sixteenth Century," III *Papers of the American Society of Church History* (1890) 145-64, 150; Horsch, John, "The Struggle Between Zwingli and the Swiss Brethren in Zürich," VII *MQR* (1933) 3:142-61; further on Anabaptist experience in Canton Zürich, see article on "Grüningen," *ME* (1956) II, 604-06. Zwingli was dealing in those compromises necessary to make the whole people officially Protestant. Of all leaders in the Continental Reformation, he was the least disturbed by a close linking of secular authorities with the life of the church, and less than three months after Zwingli's death Marpeck — in his third Strassburg debate with Butzer — criticized him for mixing religion and politics at Zürich; Wenger, John C., "The Life and Work of Pilgrim Marpeck," XII *MQR* (1938), 3:137-66, 154. In a contemporary Swiss study we read: "It is quite clear that in putting the State at the service of the Church the Reformer abandoned the ground of the New Testament." The author goes on to say that whereas in Zwingli's lifetime the civil authorities were accustomed to defer to the judgment of the theologians, afterwards the Anabaptist charge that Zwingli had betrayed the freedom of the church became more and more true. Ley, Roger, *Kirchenzucht bei Zwingli* (Zürich: Zwingli-Verlag, 1948), pp. 41, 61.

60. On GREBEL, see article by Neff in *MI.* (1937) II, 163-69; Bender, Harold S., "Conrad Grebel," in *ME* (1956) II, 566-75; Yoder, Edward, articles in XXVII *Gohsen College Record, Review Supplement* (1926) 33-37, II *MQR* (1928) 4:229-59, III *MQR* (1929) 2:132-46; Bender, Harold S., *Conrad Grebel (c. 1498-1526), The Founder of the Swiss Brethren Sometimes Called Anabaptists* (Goshen, Ind.: Mennonite Historical Society, 1950). Grebel-Vadian correspondence is found in *WtQ:Zürich*, and as translated by Edw. Yoder in MSS at Goshen College. An older treatment of Grebel and his associates is Strasser, Gottfried, "Der schweizerische Anabaptismus zur Zeit der Reformation," in Nippold, Friedrich, ed., *Berner Beiträge zur Geschichte der Schweizerischen Reformationskirchen* (Bern: K. J. Wysz, 1884), pp. 168-245.

61. On MANZ, see article in *ML* (1938) 31:22-24.

62. On REUBLIN, see Fast, Heinold, "Neues zum Leben Wilhelm Reublins," XI *Theologische Zeitschrift* (1955) 6:420-25; article in *ML* (1956) 40: 477f; Ludwig Keller's article in *ADB* (1889) XXVIII, 279.

63. *Infra*, p. 121.

64. *Infra*, p. 17.

65. *Egli*, #646 (Feb. 18 and 25, 1525), p. 289.

66. Loserth, Johann, and Beck, Josef R., "Georg Blaurock und die Anfänge des Anabaptismus in Graubündten und Tirol," VII *Vorträge und Aufsätze aus der Comenius-Gesellschaft* (1889) 1-30, 9. Blaurock, Castelberger, Joh. Brödli, and Schorant were all from the Grisons, an area also important for the Anti-Trinitarians and "evangelical rationalists."

67. For the Anabaptist teaching on Baptism, see *infra*, p. 83.

68. *ME* (1956) II, 771.

69. *Supra,* p. 8.

70. On VADIAN, see Bonorand, Conradin, "Joachim Vadian und die Täufer," XI *Schweizer Beiträge zur allgemeinen Geschichte* (1953) 43-72; article by H. Hermelink in *Real.-3* (1908) XXI, 25-29.

71. Zili challenged Zwingli for not having a similar discipline in Zürich, and also objected to the civic oath required of the preachers at ordination. Horsch, John, *Mennonites in Europe* (Scottdale, Penna.: Mennonite Publishing House, 1942), p. 92.

72. Egli, Emil, *Die St. Galler Täufer* (Zürich: Friedrich Schulthess, 1887), p. 42.

73. *ME* (1956) II, 636; also, article in *Real.-3* (1889) VII, 366-70.

74. Gratz, Delbert L., *Bernese Anabaptists* (Goshen, Ind.: Mennonite Historical Society, 1953), p. 17.

75. There were repeated mandates against Anabaptists in Bern through the years — September 3, 1585; July 29, 1597; etc. — indicating that the movement was not utterly crushed out, although cruelly persecuted and scattered. A Commission for Anabaptist Matters was set up in 1589, and an Anabaptist Chamber as late as 1699. On Bern, see *ML* (1913) I, 168-96; also, "Emmental," *ME* (1956) II, 205-10. Haller (1492-1536), the Reformer of Bern, was a tolerator; nevertheless, persecution was pressed by the Council; see article on Hans Hausmann in *ME* (1956) II, 655-56.

76. Celio Secundo Curione was a primitivist in respect to the Early Church, and was once thought to serve as a link between Swiss Anabaptism and the Italian Reformers in Naples, Venice, and the Grisons; see Benrath, Karl, "Wiedertäufer im Venetianischen um die Mitte des 16. Jahrhunderts," 58 *TSK* (1885) 9-67, 23. Henry A. DeWind has, however, called Benrath's interpretations into question; " 'Anabaptism' and Italy," XXI *CH* (1952) 1:20-38. On Curione, see article by Benrath in *Real.-3* (1898) IV, 353-57.

77. On the extraordinary group which gathered in Basel over the years, see Cantimori, Delio, "Inconti Italo-Germanici Nell'eta della Riforma"; reprint, pp. 77-78. On Giulio Gherlandi (c. 1520-1562), see article by DeWind in *ME* (1956) II, 513-14; DeWind, Henry A., "Italian Hutterite Martyrs," XXVIII *MQR* (1954) 3:163-85. See, however, Ritter, Gerhard, "Wegbahner eines 'aufgeklärten' Christentums im 16. Jahrhundert," XXXVII *ARG* (1940) 2/3:268-89; Ritter is of the opinion that the distinction between *Täufer* and *Spiritualisten* cannot be maintained in Italy as in Germany (p. 273). On the official Basel position vs. the "Rottengeister," note the "Basler Konfession" by Oecolampadius and Myconius (1488-1552) (January 21, 1534): *ML* (1941) 37:193-94.

78. Burckhardt, Paul, *Die Basler Täufer* (Basel: R. Reich, 1898), pp. 13f.

79. Oecolampadius' report on the First Disputation led to a counter-report by Hübmaier, followed by a lengthy exchange: Smithson, R. J., *The Anabaptists* (London: James Clarke & Co., 1935), pp. 176-77. On December 29, 1529, he participated in a Third Disputation with the Anabaptist leaders in jail. On OECOLAMPADIUS, see Staehelin, Ernst, ". . . zum Leben Oekolampads," X *QuFRG* (1927), XIX (1934), XXI (1939); also, article in *ML* (1951) 37:296-97.

80. On Anabaptism in other cantons, see articles in *ML* and *ME;* e.g., "Geneva," XX *ME* (1956) II, 471-73.

81. Note the planning in the Martyr Synod (1527) ; see *infra*, p. 122. Also, "Mähren," in *ML* (1937) II, 711-17; *ME* (1956) II, 826-34.

82. On HÜBMAIER, see article by Loserth in *ML* (1937) II, 353-63; Hegler, A., in *Real.-3* (1900) VIII, 418-24; Loserth, Johann, *Doctor Balthasar Hubmaier und die Anfänge der Wiedertaufe in Mähren* (Brünn: R. M. Rohrer, 1893) ; Mau, Wilhelm, *Balthasar Hübmaier* (Berlin: Dr. Walter Rothschild, 1912) ; Newman, A. H., "Balthazar Hübmaier and the Moravian Anabaptists," XXVII *Goshen College Record, Review Supplement* (1926) 10: 4-22; Sachsse, Carl, *D. Balthasar Hubmaier als Theologe* (Berlin: Trowitzsch & Sohn, 1914) ; Vedder, Henry C., *Balthasar Hübmaier: The Leader of the Anabaptists* (New York and London: G. P. Putnam's Sons, 1895) . On Waldshut, see Loserth, Johann, "Die Stadt Waldshut und die vorderösterreichische Regierung," XXXVII *Archiv für österreichische Geschichte* (1891) 93-147; Westin, Gunnar, *Der Weg der freien christlichen Gemeinden durch die Jahrhunderte* (Kassel: J. G. Oncken Verlag, 1956) , p. 63f; for documents on Waldshut, see *WtQ:Baden/Pfalz*, #365-76, pp. 387ff. Hübmaier was influenced by Müntzer on baptism, and by Karlstadt on the Lord's Supper; Sachsse, Carl, *op. cit.*, pp. 153, 154f.

83. Sachsse, *op. cit.*, pp. 187, 190.

84. *Ibid.*, pp. 153ff.

85. For a fuller discussion of the congregational principle, see Schubert, Hans von, *Revolution und Reformation im XVI. Jahrhundert* (Tübingen: J. C. B. Mohr, 1927) , p. 26.

86. *ML* (1942) 36:256-60, on Nikolsburg.

87. Heyer, Fritz, *Der Kirchenbegriff der Schwärmer* (Leipzig: M. Heinsius Nachf., 1939) , p.68. See the discussion in the present study, p. 133.

88. Horsch, *Mennonites in Europe*, p. 315.

89. *Beck*, p. 9.

90. Burckhardt, Paul, *op. cit.*, pp. 123-24; Egli, *Die Züricher Wiedertäufer*, p. 31.

91. Egli, Emil, *Die St. Galler Täufer*, pp. 44-45.

92. Neuser, Wilhelm, *Hans Hut. Leben und Wirken bis zum Nikolsburger Religionsgespräch* (Berlin: Hermann Blanke, 1913) , p. 19. On the radical circles at Nürnberg, see article on Albrecht Dürer by Karl Rembert, *ML* (1913) I, 486-93; also "Nürnberg," *ML* (1942) 36:279-81.

93. Testimony #14 (November 28, 1529) , printed in *WtQ1930*, p. 924. Further documents on Bader follow. See Bossert, Gustav, "Augustin Bader von Augsburg, der Prophet und König, und seine Genossen, nach den Prozessakten von 1530," X *ARG:Texte und Untersuchungen* (1912/13) 117-65, 209-41, 297-349. Also see, on Oswald Leber, #19, #37, and on Gall Fischer, #20, in *WtQ1930; ML* (1913) I, 107-09; *ME* (1955) I, 209-10; Peachey, Paul, *Die soziale Herkunft der Schweizer Täufer in der Reformationszeit* (Karlsruhe: Heinrich Schneider, 1954) , p. 38, fn. 13.

94. See article on "Augsburger Täufergemeinde," by Hege in *ML* (1913) I, 92-6. On Denck and the middle cities, see Keller, Ludwig, *Ein Apostel der Wiedertäufer* (Leipzig: S. Hirzel, 1882) , pp. 6-12. On the Martyr Synod, see *infra*, p. 122.

95. He desired the inner and nonsectarian truth sought by all parties. "Falsche Propheten reden nur von Schrift und nicht auch von Gegenschrift." Keller, *Ein Apostel*, p. 71. This theme was dominant in Sebastian Franck.

96. Hulshof, Abraham, *Geschiedenis van de Doopsgezinden te Straatsburg van 1525 tot 1557* (Amsterdam: J. Clausen, 1905), pp. 5f. See also Kreider, Robert J., "The Anabaptists and the Civil Authorities of Strasbourg, 1525-1555," XXIV *CH* (1955) 2:99-108.

97. Loserth, Johann, "Studien zur Pilgram Marpeck," in Neff, ed., *Gedenkschrift*, p. 140.

98. On HOFMANN, see article by Neff in *ML* (1913) I, 401-14; *ME* (1956) II, 778-85; article by A. Hegler in *Real.-3* (1900) VIII, 222-27; Krohn, Barthold Nicolaus, *Geschichte der Fanatischen und Enthusiastischen Wiedertäufer, Melchior Hofmann und die Secte der Hofmannianer* (Leipzig: Bernhard Christoph Breitkopf, 1758); zur Linden, Friedrich Otto, *Melchior Hofmann, ein Prophet der Wiedertäufer* (Haarlem: de Erven F. Bohn, 1885). Further, in *KSch:* #8518, #8521. On Hofmann's successful evangelical preaching in one area, see Krahn, Cornelius, "Anabaptism in East Friesland," XXX *MQR* (1956) 4:247-58; by the same author, *ME* (1956) II, 119-22. For Hofmann's own writings, see *BRN* V. It has been estimated that by the end of the sixteenth century, one-fourth of the population of Frisia was Mennonite; Unruh, Benjamin Heinrich, *Die niederländisch-niederdeutschen Hintergründe der mennonitischen Ostwanderunger im 16., 18., und 19. Jahrhundert* (Karlsruhe: Heinrich Schneider, 1956), p. 23.

99. See article by Neff on Amsdorf, *ML* (1913) I, 58; *ME* (1955) I, 100. See also Neff's article on "Johann Bugenhagen," *ML* (1913) I, 290; *ME* (1955) I, 463-64. Bugenhagen (1485-1558) reported the Flensburg Disputation, and was led thereby into violent controversy with Hofmann.

100. *Infra*, pp. 29f.

101. *Infra*, p. 76.

102. On DENCK, see article by Neff in *ML* (1913) I, 401-14; as expanded by Fellman, Walter, *ME* (1956) II, 32-35; article by Hegler in *Real.-3* (1898) IV, 576-80; Coutts, Alfred, *Hans Denck (1495-1527): Humanist and Heretic* (Edinburgh: Macniven and Wallace, 1927); Baring, Georg, *Quellen zur Geschichte der Taüfer, VI: Hans Denck/Schriften, 1; Bibliographie* (Gütersloh: C. Bertelsmann Verlag, 1955), XXIV *QuFRG;* Fellman, Walter, *Quellen zur Geschichte der Taüfer, VI: Hans Denck/Schriften, 2* (Gütersloh: C. Bertelsmann Verlag, 1956), XXIV *QuFRG;* Heberle, Dekan, "Johann Denck und sein Büchlein vom Gesetz," 24 *TSK* (1851) 121-94, 412-13. Denck's pupil, Christian Entfelder, started his career as a *Taüfer* preacher and became a high official in the Prussian court: *ME* (1956) II, 227.

103. On HETZER, see article by Neff in *ML* (1937) II, 225-31; article by Hegler in *Real.-3* (1899) VII, 325-29; Keim, Theodor, "Ludwig Hetzer. Ein Beitrag zur Characteristik der Sektenbewegung in der Reformationszeit," I *Jahrbücher für Deutsche Theologie* (1856) 215-88; Weis, Frederic Lewis, *The Life and Teachings of Ludwig Hetzer* (Dorchester, Mass.; Underhill Press, 1930); article by J. F. Gerhard Goeters in *ME* (1956) II, 621-26; by the same author, "Ludwig Haetzer, a Marginal Anabaptist," XXIX *MQR* (1955) 4:251-62; see also, by the same author, *Ludwig Hätzer* (Gütersloh: C. Bertelsmann Verlag, 1957), XXV *QuFRG*. For reports of his execution, see *WtQ:Baden/Pfalz*, #462 and #467. Peachey, *Die Soziale Herkunft*, p. 24, fn. 5.

104. On BÜNDERLIN, see article by Neff in *ML* (1913) I, 298-300; *ME* (1955) I, 469-70; Nicoladoni, Alexander, *Johannes Bünderlin von Linz und die oberösterreichischen Täufergemeinde in den Jahren 1525-1531* (Berlin: R. Gaertners Verlag, 1893). Stoffel and Leonhard Freisleben belonged to his circle before accommodating at the end; *ME* (1956) II, 183-84.

105. *Infra*, p. 152.

106. On SCHWENCKFELD, see the *Corpus Schwenckfeldianorum* (Norristown, Penna.: Board of Publication of the Schwenckfelder Church, 1907 — ; final editor, Elmer E. S. Johnson; (*CSchw*). Also, Ecke, Karl, *Schwenckfeld, Luther, und der Gedanke einer apostolischen Reformation* (Berlin: Martin Warneck, 1911), in abridged form (Gütersloh: C. Bertelsmann Verlag, 1952); Schultz, Selina Gerhard, *Caspar Schwenckfeld von Ossig (1489-1561)* (Norristown, Penna.: Board of Publication of the Schwenckfelder Church, 1946); Hirsch, Emanuel, "Zum Verständnis Schwenckfelds," in *Festgabe für Karl Müller* (Tübingen: J. C. B. Mohr, 1922); French, James Leslie, ed., *The Correspondence of Caspar Schwenckfeld of Ossig and the Landgrave Philip of Hesse, 1535-1561* (Leipzig: Breitkopf & Härtel, 1908); article by Grützmacher in *Real.-3* (1907) XVIII, 72-81. Further in *KSch*, #19623, #19624, #19649, #19722. See *GHW/M*, p. 161, fn. 1; p. 65, fn. 4.

107. *Infra*, p. 126.

108. Heyer, *op. cit.*, pp. 47-8.

109. Schlaffer, Hans, "Gebet und Danksagung," *WtQ1938*, pp. 96-98, 97.

110. Stadler, Ulrich, "Vom lebendig wort und geschribnen," *WtQ1938*, pp. 212-15, 214.

111. *Ibid.*, p. 212.

112. On Kautz, see *ML* (1937) II, 476-78; article by Hegler in *Real.-3* (1901) X, 192-94.

113. Arnold, Gottfried, *op. cit.*, II; XVI, XXII, 267; *WtQ:Baden/Pfalz*, #129, pp. 113-14.

114. Horsch, John, *The Mennonites in Europe*, p. 158, quoting one of Denck's associates: "I have found, as it were, a middle way between popery and Lutheranism, by which I have avoided all separation, and am striving alone for a good, upright Christian life." On his reported recantation, see Keller, Ludwig, *Ein Apostel*, p. 222; Fellmann, Walter, *Hans Denck*, pp. 18-19. Schwenckfeld's views stand out clearly in the following passage: "Since the gracious visitation by God I could not join with any party or church in the observance of the Sacraments and in other respects, nor could I allow men to rule over my faith. Nevertheless, I have not despised any church, or any man, leader or teacher. . . . I cannot at this time [1533] unite with any party or sect regardless of name; and as I have done for the last eight years, and ever since the divine visitation, have refrained from glorying in any man and have not submitted to anyone to rule over my faith, but Almighty God." Schultz, Selina Gerhard, *op. cit.*, quotation on p. 101.

115. Quoted in Keller, *Ein Apostel*, p. 55.

116. Nicoladoni, Alexander, *op. cit.*, pp. 107, 131.

117. *Ibid.*, p. 138.

118. Hegler, A., *Geist und Schrift bei Sebastian Franck* (Freiburg i. Br.: J. C. B. Mohr, 1893), pp. 262-63. Troeltsch regarded Franck as the prototype of a third church view beside the church and sect types: the individual Christian, modern and without formal attachment. Troeltsch, Ernst, *The*

Social Teaching of the Christian Churches (New York: Macmillan Co., 1931),
II, 933f. Of Schwenckfeld as a similar modern type it has been written:
"The first tenet which Schwenckfeld adopted and consistently developed was
that of individualism. . . . The more I have made of myself the better I can
help my fellows; the more rapid will be the advancement of the race. This
is the primary axiom of Schwenckfeld's system; it magnifies individualism. . . . Some of the most masterly lines in German literature are those
which Schwenckfeld wrote in defense of Christian liberty. He suffered in
its defense; he carried its cross with him to the hour of his death. He never
would yield that freedom for an instant, although it meant immeasurable
sacrifices to defend it. We dare maintain that he was an apostle of liberty
in the teeth of the established churches and servile universities. The apostle of liberty is of infinitely more significance than an apostle of impanation,
or of consubstantiation, or of ubiquity. We claim that the man who advances
the sacred standard of freedom through Christ is an immensely more significant figure than the man who preaches it and then puts shackles on his
neighbor. . . . Schwenckfeld advocated the right of religious assembly open
or private, and entirely distinct from any authorized organization. Each
believer has the right of combining with another for religious meditation,
exercises, conferences, prayer, and study." Schultz, Selina Gerhard, *op. cit.*,
pp. 370-71. One notes here the confusion of civic right and religious obligation, a sure mark of the spiritualizing tendency in any generation. Another
spiritualizer of the period was Paracelsus (1493-1541) ; in the first article
of his *De septem punctis idolatriae Christianae*, he discoursed upon the use-
lessness of going to church. All "outward forms" are idolatry; Peuckert,
Will-Erich, *Pansophie* (Stuttgart: W. Kohlhammer, 1936), p. 261. On
Paracelsus, see article by Eberhard Teufel in *ML* (1951) 37:333-34. However, some of the most significant mystics wrestled with the problem of community, and this may suggest another dividing line in our discussion of
types; Bornkamm, Heinrich, *Mystik, Spiritualismus und die Anfänge des
Pietismus im Luthertum* (Giessen: Alfred Töpelmann, 1926), p. 11. The
"nonsectarian" approach was not without influence also in the major Reformation circles; Jakob Sturm wanted to see a "non-confessional university,"
and recommended Francis Lambert of Avignon to Philipp of Hesse to get
Marburg started.

119. Wenger, John C., "Pilgram Marpeck, Tyrolese Engineer and Anabaptist Elder," IX *CH* (1940) 24-36, 24. Further on MARPECK, see articles
by Wenger in XII *MQR* (1938) 137ff, 167ff, 205ff, 269ff; Loserth, Johann,
"Studien zu Pilgram Marbeck," and Hege, Christian, "Pilgram Marbeck's
Vermahnung," in Neff, ed., *Gedenkschrift*, pp. 134f, 178f; Loserth in *ML*
(1938) 31:25-35; Bender, Harold S., "New Discoveries of Important Sixteenth
Century Anabaptist Codices," XXX *MQR* (1956) 1:72-77; Loserth, J., "Zwei
biographische Skizzen aus der Zeit der Wiedertäufer in Tirol," XI *Zeitschrift des Ferdinandeums für Tirol und Voralberg* (1895) III:39:277-302;
Quiring, Horst, "Die Anthropologie Pilgram Marpecks," II *Menn. Geschichts-
blätter* (1937) 1/2:10-17; Hege, Christian, "Pilgram Marbeck und die oberdeutschen Taufgesinnten," XXXVII *ARG* (1940) 2/3:249-58. The disputes
of Marpeck and Schwenckfeld ran into hundreds of items; Loserth, Johann,
ed., *Quellen und Forschungen zur Geschichte der oberdeutschen Taufgesinnten im 16. Jahrhundert* (Vienna and Leipzig: Carl Fromme, G. m. b. H..

1929) , p. 20. See also, Kiwiet, Jan J., *Pilgram Marbeck* (Kassel: J. G. Oncken Verlag, 1957) .

120. Burrage, Champlin, *The Church Covenant Idea* (Philadelphia: American Baptist Publication Society, 1904) , Ch. 1, and esp. pp. 15f. See also *infra,* p. 85.

121. Friedmann, Robert, *Mennonite Piety Through the Centuries* (Goshen, Ind.: Mennonite Historical Society, 1949) , p. 29.

122. Text published in Neff, ed., *Gedenkschrift,* pp. 185f.

123. Loserth, Johann, "Studien zu Pilgram Marbeck," pp. 152ff.

124. *Ibid.,* pp. 166f.

125. *CSchw* III, 830-34. This appeared after the debate in which Capito and Schwenckfeld faced Jakob Kautz; the Brethren based their cause upon the Great Commission.

126. *CSchw* VIII, 161f. This was to refute the *Vermanung* of the Brethren; it called forth the *Verantwortung.*

127. *CSchw* VII, 161f, for a discussion of the relation of Schwenckfeld to the Anabaptists, with bibliography.

128. *CSchw* III, 489-90.

129. *Infra,* p. 35. Apparently Calvin learned from the Strassburgers something of the church discipline and missionary intensity which marked the Anabaptists, and appropriated from them. See article on Calvin in *ML* (1913) I, 314-17; Hulshof, Abraham, *op. cit.,* Ch. 11; Pauck, Wilhelm, "Calvin and Butzer," IX *Journal of Religion* (1929) 237-56, 247; Schwarz, Rudolf, ed., *Johannes Calvins Lebenswerk in seinen Briefen* (Tübingen: J. C. B. Mohr, 1909) , I, #96 (March 24, 1543) , pp. 163-64. Calvin cited Matthew 28:18 to establish the church's power to excommunicate: "Now, there are three ends proposed by the Church in those corrections, and in excommunication. . . ." Kerr, Hugh Thomson, Jr., ed., *A Compend of the Institutes of the Christian Religion by John Calvin* (Philadelphia: Presbyterian Board of Christian Education, 1939) , pp. 180-81.

130. On Cellarius, see article in *ML* (1913) I, 336-38; *ME* (1955) I, 538-39; article by Bernoulli in *Real.-3* (1897) III, 332-33.

131. Capito himself opposed infant baptism, and as a chiliast divided history into three periods: 1) the Apostolic Age; 2) the reign of Anti-Christ; 3) the beginning of the absolute reign of Christ in the Reformation. He was at one time and another friend of Sattler, Denck, Hetzer, Reublin, Marpeck, but later turned more severe. Baum, Johann Wilhelm, *Capito und Butzer* (Elberfeld: R. L. Fridericks, 1860) ; *ME* (1955) I, 512-16; *Real.-3* (1897) III, 715-17.

132. Rott, Jean, ed., *Elsässischen Täuferakten: I,* not yet published; "Bucers Widerlegung des Bekenntnisses von Pilgram Marbeck" (1532) , 303:21.

133. *Infra,* p. 35.

134. For a thorough treatment of possible links between Anabaptism and Pietism, with a generally negative conclusion as to the significance of such ties, see Friedmann, Robert, *Mennonite Piety,* especially the first four chapters. Nevertheless, Hege notes (quoting Becker) : "It is noteworthy that a considerable number of villages which were known to have been centers of Anabaptism later became centers of pietism and in our day are now centers of the 'Gemeinschaften'." Hege, Christian, "The Early Anabaptists in Hesse," V *MQR* (1931) 3:157-78, 177. On rejoining the Evengelical Church

of Hesse, Peter Tesch and his group no longer cut off those outside the Anabaptist movement from fellowship, but rather adopted the position of an Ideal Community within the established church (pre-Pietist fellowship) ; Bergfried, Ulrich, *Verantwortung als theologisches Problem im Täufertum des 16. Jahrhunderts* (Wuppertal-Elberfeld: A. Martini & Grüttefien, 1938), pp. 34f.

135. Dosker, Henry Elias, *The Dutch Anabaptists* (Philadelphia: Judson Press, 1921), pp. 87-88.

136. Kühler, W. J., *Geschiedenis der Nederlandsche Doopsgezinden in de Zestiende Eeuw* (Haarlem: H. D. Tjeck Willink & Zoon, 1932), Ch. 3.

137. On HUT, see article by Loserth in *ML* (1937) II, 370-75; as expanded by Friedmann, *ME* (1956) II, 646-50; article by Hegler in *Real.-3* (1900) VIII, 489-91; Neuser, Wilhelm, *op. cit.*

138. Testimony #19 (March 26, 1527, at Nürnberg), in *WtQ1934*, p. 19.

139. Wappler, Paul, *Die Täuferbewegung in Thüringen von 1526-1584* (Jena: Gustav Fischer, 1913), pp. 26f.

140. Testimony #45 (September 22, 1527), in *WtQ1934*, p. 37.

141. #51 (Hut's answers to questioning), in *WtQ1934*, p. 55.

142. In his final deposition of October 5, 1527, he said that he gave up revolution through Denck's influence; Keller, *Ein Apostel*, pp. 41-42.

143. Meyer, Christian, "Zur Geschichte der Wiedertäufer in Oberschwaben: 1. Die Anfänge des Wiedertäuferthums in Augsburg," I *Zeitschrift des Historischen Vereins für Schwaben und Neuberg* (1874) 207-56, 231ff.

144. *WtQ1938*, p. 10ff.

145. Rembert, Karl, *Die 'Wiedertäufer' im Herzogtum Jülich* (Berlin: R. Gaertners Verlag, 1899), p. 207. Other "Wassenburgers" were Dionysius Vinne, Hermann Staprade, Heinrich Schlatscaef, Johann Klopreiss; on the latter, *ML* (1937) II, 513. On CAMPANUS, whose *Restitutio* was in answer to Melanchthon's *Loci Communes*, see article by Rembert in *ML* (1913) I, 317-24; also Robert Friedmann in *ME* (1955) I, 499-500; article by Hegler in *Real.-3* (1897) III, 696-98; note "Dissertatio de Joanne Campano Anti-Trinitario" in Schelhorn, J. G., ed., *Amoenitates Literariae* (Frankfurt and Leipzig: Daniel Bartholomew & Söhne, 1729), Vol. 11, pp. 1-92; Campanus' letter via Butzer and Tesch to Philipp of Hesse justifying his Di-Theism and expressing his primitivism is printed in Lenz, Max, ed., *Briefwechsel Landgraf Philipps . . . mit Bucer* (Leipzig, 1880, 1887, 1891), V *Kgl. Preuss. Staatsarchiven*, Vol. 2, pp. 434-37, fn. On Henric Rol (? - 1534), see article by van der Zijpp in *ME* (1956) II, 704-05.

146. *Infra*, p. 77.

147. Sixteen Articles (August 10, 1532) ; Detmer, Heinrich, and Krumbholtz, Robert, ed., *Zwei Schriften des Münsterischen Wiedertäufers Bernhard Rothmann* (Dortmund: Fr. Wilh. Ruhfus, 1904), p. LIII. On ROTHMANN, see Köhler, Walther, on "Münster, Wiedertäufer," in *Real.-3* (1903) XIII, 539-53, 542. For Philipp of Hesse's efforts to win back the Wassenburgers and Rothmann, see article on Theodor Fabricius (1501-1570), in *ME* (1956) II, 287.

148. In the *Bekentnisse van beyden Sacramenten*, in which Rothmann also portrayed the Lord's Supper as a symbol of Christian communism. Schiedung, Hans, *Beiträge zur Bibliographie und Publizistik über die Münsterischen Wiedertäufer* (Münster: Heinrich Buschmann, 1934), p. 11.

149. Quoted and discussed in Bergfried, Ulrich, *op. cit.*, p. 45.

150. Confession of Dionisius of Diest (1534); Niesert, Joseph, *Münsterische Urkundensammlung* (Coesfeld: Bernhard Wittneven, 1826), p. 48.

151. See the discussion of eschatology in Hase, Karl, *Neue Propheten: Drei historische-politische Kirchenbilder* (Leipzig: Breitkopf & Härtel, 1851), III ("Das Reich der Wiedertäufer"), pp. 145f, 244.

152. Burrage, Champlin, *op. cit.*, p. 22.

153. Cornelius, C. A., *Die Niederländischen Wiedertäufer während der Belagerung Münsters 1534 bis 1535* (Munich: Kgl. bayer. Akademie, 1861). reprint, p. 5.

154. Bouterwek, K. W., "Zur Wiedertäufer-Literatur," I *Zeitschrift des Bergischen Geschichtsvereins* (Bonn, 1864) 3:280-344; also, article by Keller in *ADB* (1889) XXIX, 362-70.

155. Geisberg, Max, *Das Wiedertäuferreich* (Munich: Hugo Schmidt Verlag, 1929), plate. The key city implies a total pattern of social and religious reorganization combined with the impending world sovereignty of the elect; Schiedung, Hans, *op. cit.*, p. 75. See Reichel, Ernst, *Die Vorstellung der Münsterischen Wiedertäufer über ihr Verhältnis zur Welt und zu ihren Mitmenschen*, N. F. 18 *Theol. Arbeiten aus dem Rheinischen Wissenschaftlichen Predigerverein* (1919); article by Köhler in *Real.-3* (1903) XIII, 539-53; Blanke, Fritz, "Das Reich der Wiedertäufer zu Münster, 1534/35," XXXVII *ARG* (1940) 1:13-37.

156. As reported by Jonas to Duke George of Anhalt (Dec. 20, 1534); Kawerau, Gustav, ed., *Der Briefwechsel des Justus Jonas* (Halle: Otto Hendel Verlag, 1884-85), I, 220.

157. Liefmann, Robert, *Die Kommunistischen Gemeinden in Nord-Amerika* (Jena: Gustav Fischer, 1922), p. 7, depending upon Kautsky's interpretation.

158. Von Schubert, Hans, "Der Kommunismus der Wiedertäufer in Münster und seine Quellen," X *Sitzungsberichte der Heidelberger Akademie der Wissenschaften. Phil.-Hist. Klasse* (1919) 11:3-7.

159. Detmer, Heinrich, *Bilder aus den religiösen und sozialen Unruhen in Münster während des 16. Jahrhunderts* (Münster: Coppenrathsche Buchh., 1903-04), Vol. II ("Bernhard Rothmann"), p. 156.

160. The parallelism with early Mormon experience and teaching will not escape the reader. Ochino was banishd from Zürich at the age of 76 for saying that polygamy might be practiced by divine special permission, although he was probably only using a traditional formula to cover the patriarchs; Bainton, Roland H., "The Immoralities of the Patriarchs According to the Exegesis of the Late Middle Ages and of the Reformation," XXIII *Harvard Theological Review* (1930) 39-49, 45. See discussion with much detail in Rockwell, William Walker, *Die Doppelehe des Landgrafen Philipp von Hessen* (Marburg: N. G. Elwert'sche Verlagsbuchh., 1904).

161. Detmer, Heinrich, *op. cit.*, I ("Johann von Leiden"), 46. There is no Anabaptist source for polygamy; witness Hofmann's excommunication of Klaus Frey. *Ibid.*, III ("Uber die Auffassung von der Ehe und die Durchführung der Vielweiberei in Münster während der Täuferherrschaft"), 230f.

162. See long lists of regulations under "Mandate," *ML* (1938) 31: 4-11; also, "Landesverweisung," *ML* (1937) II, 610-12. See article on Berthold Aichele, in *ME* (1955) I, 27; see also article on Ferdinand I (1503-1564),

ME (1956) II, 322-23; on "Dietrichstein," *ME* (1956) II, 59-60; "Bavaria," *ME* (1955) I, 251-53; "George the Bearded" (1471-1539), *ME* (1956) II, 476-77.

163. On Philipp see my *Landgraf Philipp und die Toleranz* (Bad Nauheim: Christian Verlag, 1957); *ML* (1952) 38:363-67; also, "Hessen," *ML* (1937) II, 294-303; *ME* (1956) II, 719-27. Philipp's policy can be seen in stark contrast to the general line of persecutors in the exchanges over treatment of heretics in the Condominium Hausbreitenbach. Wappler, Paul, *op. cit.*, pp. 30-44, 94-102; "Reinhardsbrunn," in *ML* (1956) 40:455-56; "Christoph von der Eichen," *ME* (1956) II, 167; "Fritz Erbe," *ME* (1956) II, 241.

164. #224 in *WtQ:Zürich*, p. 252.

165. Lenz, W., "Zwingli und Landgraf Philipp," III *Brieger's Zeitschrift für Kirchengeschichte* (Gotha, 1879), quotation on p. 462.

166. Cited in Köhler, *Reformation und Ketzerprozess*, p. 43.

167. The Wittenbergers distinguished three types of Anabaptists, two of which deserved the death penalty; *ML* (1913) I, 203. See *WtQ:Hessen*, p. 105 (Lüneburg), p. 117 (Tübingen).

168. *WtQ:Hessen*, #148 (May 13, 1560), p. 341.

169. *Ibid.*, #13a (c. 1530), p. 31. For the data on Rinck's hearings, *WtQ:Hessen*, #5, #14. On RINCK, see article by Mirbt in *Real - 3* (1906) XVII, 17-19; also Köhler, in *RGG-2*, IV, 2039.

170. Hermann, Fritz, *Das Interim in Hessen* (Marburg: N.G. Elwert'sche Verlagsbuchh., 1901), p. 213. Note further his word: "It is of course necessary to have authority for the sake of good order, but to improve the church and not to corrupt it, also not to make law against God's word — as though He had left it free to bind the conscience against His word and command. Even more it is not right to kill people for their faith, even heretics. For I have never read that in the Early Church; it is utterly opposed to John Chrysostom and Holy Writ, the Christian fathers. And it is even more unjust to murder Christian people for the sake of right faith and teaching, even if they err in something" (p. 211). "The name Pope is new. In the Early Church he was known as the Bishop of Rome" (p. 212).

171. *Ibid.*, p. 177.

172. *ML* (1937) II, 535.

173. Ridemann was imprisoned in Wolkersdorf in 1540, and wrote there his great *Rechenschaft*. After his return he was for twenty-four years leader of the Hutterite colonies; *Z*, pp. 212-13, 217-18.

174. On BUTZER, see article in *ML* (1913) I, 307-13; *ME* (1955) I, 455-60; Eells, Hastings, *Martin Bucer* (New Haven and London: Yale University Press/Humphrey Milford-Oxford University Press, 1931), esp. p. 239f; article in *Real - 3* (1897) III, 603-12; Pauck, Wilhelm, "Martin Bucer's Conception of a Christian State," XXVI *Princeton Theological Review* (1928) 80-88.

175. On TESCH, see Wappler, Paul, *op. cit.*, pp. 181ff; by the same author, *Die Stellung Kursachsens und des Landgrafen von Hessen zur Täuferbewegung* (Münster: Aschendorffsche Buchh., 1910), pp. 73f; Rembert, Karl, *op. cit.*, pp. 471ff.

176. Lenz, Max, ed., *op. cit.*, #62 (April 19, 1540).

177. *WtQ:Hessen,* #92, for Ridemann's report on the decline of the Anabaptist movement in Hesse.

178. *WtQ:Baden/Pfalz,* #44, pp. 30f.

179. Hege, Christian, "The Early Anabaptists in Hesse," V *MQR* (1931) 3:157-78, citing Walter Sohm's judgment, pp. 163-66.

180. "Konfirmation," in *ML* (1937) II, 533-36; *ME* (1955) I, 686-88. On its appearance among Anabaptists, *ME* (1955) I, 699-700.

181. On the centrality of the idea of the Covenant, which distinguished them from other Protestants, see Friedmann, Robert, "Anabaptism and Protestantism," XXIV *MQR* (1950) 1:12-24; also, "Covenant Theology," in *ME* (1955) I, 726-27. In the Swiss situation also: Zwingli is credited with introducing emphasis on the Covenant into Reformed theology, and he is said to have gotten it from the Anabaptists; Wenger, John C., "The Theology of Pilgram Marpeck," p. 209.

182. *Z,* p. 87. See article by Loserth on the *Diener der Notdurft,* in *ML* (1913) I, 440-42; as expanded by Friedmann, *ME* (1956) II, 54-55.

183. On HUTER, see article by Loserth in *ML* (1937) II, 375-78; *ME* (1956) II, 851-54; also, in Horsch, John, *The Hutterian Brethren, 1528-1931* (Goshen, Ind.: Mennonite Historical Society, 1931); Fischer, H. G., *Jakob Huter, Leben, Frömmigkeit, Briefe* (Newton, Kans.: Mennonite Publishing Office, 1956); "Hutterian Brethren," by Friedmann, in *ME* (1956) II, 854-65.

184. On BRANDHUBER, see *ML* (1913) I, 255-56; *ME* (1955) I, 404-05.

185. *Z,* p. 65.

186. Müller, Lydia, *Der Kommunismus der mährischen Wiedertäufer,* pp. 53f.

187. Several letters and reports are published in *WtQ1930,* pp. 1086ff.

188. *Infra,* p. 95.

189. *Infra,* Chapter 4.

190. *Supra,* p. 20.

191. Krohn, *Melchior Hofmann,* p. 248. On OBBE PHILIPSZ, see article by Schowalter and van der Zijpp in *ML* (1952) 38:369-71.

192. Braght, T. J. van, *A Martyrology of the Churches of Christ Commonly Called Baptist* (London: Hanserd Knollys Society, 1850-53), II, 195ff. On the Heavenly Flesh of Christ, see *GHW/M,* p. 182f.

193. Philipsz, Obbe, "A Confession (c. 1560)," in *GHW/M,* p. 224.

194. Kühler, W. J., *op. cit.,* p. 4.

195. On JORIS, in addition to Roland H. Bainton's standard biography, see Neff in *ML* (1913) I, 235-36; Gerhard Hein in *ME* (1956) II, 17-19; see also article on Blesdijk (? - 1584), *ME* (1955) I, 360-61; "Jurgen Ketel," *ML* (1937) II, 484.

196. On PASTOR, see Newman, A. H., "Adam Pastor, Anti-trinitarian, Antipaedo-Baptist," V *Papers of the American Society of Church History* (1917) 75-99; *BRN* V, 317-59; K. Vos in *DB* (1909) 104-26; *Real. - 3* (1904) XIV, 759-60; VII *MQR* (1933) 105-07; *ML* (1951) 37:336.

197. On MENNO, see article by Cramer in *Real. - 3* (1903) XII, 586-94; Vos, K., *Menno Simons* (Leiden: E. J. Brill, 1914); Horsch, John, *Menno Simons* (Scottdale, Penna.: Mennonite Publishing House, 1916); Krahn, Cornelius, *Menno Simons (1496-1561)* (Karlsruhe: Heinrich Schneider, 1936). A fine new translation and edition of his works has been published: *The Complete Writings of Menno Simons (c. 1496-1561)* (Scottdale, Penna.: Herald

Press, 1956) ; translated by Leonard Verduin, edited by John Christian Wenger, with a biography by Harold S. Bender. On Menno's most important writing, *Dat Fundament* (1539) , see article by Krahn in *ME* (1956) II, 358. On DIRCK PHILIPSZ (1504-1568) , who remained a true elder of the churches, see Neff in *ML* (1938) 32:77-90; *ML* (1952) 38:368-69; van der Zijpp in *ME* (1956) II, 65-66. His complete writings are in *BRN*, Vol. 10. Dirck's *Van de geestelijke Restitution* was written in answer to Rothmann's *Restitution* (1534) ; Dirck was also important as chief theological opponent of Adam Pastor and Sebastian Franck. *GHW/M*, p. 226, fn. 1. On his *Enchiridion* (1564) , see Krahn in *ME* (1956) II, 213.

198. Brons, A., *Ursprung, Entwicklung und Schicksale der Taufgesinnten oder Mennoniten* (Norden: Diedr. Soltau, 1884) , p. 64.

199. Van der Zijpp, N., "The Conception of Our Fathers Regarding the Church," XXVII *MQR* (1953) 2:91-99.

200. Mrs. Brons attributes the glorification of the Early Church primarily to the continuing tradition of the Brethren of the Common Life; *op. cit.,* pp. 56f.

201. Bergfried, Ulrich, *op. cit.,* pp. 49-50.

202. See *ME* (1955) I, 376-77.

203. Krahn, *Menno Simons,* pp. 124f.

204. *Ibid.,* pp. 104-05.

205. Horsch, John, *Menno Simons,* p. 50.

206. Quoted in Horsch, John, "Menno Simons' Attitude toward the Anabaptists of Münster," X *MQR* (1936) 1:55-72, 57. "In the first case only the cross and persecution are known until the imminent coming again of Christ. The coming judgment is administered by Christ himself. On the other hand, the chiliastic mind twists the coming again and moves over to execute judgment itself with the claim that the kingdom of God has arrived. Münster was an example of this. Through this development came the clear division which must be carefully observed. In the first case judgment is left to *God* and all help is awaited from *Him* in the time of persecution and its future. In the second, the judgment and God's rule are anticipated by one's own self-confident action." Krahn, Cornelius, *Der Gemeindebegriff des Menno Simons im Rahmen seines Lebens und seiner Theologie* (Karlsruhe: Heinrich Schneider, 1936) , p. 12. Nevertheless, a small remnant of "Schwertgeister" hung on for a time in the Netherlands; see J. Loosjes on Johann von Batenburg (1495-1538) , *ME* (1955) I, 247-48. On John á Lasco (1499-1560) , see article by Krahn in *ML* (1937) II, 621-22; also, *Real.- 3* (1902) XI, 292-96.

207. Krahn, Cornelius, *Menno Simons,* pp. 143ff.

208. A section of "The Church of God," in the *Enchiridion; GHW/M,* Selection 11, pp. 226-60.

209. The degree to which this leveling off of testimony was due to theological looseness is a topic worthy of study. The spiritualizing tendency was a continuing strain in some Dutch circles; the spiritual prophecy of Sebastian Franck and Adam Pastor never fully disappeared from the Dutch wing of Anbaptism. See Meihuizen, H. W., "Spiritualistic Tendencies and Movements among the Dutch Mennonites of the 16th and 17th Centuries,"

XXVI *MQR* (1953) 4:259-304; also, "Confessions of Faith," *ME* (1955) I, 679-86.

210. See my study, *The Free Church* (Boston: Starr King Press, 1957), Ch. 4.

211. "Conception of the Anabaptists," IX *CH* (1940) 4:341-65. For a stimulating classification of the Anabaptists in terms of radical Christian discipleship, see Bender, Harold S., "The Anabaptist Vision," XIII *CH* (1944) 1:3-24; by the same author, "The Anabaptist Theology of Discipleship," XXIV *MQR* (1950) 1:25-32. For another discussion of the various schools of thought in interpreting and classifying Anabaptism, see Smucker, Donovan E., "Anabaptist Historiography in the Scholarship of Today," XXII *MQR* (1948) 2:116-27. The same author, writing from modern Free Church perspectives, has proposed that the unique contribution of the Anabaptists was the rediscovery of the theology of the Bible; "The Theological Principles of the Early Anabaptist Mennonites," XIX *MQR* (1945) 1:5-26. For a conservative statement of interrelationships in the early period, see Friedmann's "The Encounter of Anabaptists and Mennonites with Anti-Trinitarianism," XXII *MQR* (1948) 3:139-62. Nevertheless, Kot has concluded of Anabaptism: "Its chief leaders did not attack directly the dogma of the Trinity, but by the fact of discarding philosophical and theological terms and holding strictly to what the Scripture says, they undeniably contributed to the weakening of the foundations." Kot, Stanislas, *Le Mouvement Antitrinitaire au XVIe et au XVIIe Siècle* (Paris: Collège de France, 1937), p. 24. According to another student of Anti-Trinitarianism: "The original Anti-Trinitarian point of departure in the 16th century was not philosophical but Biblical. The intention was to use exclusively the terminology which the Bible uses about God, and throw out everything else as 'Greek' and 'scholastic'." Dunin-Borkowski, Stanislas von, "Die Gruppierung der Antitrinitarier des 16. Jahrhunderts," VII *Scholastik* (1932) 4:481-523, 495.

212. Jones, Rufus M., "The Anabaptists and Minor Sects in the Reformation," XI *Harvard Theological Review* (1918) 3:223-46.

213. According to a suggestive discussion in an article of that title by Roland H. Bainton, in XXI *Journal of Religion* (1941) 2:24-34.

CHAPTER 2

THE FALL OF THE CHURCH

1. See my *The Free Church* (Boston: Starr King Press, 1957), Ch. 4.

2. They were opposed to all forms of what George Huntston Williams has recently classified under the term, "magisterial Protestantism": *GHW/M*, p. 21.

3. Lovejoy, Arthur O., *et. al.*, *A Documentary History of Primitivism and Related Ideas . . . in Antiquity* (Baltimore: Johns Hopkins Press, 1935), p. ix. Lovejoy also made representative studies of primitivism in the Church Fathers; see his "The Communism of St. Ambrose," III *Journal of the History of Ideas* (1942) 4:458-68, and " 'Nature' as Norm in Tertullian," reprinted

in *Essays in the History of Ideas* (Baltimore: Johns Hopkins Press, 1948), pp. 308-38. For the use of primitivist motifs in the Middle Ages, see Boas, George, *Essays on Primitivism and Related Ideas in the Middle Ages* (Baltimore: Johns Hopkins Press, 1948).

    4. According to Hans von Schubert, Sebastian Franck drew upon a source which defended theft on the ground that all things are common "as the Greek philosophers say." Von Schubert suspected Seneca's Epistle 90 was the source, and also showed the influence of Seneca's primitivism upon Erasmus, Colet, and More. Von Schubert, "Der Kommunismus der Wiedertäufer in Münster und seine Quellen," X *Sitzungsberichte der Heidelberger Akad. der Wiss. Phil.-Hist. Klasse* (1919) 11:46-47.

    5. Burdach, Konrad, *Reformation, Renaissance, Humanismus* (Berlin and Leipzig: Paetel Brothers, 1926), 2nd ed., pp. 174f.

    6. Pastor, Antonio, *The Idea of Robinson Crusoe* (Watford, Herts., England: Gongōra Press, 1930), p. 302.

    7. Bissell, Benj., *The American Indian in English Literature of the Eighteenth Century* (New Haven: Yale University Press, 1925), pp. 17-19; Chinard, Gilbert, *L'Exoticisme Amèricain dans la Litterature Française au XVIe Siècle* (Paris: Libraire Hachette et Cie, 1911), p. xvi.

    8. *Egli*, #691, p. 307. When a group escaped from Zürich prison, March, 1526, some suggested going to "den roten Juden" over the sea. Correll corrected the date (given by Egli as April, 1525) and the phrase by reference to the material in the Zürich canton archives. It should read "Inden" instead of "Juden," and Correll considers the report to cover a serious suggestion. Correspondence of 5/4/44.

    9. Stadelmann, Rudolph, *Vom Geist des ausgehenden Mittelalters* (Halle: Max Niemeyer, 1929), p. 223.

    10. Ferguson, Wallace K., "Humanist Views of the Renaissance," XLV *American Historical Review* (October, 1939) 1: reprint, pp. 3f.

    11. Hyma, Albert, *The Christian Renaissance* (New York and London: Century Co., 1925). See also Ullmann, C., *Reformers before the Reformation* (Edinburgh: T. & T. Clark, 1855), two volumes translated.

    12. On ERASMUS, see Hyma, Albert J., *The Youth of Erasmus* (Ann Arbor: University of Michigan Press, 1930); Mestwerdt, Paul, *Die Anfänge des Erasmus* (Leipzig: Rudolph Haupt, 1917); R. Stähelin in *Real.-3* (1898) V, 434-44; K. Vos and Neff in *ML* (1913) I, 599-600; Neff and Bender in *ME* (1956) II, 239-40. For a statement on his relation to Anabaptism, see Rembert, Karl, *Die 'Wiedertäufer' im Herzogtum Jülich* (Berlin: R. Gaertners Verlag, 1899), p. 194.

    13. Burckhardt-Biedermann, Th., *Bonifacius Amerbach und die Reformation* (Basel: R. Reich, 1894), "Good God! What unchristian strife has sprung from books when simple Love alone is 'Christian'!" (p. 37). Erasmus was often cited by Denck, Campanus, Thomas von Imbroich, Menno Simons, Adam Pastor, Dirck Philipsz.

    14. On ZWINGLI, see I:57-59.

    15. On Humanism, see article by Emil Händiges in *ME* (1956) II, 841-43. The Dutch Mennonites have been more ready to claim Humanist affiliations than have other wings; according to John Horsch, however, this did not extend even among the Waterlanders to freedom on doctrine. See

"Is Dr. Kühler's Conception of Early Dutch Anabaptism Historically Sound?" VII *MQR* (1933) 2:97-126. Robert Kreider ends his study, "Anabaptism and Humanism: An Inquiry into the Relationship of Humanism to the Evangelical Anabaptists," XXVI *MQR* (1950) 2:123-41, with the sentence: "The Humanist was a scholar, the Anabaptist a disciple." However, it has been concluded: "In a wider respect the aim of the Reformation can be interpreted as the final break of the medieval synthesis between Christianity and Hellenism; and, on the other hand, an authoritative humanist scholar today ascribes to Huguenot France and Protestant Germany 'the break through to Hellenism.' Indeed, the cry 'Ad Fontes' indicates a parallel move in the Reformation and in Humanism. . . ." Hildebrandt, Franz, *Melanchthon: Alien or Ally?* (Cambridge, Eng.: University Press, 1946), p. 3. The truth would seem to be that direct influence on Anabaptism by Humanism cannot be established; certainly the Anabaptists did not have an emancipated view of Biblical truth. Nevertheless, like the Humanists the Anabaptists had a certain attitude to the origins and to the authority of primary sources.

16. Benz, Ernst, *Ecclesia Spiritualis* (Stuttgart: W. Kohlhammer, 1934); Grundmann, Herbert, *Studien über Joachim von Floris* (Leipzig and Berlin: B. G. Teubner, 1927); Douie, Decima L., *The Nature and Effect of the Heresy of the Fraticelli* (Manchester, Eng.: University Press, 1932). On Joachim's interpretation of history as an attempt to establish independence of the medieval Corpus Christianum, see Taubes, Jakob, *Abendländische Eschatologie* (Berlin: A. Francke, 1947), p. 81.

17. Benz, p. 22.

18. *Ibid.*, p. 27.

19. *Ibid.*, p. 36.

20. *Ibid.*, p. 37.

21. *Ibid.*, p. 310.

22. *Ibid.*, pp. 313, 362f.

23. *Ibid.*, p. 357.

24. *Ibid.*, p. 66.

25. Hobhouse, Walter, *The Church and the World in Idea and in History* (London: Macmillan & Co., 1910), pp. ix-x.

26. Heering, G. J., *The Fall of Christianity* (New York: Fellowship Publications, 1943). First published in Dutch, 1928.

27. *Ibid.*, p. 33.

28. Townsend, Henry, *The Claims of the Free Churches* (London: Hodder & Stoughton, 1949), p. 45.

29. Jacob, Günter, "Der Raum für das Evangelium in Ost und West," in *Bericht über die ausserordentliche Synode der evangelischen Kirche in Deutschland, 1956* (Hannover-Herrenhausen: Evang. Kirchenkanzlei, 1956), pp. 17-29.

30. Hyma, Albert, *The Christian Renaissance*, p. 61.

31. Lovejoy, *et. al.*, *op. cit.*, pp. 32f, 61f.

32. Z, p. 298.

33. Lovejoy, *et. al.*, *op. cit.*, p. 53. See also Boas, George, *op. cit.*, pp. 103, 119.

34. "Ein Epistl an die gmain zu Rottenburg geschrieben, darinnen hübsche erklärungen der 12 haupt stück unsers christlichen glaubens begriffen sein," *WtQ1938*, p. 56.

35. Spitalmeier's court testimony, Nürnberg; #70 (Dec., 1527), in *WtQ1934*, p. 64.

36. *Beck*, pp. 169-73.

37. Rideman, Peter, *Account of Our Religion, Doctrine and Faith . . .* (London: Hodder & Stoughton/Plough Publishing House, 1950), pp. 88f.

38. "Eine liebe unterrichtung Ulrichen Stadlers, diener des worts, der sünd halben und des ausschluss, wie er darinen stehe, auch gemainschaft der zeitlichen güeter halben. Wider die, so des Herrnwerk pand und strick schelten, mit warhaftiger zeugnus heiliger geschrift, wie hernach volget," in *WtQ1938*, pp. 215-27, 225.

39. Lovejoy, *et. al., op. cit.,* pp. 96, 119f, 140f. Boas, George, *op. cit.,* pp. 43, 111, 122, 212-13. See Boas on the monks' use of New Testament texts: "Such texts give us a verbal picture of the Christian who is ascetic, poor in worldly goods, free even when enslaved by a terrestrial master, careless of the future, wise without learning. It is not to be wondered that such a person was confused with the pagan Sage of the 'ethical period' nor that the monastic life was described as 'the life of philosophy'" (p. 107). On the other hand, medieval Christian primitivism also had its anti-intellectual expressions; Gregory the Great spoke contemptuously of those "who revere more the talents of the learned than the simple life of the innocent" (p. 122). For specialized aspects of determined simplicity, see articles by John C. Wenger on "Dress," in *ME* (1956) II, 99-104; by Bender, on Footwashing, *ME* (1956) II, 347-51; on "Alcohol," *ME* (1955) I, 36-40.

40. Given May 12, 1531; printed in *WtQ1934*, #267, pp. 243-47, 244.

41. Lovejoy, *et. al., op. cit.,* p. 112. Boas, George, *op. cit.,* pp. 30, 127-28, 187.

42. Hut, Hans, "Vom geheimnus der tauf, baide des zaichens und des wesens, ein anfang eines rechten warhaftigen Christlichen lebens; Joan:5," printed in *WtQ1938*, pp. 14-27, 17: "He teaches the Gospel to the gardener by the trees, to the fisher by the catching of fish, to the carpenter by the building, to the goldsmith by the testing of gold . . . the women by the leaven. . . ." See also Schlaffer, Hans, "Ein kurzer bericht und leer eines recht christlichen lebens," *ibid.*, pp. 14-27, 17. In Sebastian Franck's writing, Nature was extolled as Life and Being, and art was condemned as appearance and sham; he favored the peasants, and liked the fable of the town and country mouse. Reimann, Arnold, *Sebastian Franck als Geschichtsphilosoph* (Berlin: Alfred Unger, 1921), p. 97.

43. *Infra*, p. 150.

44. Mestwerdt, Paul, *op. cit.,* pp. 32, 43. The normative use of the Early Church probably came to the Anabaptists largely from Zwingli; Köhler, Walther, "Ulrich Zwingli und die Reformation in der Schweiz," in Pflugk-Harttung, Julius von, *Im Morgenrot der Reformation* (Hersfeld: Vertriebsanstalt christl. Kunstwerk, 1912), pp. 669-715, 675.

45. Lovejoy, *et. al., op. cit.,* p. 19. Boas, George, *op. cit.,* p. 21.

46. "Eine liebe unterrichtung Ulrichen Stadlers . . . ," *WtQ1938*, p. 226.

47. *WtQ1938*, p. xxi.

48. Stauffer, Ethelbert, "Märtyrertheologie und Täuferbewegung," LII *ZKG* (1933) 545-98, 549. Translated in large part by Friedmann, XIX *MQR* (1945) 3:179-214.

49. Schlaffer, Hans, *WtQ1938*, p. 84.

50. The Polish Brethren provide one of the most romantic chapters in the history of the Left Wing, with sections of the movement Anti-Trinitarian, Anabaptist, and both. On Anabaptism in the Polish Minor Church, see Wotschke, Theodor, *Geschichte der Reformation in Polen* (Leipzig: R. Haupt, 1911), I, 219f. On the parallelism of Anabaptist and Anti-Trinitarian primitivism in Poland, see Trechsel, Fr., *Die protestantischen Antitrinitarier vor Faustus Socin* (Heidelberg: Karl Winter, 1844), pp. 8-9. Servetus' theme was *Restitutio Christianismi;* Campanus' *Restitutio und Besserung Göttlicher und heiliger Schrift* (1532) influenced both Anabaptists and Anti-Trinitarians. Efforts at union with the settlements in Moravia, 1569, and the Dutch Mennonites, 1612, however, failed; Kot, Stanislas, *Le Mouvement Antitrinitaire au XVIᵒ et au XVIIᵉ Siècle* (Paris: Collège de France, 1937), pp. 47f.

51. Wilbur, Earl Morse, *A History of the Polish Reformation by Stanislaus Lubieniecki;* MSS, p. 33. Text is in Book III, Chapter 32, in Eusebius' *Historia Ecclesiae.* On the Anabaptists' use of Eusebius, see *ME* (1956) II, 261-62. Butzer referred to Eusebius' report on Constantine and Theodosius: "En ces temps donc les Églisès de Christ ont abandannent experimenté la liberté et benignité du Seigneur predite par les Prophetes"; p. 39 in Wendel, François, *Du Royaume de Jésus-Christ* (Gütersloh: C. Bertelsmann Verlag, 1954); companion volume to *De regno Christi,* Vol. XVbis in *Martini Bvceri Opera Latina,* Book I, Chapter IV. The Reformers in general accepted the medieval assumption that the Christian triumph with Constantine's establishment marked the high tide of the faith, and not a "fall."

52. Wilbur, E. Morse, *A History of Unitarianism* (Cambridge: Harvard University Press, 1945), I, 142-43. Also Trechsel, Fr., *op. cit.,* I, 123.

53. Krahn, Cornelius, *Menno Simons (1496-1561)* (Karlsruhe: Heinrich Schneider, 1936) p. 136.

54. Bainton, Roland H., "The Left Wing of the Reformation," XXI *Journal of Religion* (1941) 2:124-34, 125, 128. In Sebastian Franck's scheme of history, there is a Fall every time when the "church" and "world" are co-extensive, amalgamated: with Constantine, when the Saxons were "converted" by Charlemagne, or in the territorial principle of the Reformers. Endriss, Julius, *Sebastian Francks Ulmer Kämpfe* (Ulm: Dr. Karl Hohn, 1935), p. 5. Significantly, Franck was the first historian to prefer Celtic Christianity to the Roman, and to criticize Boniface's mission; he regarded the whole imperial idea as a national calamity. Reimann, Arnold, *op. cit.,* pp. 69-71.

55. Z, p. 34.

56. *Supra,* p. 43.

57. Seeberg, Erich, *Gottfried Arnold: die Wissenschaft und die Mystik seiner Zeit* (Meerane i. Sa.: E. R. Herzog, 1923), p. 435.

58. It is interesting to note that the periodization of Christian history remains the same whether the triumph of the Eusebian martyr-history under Constantine is regarded with delight or dismay. Luther took the triumph at face value, the radicals looked behind it to perceive the inward meaning of corruption and compromise in the apparent glory. William Cave (1637-1713) took the reign of the Great Emperor for the heyday of Christianity; Gottfried Arnold used Cave's periodization of history, but deplored the consequent institutionalization and confessionalism. Schröder, William Freiherr

von, *Gottfried Arnold* (Heidelberg: Carl Winters Univ.-Buchh., 1917), p. 20.

59. Baur, August, *Zwinglis Theologie* (Halle: Max Niemeyer, 1885-89), II, p. 68, fn.

60. Seeberg, Erich, *op. cit.,* p. 455.

61. Here was the inevitability of the Anabaptist attack upon the Reformers, who also belonged to the fallen condition of the church; Heyer, Fritz, *Der Kirchenbegriff der Schwärmer* (Leipzig: M. Heinsius Nachf., 1939), pp. 13-15.

62. See Wenger, John C., "The Doctrinal Position of the Swiss Brethren as Recalled in their Polemical Tracts," XXVI *MQR* (1950) 1:65-72.

63. Z, p. 183.

64. True religion can never be popular, peddled on the marketplace. Hegler, A., *Geist und Schrift bei Sebastian Franck* (Freiburg: J. C. B. Mohr, 1892), p. 254.

65. "Artikel und handlung, so Michael Sattler zu Rotenburg am Neckar mit seinem blut bezeuget hat," in *WtQ1938,* p. 39. "No, . . . we shall arm and equip ourselves with the prayer that God strive for us. Also I say the Turk remains a Turk and is a Turk; but the so-called Christians remain Christians according to the flesh but persecute the true Christians, drive them from house and home; they are Turks in spirit." Quoted from the Testimony of Hans Schmidt in Württemberg (1550), in *WtQ1930,* p. 656. Jörg Haug von Juchsen, in "Ein christliche ordnung aines warhaftigen Christen zu verantworten die ankunft seines glaubens" (1524): "Both tyrants, spiritual and worldly, devour with their lust flesh and blood, strength and life with all the work of the poor. These are the ravenous beasts, who are by nature born to plunder." *WtQ1938,* p. 6.

66. Marginal note in Z, p. 75: "Wir zwingen niemands zum glauben . . ." — a proud boast! Manz, in his death hymn "Bey Christo wil ich bleiben" *(WtQ:Zürich,* #202, pp. 220-21), sang:

> "They call out the magistrate
>   to put us to death,
> For Christ has abandoned them.
> "To shed innocent blood
>   is the most false love of all."

67. Evans, Austin P., *An Episode in the Struggle for Religious Freedom: the Sectaries of Nuremberg, 1524-1528* (New York: Columbia University Press, 1924), pp. 53f. Denck at other times went beyond the appeal to private interpretation and spoke for the rights of the independent meeting; see Harder, Ernst, "Die Frühesten Vorkämpfer der Toleranzgedankens," XXIII *Monatsschriften der Comenius-Gesellschaft* (1914) 9:173-79.

68. Marpeck, Pilgram, "Confession of Faith Composed at Strasburg . . . ," edited by John C. Wenger, XII *MQR* (1938) 3:167-202, 171, 197. See also Bender, Harold S., "The Anabaptists and Religious Liberty in the 16th Century," XXIX *MQR* (1955) 2:83-100.

69. Hans Denck, quoted in Baring, Georg, *Quellen zur Geschichte der Täufer, VI: Hans Denck/Schriften, 1: Bibliographie* (Gütersloh: C. Bertelsmann Verlag, 1955), XXIV *QuFRG,* p. 51.

70. Egli, Emil, *Analecta Reformatoria* (Zürich: Zürcher & Furrer, 1899), I, 103. Lord Acton once stated that Anabaptists and Catholics shared a common conviction at this point, that the state is not responsible for religion.

"The Protestant Theory of Persecution," in *Essays on Freedom and Power* (Boston: Beacon Press, 1948), edited by Gertrude Himmelfarb, Ch. IV, p. 95.

71. *Beck,* pp. 14-15.

72. #247 (1564), reported in *WtQ1930,* p. 242. "Christ alone is King!": Heyer, Fritz, *op. cit.,* p. 89.

73. Bainton, Roland H., *David Joris: Wiedertäufer und Kämpfer für Toleranz im 16. Jahrhundert* (Leipzig: M. Heinsius Nachf., 1937), p. 87. Meyer von Buchs, in his court hearing, accused the evangelical pastors of killing and drowning the good and pious, and letting all drunkards, swindlers, gamblers and whores go free: *WtQ:Zürich,* #358 (Dec. 6, 1532 — March 5, 1533), pp. 370-72, 372.

74. The "Seven Articles" (Feb. 24, 1527): *Beck,* pp. 41-44.

75. *Infra,* p. 101.

76. Heyer, Fritz, *op. cit.,* p. 15. According to Heyer the Reformers allowed more freedom in "forms" than did the Anabaptists. Heyer fails to distinguish between the radicals' initial protest against all formalism and the Anabaptists' final insistence upon certain disciplines to maintain the integrity of the congregation. See *infra,* p. 37.

77. Although the assertion of the importance of the inner experience was pronounced, the Anabaptists proper did not go as far as the spiritualizers in eliminating "forms." A great exchange between Marpeck and Schwenckfeld on baptism and the Ban clarified the two positions in this respect. Marpeck said his opponent was so hypercritical that he would not have followed even Jesus in a group when He was on earth. The command to gather a people could not, believed Marpeck, be avoided. The sense of the meaning of history and its fulfillment lay strongly upon the Anabaptists, while the spiritualizers tended to hang issues upon the philosophical speculation in which historical choices were little seen. Loserth, Johann, "Studien zur Pilgram Marpeck," in Neff, Christian, ed., *Gedenkschrift zum 400. Jährigen Jubiläum der Mennoniten oder Taufgesinnten, 1525-1925* (Ludwigshafen: Konferenz der Süd-deutschen Mennoniten E. V., 1925), pp. 134f, 150.

78. Thomas Müntzer, quoted in Seidemann, J. R., *Thomas Münzer* (Dresden and Leipzig: Arnoldsche Buchh., 1842), p. 124.

79. For discussion of their positive teaching on the Supper, see *infra,* p. 98.

80. On KARLSTADT, see article by G. Hein in *ML* (1937) II, 463-65; also, *ME* (1955) I, 519f; article by Barge in *Real.-3* (1901) X, 73-80; Barge, Hermann, *Andreas Bodenstein von Karlstadt* (Leipzig: Fr. Brandstetter, 1905). Further, *KSch:* #9627, #9636, #9638. His commentary on Augustine, *De spiritu et litera . . . , 1517/19,* recently has been edited by Ernst Kähler: *Karlstadt und Augustin* (Halle: Max Niemeyer, 1952).

81. #73 (Dec. 25, 1521), in Müller, Nikolaus, *Die Wittenberger Bewegung, 1521 und 1522* (Leipzig: M. Heinsius Nachf., 1911), 2nd ed., p. 170.

82. Barge, Hermann, *op. cit.,* II, 259.

83. *WtQ1938,* p. xiv. Also, Müller, Lydia, *Der Kommunismus der mährischen Wiedertäufer* (Leipzig: M. Heinsius Nachf., 1927), p. 38. There is, however, a Mennonite tradition that Zwingli's interpretation was due to the influence of the Anabaptists; *supra,* I:58.

84. *WtQ1930,* pp. 200, 204.

85. Confession of the Ansbach Anabaptists, #176 (May 10, 1529), in *WtQ1934,* p. 166. Also, "Urlaub brüeff Anthoni Erdtfordters an die zu Clagen fort beschrieben in Kärnten und überantwort," printed in *WtQ1938,* pp. 258-62, 262. On Antoni Erfordter (? - 1541), see Loserth in *ME* (1956) II, 242-43.

86. Many of the old monks attributed the "Fall" to the rise of the hierarchy. We have here a link between monachism and radical Protestantism. Seeberg, Erich, *op. cit.,* p. 279.

87. Matthew 18:20 was always a favorite text of the *Täufer!*

88. *Z,* p. 36.

89. One testified that they met "by the oak in Esslingen wood"; #99 (July 10, 1539), *WtQ1930,* p. 71. For constitutive discussion, *infra,* p. 130.

90. Harder, Ernst, *loc. cit.,* p. 177. See J. Warns on "Kindertaufe," in *ML* (1937) II, 488-94.

91. *WtQ1930,* #174, p. 148f.

92. Testimony of Ambrose Spitalmeier, #31 (c. Sept. 9, 1527), in *WtQ1934,* p. 27.

93. Krahn, Cornelius, *op. cit.,* p. 130.

94. Hans Schlaffer, quoted in *WtQ1938,* p. 93.

95. Egli, Emil, *Die Züricher Wiedertäufer zur Reformationszeit* (Zürich: Friedrich Schulthess, 1878), p. 23.

96. *Infra,* p. 85.

97. There were various attempts made, all unsuccessful with the exception of the introduction of the use of confirmation on a wide scale; the Church of Land Hessen also adopted a certain minimum of discipline as a result of encounter with the Anabaptists. See the author's *Landgraf Philipp und die Toleranz* (Bad Nauheim: Christian Verlag, 1957), p. 28; also, "Bann," by Neff in *ML* (1913) I, 115-19; *ME* (1955) I, 219-23.

98. *ME* (1955) I, 27. Further, I:162.

99. The "Five Articles," in *WtQ1938,* pp. 236-57, 245.

100. #623 (c. Jan. 20, 1525), in *Egli,* p. 276f.

101. *WtQ1938,* pp. 236-57, 256. The positive form of this discussion will be found below, p. 123.

102. Müller, Lydia, *op. cit.,* p. 59.

103. Haupt, Hermann, "Ein oberrheinischer Revolutionär aus dem Zeitalter Kaiser Maximilians I.," Erg. Bd. VIII *Westdeutsche Zeitschrift für Geschichte und Kunst* (1893) 77-228, quotation on p. 115.

104. *Ibid.,* quotation on p. 201.

105. *Supra,* p. 21. We may note parallel thinking in later radicals: Francis Hotman dated the "Fall" of France with the end of the grand old Frankish kingdom, the going over to Rome. Gerard Winstanley dated the "Fall" of England with the Norman Conquest, the beginning of the system of rents and tithes. Even Karl Marx had a primitivist myth in the explanation he gave for the shift from primitive collective to private ownership of land.

106. *Infra,* p. 133.

107. According to John Horsch, the late American Mennonite scholar, their attitude has always been soundly Biblical and pessimistic toward the world to this day. "The Hutterians . . . believe that modern progress has changed neither the individual human heart nor the character of the

world. . . . The modern idea of Christ as the saviour of the world, in the sense that he is the leader in movements for world regeneration through reform, falls short by far of representing his true saviourhood. He is the Redeemer of those only who have been personally saved, and in consequence own and follow him as their Lord. The world is to be overcome — not assimilated." Horsch, John, *The Hutterian Brethren*, p. 134, fn. 128.

108. Seeberg, Erich, *op. cit.*, pp. 262f.

109. Bainton, Roland H., *David Joris*, p. 30.

110. Bouterwek, K. W., *loc. cit.*, p. 299. This dualism of churchly and social restitution is familiar in St. Augustine.

111. *Z*, pp. 35f. Also, *Beck*, p. 11. On the relation of the Anabaptists to the Waldenses, see Dosker, Henry Elias, *op. cit.*, pp. 16f. Also, for an argument that the South Germans were uniquely influenced, see Nicoladoni, Alexander, *Johannes Bünderlin von Linz* (Berlin: R. Gaertners Verlag, 1893) , pp. 45f. On the general question of classification, see *infra*, p. 154.

112. Bouterwek, K. W., *loc. cit.*, p. 304: "Thus unhappily for fourteen hundred years this truth has been so completely falsified, impeded and suppressed, and that most of all by the Pope and his hangers-on, that you can hardly find the spoor of a true Christian church on earth. . . ."

113. For general discussion, see Heyer, Fritz, *op. cit.*, pp. 24f. Complete pessimism is expressed in the "Nineteen Articles" of Galenus Abrahams and Spruyt (c. 1650) , wherein all hope of erecting an apostolic church is abandoned. John Smyth represented a similar despair of reclaiming the lost thread of authority. Troeltsch, Ernst, *The Social Teaching of the Christian Churches* (New York: Macmillan Co., 1931) , II, 766.

114. *Infra*, Ch. 4.

115. Heyer, Fritz, *op. cit.*, p. 22.

116. *Supra*, p. 51.

117. Quoted in Rembert, Karl, *op. cit.*, p. 197.

118. Ritschl, Albrecht, "G. Witzels Abkehr vom Luthertum," II *ZKG* (1877./78) 386-417, 396f. Ritschl, whose own use of the theme is so well known, traces the normative use of the apostolic community back to Joachim of Fiore. On WITZEL, see article by Tschackert in *ADB*, XLIII, 657-62; article by Kawerau in *Real.-3* (1908) XXI, 339-409; Schmidt, G. L., *Georg Witzel: Ein Altkatholik des XVI. Jahrhunderts* (Vienna: Wm. Braumüller, 1876) . Further, *KSch:* #22711a, #22712, #22736.

119. Detmer, Heinrich, and Krumbholtz, Robert, ed., *op. cit.*

120. Schiedung, Hans, *Beiträge zur Bibliographie und Publizistik über die Münsterischen Wiedertäufer* (Münster: Heinrich Buschmann, 1934) , p. 11.

121. Rembert, Karl, *op. cit.*, p. 244, fn. 2. Franck's writings were widely read among the Anabaptists. On the popularity of the theme "Restitution" see Bainton, Roland H., "Changing Ideas and Ideals in the Sixteenth Century," VIII *Journal of Modern History* (1936) 4:417-43; p. 428, fn. See also: article by same author, "The Church of the Restoration," VIII *Mennonite Life* (1953) 3:136-43; article by Neff and Crous in *ML* (1956) 40:476-77.

122. Dolan, John P., "Georg Witzel: Liturgiker und Kirchenreformer," XI *Una Sancta* (1956) 4:196-204.

123. Whitney, Lois, *Primitivism and the Idea of Progress* (Baltimore: Johns Hopkins Press, 1934) , p. 1.

CHAPTER 3

THE RESTITUTION OF THE TRUE CHURCH

1. See the author's article, "The Anabaptist Doctrine of the Restitution of the True Church," XXVI *MQR* (1956) 1:33-52; Wray, Frank J., "The Anabaptist Doctrine of the Restitution of the Church," XXVIII *MQR* (1954) 3:186-96; Bender on "Church," *ME* (1955) I, 594-97.

2. For two interesting attempts at new typology see Müller-Gangloff, Erich, "Gottes Drittes Volk — Aus den Heiden?" I *Kommunität* (1957) 3: reprint; Thadden-Trieglaff, Reinold von, "Das Ende des protestantischen Individualismus," XXVIII *Zeitwende/Die Neue Furche* (1957) 3:152-60.

3. See "Apostolic Succession," *ME* (1955) I, 139-41.

4. Heyer, Fritz, *Der Kirchenbegriff der Schwärmer* (Leipzig: M. Heinsius Nachf., 1939), p. 18.

5. *WtQ1934*, p. 61.

6. Heyer, Fritz, *op. cit.*, pp. 99-102.

7. Schlaffer, Hans, "Ein Kurzer Underricht zum Anfang Eines Recht Christlichen Lebens," in *WtQ1938*, p. 92.

8. Hut, Hans, "Vom geheimnus der tauf . . . ," in *WtQ1938*, p. 14.

9. Westin, Gunnar, *Der Weg der freien christlichen Gemeinden durch die Jahrhunderte* (Kassel: J. G. Oncken Verlag, 1956), p. 16.

10. On the Anabaptist attitude to the Bible and its authority, see Kaufman, Gordon D., "Some Theological Emphases of the Early Swiss Anabaptists," XXV *MQR* (1951) 2:75-99; Wiswedel, Wilhelm, "The Inner and the Outer Word," XXVI *MQR* (1952) 3:171-91. It is significant that almost the only tendency to literalism/formalism in the movement was also a product of primitivism in relation to Biblical institutions: i.e., Sabbatarianism; see article on Oswald Glait, *ME* (1956) II, 522-23; "Bible," *ME* (1955) I, 322-28.

11. *Beck*, pp. 41-44. The "Seven Articles" were defined at a noted conference called under the direction of Michael Sattler, an important leader in the new movement, to serve the Anabaptist congregations as a guide against false teaching. See Blanke, Fritz, "Beobachtungen zum ältesten Täuferbekenntnis," XXXVII *ARG* (1940) 2/3:242-49; McGlothlin, M. J., *Baptist Confessions of Faith* (Philadelphia: American Baptist Publication Society, 1911), pp. 2-9; Jenny, Beatrice, *Das Schleitheimer Täuferbekenntnis 1527* (Thayngen, Switzerland: Verlag Karl Augustin, 1951); Wenger, John C., "The Schleitheim Confession of Faith," XIX *MQR* (1945) 4:243-53; Friedmann, Robert, "The Schleitheim Confession (1527) and other Doctrinal Writings of the Swiss Brethren in a Hitherto Unknown Edition," XVI *MQR* (1942) 2:82-98; Köhler, Walther, ed., *Brüderlich Vereinigung etzlicher Kinder Gottes sieben Artikel betreffend. Item ein Sendbrief Michael Sattlers . . . 1527*, 2 *Flugschriften aus dem ersten Jahren der Reformation* (Otto Clemens, ed.); *ME* (1955) I, 447-48. "Anabaptism was shaped by its Biblical antithesis to both the Churches and the extra-church spiritual movements of its time": Friedmann, Robert, *loc. cit.*, p. 93. On SATTLER, see *GHW/M*, pp. 138f.

12. Hut, Hans, *loc. cit.*, p. 27.

13. This was a favorite Anabaptist argument. See Schlaffer, Hans, "Kurtze und ainfältige vermanung vom kindertauf, wie derselbig nit mag beibracht werden auss heiliger schrift" (1528), in *WtQ1938*, p. 100; Stadler, Ulrich, "Etlich schöne tröstliche sendbrief, underrichtungen und leeren. . . . Vom der erbsünd, tauf, urtl der sünd zum tod, gemainschaft und andern nutzlichen sachen," *ibid.*, p. 233; reported in the Disputation at Lütisberg (1533), in Egli, Emil, *Die St. Galler Täufer* (Zürich: Friedrich Schulthess, 1887), p. 54, fn. 5; Testimony of the Grüninger Täufer (June 4, 1527), #1201 in *Egli*, II, 547. See Mecenseffy, Grete, "Das Verständnis der Taufe bei den süddeutschen Täufern," in Wolf, Ernst, *et al.*, *Antwort: Karl Barth zum siebzigsten Geburtstag* (Zollikon-Zurich: Evangelischer Verlag, 1956), pp. 642-46.

14. Testimony in *WtQ1930*, p. 240.

15. Dosker, Henry Elias, *The Dutch Anabaptists* (Philadelphia: Judson Press, 1921), pp. 106f.

16. *Z*, p. 27.

17. Testimony of Sept. 22, 1527, #25 in *WtQ1934*, p. 38.

18. The oldest was by Hübmaier, and the second came thirteen years later from the hand of Peter Ridemann; Heyer, Fritz, *op. cit.*, p. 9.

19. Müller, Lydia, *Der Kommunismus der mährischen Wiedertäufer* (Leipzig: M. Heinsius Nachf., 1927), p. 37.

20. Hut, Hans, *loc. cit.*, p. 21.

21. Testimony (Feb. 7, 1525), #636 in *Egli*, I, 284.

22. Krahn, Cornelius, *Menno Simons (1496-1561)* (Karlsruhe: Heinrich Schneider, 1936), pp. 124f.

23. Hut, Hans, *loc. cit.*, p. 25.

24. Loserth, Johann, *Doctor Balthasar Hubmaier und die Anfänge der Wiedertäufer in Mähren* (Brünn: R. M. Rohrer, 1893), p. 2.

25. *Supra*, p. 14.

26. Only an adult might qualify under the Great Commission; see *infra*, Ch. 4.

27. Bergfried, Ulrich, *Verantwortung als Theologisches Problem im Täufertum des 16. Jahrhunderts* (Wuppertal-Elberfeld: A. Martini & Grüttefien, 1938), p. 98. It has been wrongly asserted that the Anabaptists were "Confessionless" groups. This is only true in the sense that ethical rather than doctrinal issues generally concerned them, and that they used the Ban for moral government but rarely to enforce intellectual conformity. Schwenckfeld and Franck are the true points of departure for Confessionless Christianity; Heyer, Fritz, *op. cit.*, p. 47. See also "Doctrinal Writings of the Anabaptists," *ME* (1956) II, 77-79.

28. "Ein Ausschnitt aus Peter Walpots 'Kinderlehre'," printed in *WtQ1938*, p. 257. "I Peter 3 speaks not just of a union, but of a good conscience with God. Then baptism is a good conscience with God, all that by the adults . . . and may not be by children." *Acta des Gesprächs zwüschenn predicanntenn Vnnd tauffbruederenn Ergangen, Inn der Statt Bernn. . . ;* typed MSS in Mennonite Historical Library, Goshen, Indiana, from Vol. 80 of *Unnützen Papiere* in Staatsarchiv Kantons Bern, p. 191. Also, "Baptism," *ME* (1955) I, 225-28.

29. A Hutterite observer condemned the quality of Nikolsburg congregational life because Hübmaier baptized into the church every Sunday

large numbers who certainly did not know the full meaning of their commitment; nor were the members subject to any system of congregational government. Testimony at Erlangen (Jan. 17, 1529), #145, in *WtQ1934*, p. 132.

30. Müller, Lydia, *op. cit.*, pp. 42-43.

31. "Rechenschaft und bekanntnus des glaubens . . ." (Trieste, 1539), in *WtQ1938*, p. 204; "Ein Rechenschaft von unsern lieben brüedern Jeronime, Michel und Hänssl" (1536), p. 209.

32. Quoted in Nicoladoni, Alexander, *Johannes Bünderlin von Linz* (Berlin: R. Gaertners Verlag, 1893), p. 155.

33. Z, pp. 110-12. ". . . Christ gave his congregation the Keys of the Kingdom of Heaven (Matth. 16:19) . . ." Philipsz, Dirck, "The Church of God," in *GHW/M*, pp. 226-60, 247.

34. Z, pp. 83f.

35. *WtQ1938*, p. xvii.

36. #174 (August 1557?), *WtQ1930*, p. 148.

37. See "Rechenschaft und bekanntnus . . ." (Trieste, 1539), *WtQ1938*, p. 197.

38. See Bender on "Excommunication, Procedure and Grounds," *ME* (1956) II, 277-79; also, "Gemeindezucht," *ML* (1937) II, 61-65.

39. Letter of Grebel and associates to Müntzer (Sept. 5, 1524); Rauschenbusch, Walter, "The Zürich Anabaptists and Thomas Müntzer," IX *American Journal of Theology* (1905) 91-106, 94, 95.

40. *WtQ:Bayern II*, #19 (1536), pp. 193-209, 206.

41. *Beck*, pp. 41-44.

42. "Von der Eeschaidung zwischen glaubigen und unglaubigen," in *WtQ1938*, pp. 253f. Separation was possible, but not a commandment; p. 255. See "Ehemeidung," *ML* (1913) I, 526-28; "Divorce," and "Divorce from Unbelievers," in *ME* (1956) II, 74-76.

43. Quotation from Hübmaier in Newman, A. H., "Balthazar Hübmaier and the Moravian Anabaptists," 27 *Goshen College Record, Review Supplement* (1926) 10:4-22, 12.

44. Quotation from Hübmaier in Vedder, Henry C., *Balthasar Hübmaier* (New York and London: G. P. Putnam's Sons, 1905), pp. 212-14. Hübmaier intrigued Baptist scholars of an earlier generation, perhaps in part because he took a more orthodox view of the use of the sword than most Anabaptists. Today, his significance as an Anabaptist leader is generally depreciated by students of the movement.

45. On Bouwens, see article by Vos in *ML* (1913) I, 250-51; also article on Groningen, *ME* (1956) II, 589-92.

46. Bergfried, Ulrich, *op. cit.*, p. 20. Abuse of the Ban is to be avoided; Menno Simons, "On the Ban: Questions and Answers" (1550), in *GHW/M*, pp. 261-71, 267-68.

47. Testimony at Kirchheim (March 24, 1566), #120, in *WtQ1930*, p. 1084.

48. Testimony of Wolfgang Wüst at Beiersdorf (Jan. 3, 1528), #78 and #79, in *WtQ1934*, p. 71.

49. Fourth in the "Seven Articles" (Feb. 24, 1527), in *Beck*, pp. 41-44; also, article by Hege on "Absonderung," *ML* (1913) I, 11-12; *ME* (1955) I, 100-01.

50. Böhmer, H., ed., *Urkunden zur Geschichte des Bauernkrieges und der Wiedertäufer,* 50/51 *Kleine Texte für Theologische und Philologische Vorlesungen und Übungen* (1910) 25f, 30.

51. *Der Widertoeuffern ursprung/ fürgang/ Secten/wäsen/* . . . . (Zürich: Christoffel Froschower, 1541) , p. 69a. In the *Martyrs Mirror* the case for separation is stated: "These times are certainly more dangerous; for then Satan came openly, through his servants, even at noon-day, as a roaring lion, so that he could be known, and it now and then was possible to hide from him; besides, his chief design then was to destroy the body: but now he comes as in the night, or in the twilight, in a strange but yet pleasing form, and, in a two-fold way, lies in wait to destroy the soul: partly, to trample under foot, and annihilate entirely, if this were possible, the only saving Christian faith; partly to destroy the truly separated Christian life which is the outgrowth of faith." Braght, Thielman J. van, *The Bloody Theatre or Martyrs Mirror* (Scottsdale, Penna.: Mennonite Publishing House, 1950) , p. 8.

52. *Z*, p. 357.

53. A late criticism, quoted in Wotschke, Theodor, *Geschichte der Reformation in Polen* (Leipzig: R. Haupt, 1911) , I, 225.

54. Huter, Jakob, "Anschleg und fürwenden der blinden und verkerten welt, und aller gottlosen gegen den fromen," *WtQ1938,* p. 170.

55. *Ibid.,* p. 153.

56. Hege, Christian, "The Early Anabaptists in Hesse," V *MQR* (1931) 3:157-78, 159.

57. *Z*, pp. 250, 307. *Infra,* p. 126.

58. See article by Ernst Correll, "Ehe," *ML* (1913) I, 509-26.

59. Heyer, Fritz, *op. cit.,* p. 58.

60. On this particular aspect of the Brethren's radicalism, see Egli, Emil, *Die Züricher Wiedertäufer,* p. 12. Also, Unruh, B. H., "Die Revolution 1525 und das Täufertum," in Neff, Christian, ed., *Gedenkschrift zum 400. Jährigen Jubiläum der Mennoniten oder Taufgesinnten, 1525-1925* (Ludwigshafen: Konf. der Süddeutschen Mennoniten, 1925) , pp. 19-47, 42. This was perhaps not a social attack so much as part of their frontal attack on the whole pattern of religious establishment.

61. Testimony of Ambrosius Spitalmeier (c. Sept. 9, 1527) , #31, *WtQ1934,* pp. 27, 28. "Talking it up" is still more important than the actual vote among the Hutterites. An elder explained to Lee Emerson Deets: "I put questions to the members. If anybody is against it, he is to say so. They talk it up in small groups. If the (whole) group gets quiet, then it means, 'yes.' I can tell by the quietness whether they are for it." *The Hutterites: A Study in Social Cohesion* (Gettysburg, Penna.: privately published, 1939) , p. 35.

62. *Supra,* p. 40. Also, Peters, Frank C., "The Ban in the Writings of Menno Simons," XXIX *MQR* (1955) 1:16-33.

63. *Z*, pp. 107f; also, Heyer, Fritz, *op. cit.,* pp. 81f.

64. *Z*, pp. 212f. Ridemann was imprisoned during a period when missioners had been sent out to encourage the Brethren in Hesse after the damage done to the movement by the Butzer-Tesch debates and subsequnt reconversions; *WtQ:Hessen,* #92, #105.

65. Article by Neff, "Älteste," *ML* (1913) I, 39-40; Krahn, "Elder," in

ME (1956) II, 178-81; by the same author, "The Office of Elder in Ana-
baptist-Mennonite History," XXX *MQR* (1956) 2:120-27; Correll, Ernst,
Das Schweizerische Täufermennonitentum (Tübingen: J. C. B. Mohr, 1925),
p. 37.

66. "Diener am Wort," *ML* (1913) I, 438-40; *ME* (1956) II, 53-54.

67. *WtQ:Bayern II*, #49, pp. 63-71, 66. Of Umlauft the officials reported: "Item: he will not point out his comrades in baptism, but rather
first let himself be torn asunder," *ibid.*, #54, p. 54.

68. *Menno Simons, The Complete Writings of* . . . (Scottdale, Penna.:
Herald Press, 1956), p. 65.

69. *Ibid.*, p. 161.

70. Heimann, Franz, "The Hutterite Doctrines of Church and Common Life," XXVI *MQR* (1952) 1:22-47, 2:142-60, 39.

71. Peachey, Paul, "Anabaptism and Church Organization," XXX *MQR*
(1956) 3:213-28, 217.

72. Correll, Ernst, *op. cit.*, p. 45; "Community of Goods," *ME* (1955)
I, 658-62.

73. Wolkan, Rudolph, ed., *Geschicht-Buch der Hutterischen Brüder*
(Vienna and Macleod, Alta.: Carl Fromme G. m. b. H. 1923) p. 220.

74. *WtQ1938*, p. 246.

75. The Articles of Kyburg (May 2, 1525), #703, *Egli*, I, 320; the
Regensperg Articles (May E., 1525), #729, *Egli*, I, 340-43.

76. Rideman, Peter, *Account of Our Religion, Doctrine and Faith*
(London: Hodder & Stoughton/Plough Publ. House, 1950), pp. 90-91.

77. "Eine liebe unterrichtung Ulrichen Stadlers . . ." *WtQ1938*, p. 222.
For Stadler's "Cherished Instructions . . ." (c. 1537) in English, see *GHW/M*,
pp. 272f.

78. Conclusion to the Third of the "Five Articles" (c. 1547), *WtQ1938*,
p. 247.

79. Horsch, John, *The Hutterian Brethren, 1528-1931* (Goshen, Ind.:
Mennonite Historical Society, 1931), pp. xvi, 4.

80. In the "Five Articles" (c. 1547), printed in *WtQ1938*, p. 244. On
their practice of community of goods, see Friedmann, Robert, "Economic
Aspects of Early Hutterite Life," XXX *MQR* (1956) 4:259-66. Peter Walpot's
classical statement (c. 1577) has recently been translated and edited: Hasen-
berg, Kathleen E., and Friedmann, Robert, "A Notable Hutterite Document:
Concerning True Christian Surrender and Christian Community of Goods,"
XXXI *MQR* (1957) 1:22-62. See also "Gutergemeinschaft," article by Neff
and Loserth, *ML* (1937) II, 204-10.

81. Testimony of Hans Hut (1527), #51, *WtQ1934*, pp. 41-44.

82. Letter to the authorities at Zürich (March, 1526), #940, *Egli*, II,
449; also (Dec. 22, 1525) #147, *WtQ:Zürich*, pp. 148-49.

83. Certain groups frowned upon the rigor which developed in Hutterite
discipline: Confession of the Windesheim Anabaptists (April 16, 1531),
#242, *WtQ1934*, pp. 219, 238.

84. *WtQ1938*, p. 109.

85. Rideman, Peter, *op. cit.*, p. 43.

86. Brandhuber, Wolfgang, "Ein sendbrief an die gmain Gottes zu
Rottenburg am In" (1529), in *WtQ1938*, p. 138.

87. *WtQ1934*, p. 36.

88. Smith, C. Henry, *The Story of the Mennonites* (Newton, Kansas: Mennonite Publication Office, 1950), p. 55.

89. *Beck*, pp. 41-44.

90. The second of the "Five Articles" (c. 1547), *WtQ1938*, p. 242.

91. Confessions of several newly baptized at Beiersdorf (1528), #82, *WtQ1934*, p. 84.

92. Confession of Ansbach Anabaptists (May 10, 1529), #176, *WtQ1934*, p. 165. Also in Langenmantel, Hans, "Ein anders gespräch vom abentmahl Christi und seiner gemeinschaft auf kurzeste," in *WtQ1938*, p. 135; Zaunring, Georg, "Ain kurtze annzaigung des abentmals Christy," *WtQ1938*, p. 145.

93. *Z*, p. 186.

94. Schiemer, Leonhard, "Ein Epistl an die gmain zu Rottenburg geschrieben. . . ," in *WtQ1938*, p. 54.

95. #369 (June 23, 1523), in *Egli*, I, 133.

96. See "Abendmahl," in *ML* (1913) I, 6-9; as expanded by Krahn, *ME* (1955) I, 651-55.

97. "The Donatist peasant rising believed only in the sacramental power of 'pure' priests, and not in its character *indelibilis*: this was the beginning of the great series of sect-movements, with their hostility to the Church. . . ." Troeltsch, Ernst, *The Social Teaching of the Christian Churches* (New York: Macmillan Co., 1931), I, 209f; p. 338, fn.

98. Repeatedly the Anabaptist before the court would testify that he avoided the communion because he was unworthy; see instances in *WtQ1930*, pp. 199, 240, 252f. As a True Church was established this reservation disappeared, but objection to promiscuous Masses remained.

99. Confession of Simon Krausshaar of Neckar-Gröningen (May, 1559), #190, *WtQ1930*, pp. 178f.

100. Georg Zaunring in *WtQ1938*, p. 147.

101. *WtQ1938*, p. xiv. Menno used the same simile: see Krahn, Cornelius, *Menno Simons*, p. 142.

102. #247 (1564), *WtQ1930*, p. 241.

103. "Rechenschaft und bekanntnus des glaubens . . ." (Trieste, 1539), in *WtQ1938*, p. 201.

104. Waltner, Erland, "The Anabaptist Conception of the Church," XXV *MQR* (1951) 1:5-16, 15.

105. #38 (Rothenburg), *WtQ:Bayern II*, pp. 229-30.

106. "Contra Anabaptistarum opinionem" (August, 1557?), #174, *WtQ1930*, pp. 148ff; also, *WtQ:Hessen*, #28, p. 64. Grebel said that he wanted to obey the Town Council in all worldly things: *WtQ:Zürich*, #170, p. 175.

107. *WtQ1938*, p. 210.

108. Newman, A. H., *A History of Anti-Pedobaptism* (Philadelphia: American Baptist Publication Society, 1897), p. 88.

109. Correll, Ernst, *op. cit.*, p. 28, fn.

110. Burckhardt-Biedermann, Th., *Bonifacius Amerbach und die Reformation* (Basel: R. Reich, 1894), p. 91.

111. On Jakob Grebel, see *ME* (1956) II, 575.

112. Heyer, Fritz, *op. cit.*, p. 85.

113. *Ibid.*, p. 89.

114. My own translation from the German; for authorized translation and related sections, see Rideman, Peter, *op. cit.*, pp. 111-12.

115. "Anschleg und fürwenden der blinden und verkerten Welt. . . ," *WtQ1938,* p. 186.

116. *Ibid.*, p. 186; see also article by Hege, "Krieg," *ML* (1937) II, 569-72.

117. *Ibid.*, p. 199.

118. *WtQ1938*, p. 186.

119. Fourth of the "Five Articles" (c. 1547), *ibid.*, p. 252.

120. #623 (c. Jan. 20, 1525), *Egli*, I, 276f.

121. See article by Neff, "Eid," in *ML* (1913) I, 535-46.

122. *WtQ1938*, p. 249.

123. #205 (May 18, 1560), *WtQ1930*, p. 198.

124. *WtQ1938*, p. 97.

125. From the testimony of some who came from the Swiss to join the Hutterites (1543); *WtQ1938*, p. 265.

126. Smithson, R. J., *The Anabaptists* (London: James Clarke & Co., 1935), p. 125, with a reference to *BRN*.

127. *Z*, p. 205.

128. *Supra*, p. 66.

129. *Supra*, p. 142. See the report of the Colloquy of Emden (1578) in Arnold, Gottfried, *Kirchen- und Ketzer-Historie* (Frankfurt: Thomas Fritsch, 1700), II:XVI, XXI, 272a.

130. *Z*, p. 307.

131. Fourth in the "Five Articles" (c. 1547), *WtQ1938*, p. 249.

132. Stauffer, Ethelbert, "Märtyrertheologie und Täuferbewegung," LII *ZKG* (1933) 545-98, 588. The baptismal formulae were martyr-confessionals. See also Bender, on "Eschatology," *ME* (1956) II, 247-48.

133. Mannhardt, W., *Die Wehrfreiheit der Altpreussischen Mennoniten* (Marienburg and Danzig: B. Hermann Hemmpels Wwe., 1863); van der Smissen, H., "Der Grundsatz der Wehrlosigkeit in seiner historischen Entwicklung, dargestellt," 35 *Mennonitische Blätter* (1888) 21:121-24, 22:129-30; Vos, K., *De Weerlosheid der Doopsgezinden* (Amsterdam: J. H. DeBussy, 1924). In general, these writers assert that the Anabaptist nonresistance was not a dogmatic question but a matter of historical development and decline. An interesting illustration of the consequences of such relativism may be found in the conduct of Hermann von Beckerath in the 1848 Frankfurt Parliament: *ME* (1956) II, 376-77.

134. See Horsch, John, "An Historical Survey of the Position of the Mennonite Church on Nonresistance," I *MQR* (1927) 3:5-22, 4:3-20; Bender, Harold S., "The Pacifism of the Sixteenth Century Anabaptists," XXX *MQR* (1956) 1:5-18. For the definite contemporary treatment of the Mennonite peace testimony, see Hershberger, Guy Franklin, *War, Peace and Nonresistance* (Scottdale, Penna.: Herald Press, 1944), esp. pp. 219f. For a further exposition of the distinction between nonresistance and pacifism, see Littell, Franklin H., "The Inadequacy of Modern Pacifism," XI *Christianity and Society* (1946) 2:18-23.

CHAPTER 4

THE GREAT COMMISSION

1. Rideman, Peter, *Account of Our Religion, Doctrine and Faith* (London: Hodder & Stoughton/Plough Publishing House, 1950), pp. 38, 39.

2. "Foundation of Christian Doctrine" (1539), in *Menno Simons, The Complete Writings of* . . . (Scottdale, Penna.: Herald Press, 1956), pp. 103-226, 178.

3. *Infra*, p. 133. See article by the author, "The Anabaptist Theology of Missions," XXI *MQR* (1947) 1:5-17; Wiswedel, Wilhelm, "Die alten Täufergemeinden und ihr missionarisches Wirken," 40 *ARG* (1943) 183-200, 45 *ARG* (1948) 115-32; Bainton, Roland H., "The Great Commission," VIII *Mennonite Life* (1953) 4:183-89; Bender, Harold S., "Evangelism," *ME* (1956) II, 269-73.

4. "Meditation on the Twenty-fifth Psalm" (c. 1537), *The Complete Writings of Menno Simons*, pp. 63-86, 71.

5. This name has been given them by certain authors who rightly find the terms "Wiedertäufer" and "Täufer" inaccurate and restrictive. See Introduction, *supra*. "Evangelical Anabaptists" would seem best to indicate their overwhelming sense of mission. See Friedmann, Robert, "Conception of the Anabaptists," IX *CH* (1940) 4:341-65, 362.

6. Benz, Ernst, *Ecclesia Spiritualis* (Stuttgart: W. Kohlhammer Verlag, 1934), pp. 25-26.

7. *Egli*, #674 (March 16-25, 1525), I, 299: one testified that he slept home during the services; and besides he read in his testament, "who believes and is baptized. . . ." See also #1631 (Dec. 26, 1529); here the Great Commission (Mark 16) and the Ban (Matt. 18) are linked together as the basic Anabaptist ordinances; II, 692. In the "Rechenschaft und bekanntnus des glaubens . . ." (Trieste, 1539) we find Mark 16 stressed; *WtQ1938*, p. 193. When Hans Schlaffer was called up before the authorities at Schwatz, 1528, he based his answer on Matt. 28, Mark 16; Braght, T. J. van, *A Martyrology of the Churches of Christ Commonly Called Baptist* (London: Hanserd Knollys Society, 1850-53), I, 50. The central proof text in Hübmaier's "Von dem christl. Tauff der Gläubigen" is Matt. 28:19; Sachsse, Carl, *D. Balthasar Hubmaier als Theologe* (Berlin: Trowitsch & Sohn, 1914), pp. 19-20. With Menno Simons the demand for righteousness was primary, and the second order was Matt. 28:19, Mark 16:15; quotation in Horsch, John, *Menno Simons* (Scottdale, Penna.: Mennonite Publishing House, 1916), p. 50. See also *WtQ1934*, p. 186. Questions prepared by the authorities for the Windesheimer Wiedertäufer indicate an expectation that their testimony would be based on the Great Commission and Acts; *WtQ1934*, #260 (May, 1531), pp. 236-37. The testimony of Julius Lober, who had a brother in Moravia, was built on the promise of salvation to him who believes and is baptized. His proof texts were Matt. 5, Matt. 28 and Mark 16, Luke 3, Acts 3, 8, 19; *WtQ1934*, #267 (April 18, 1548), pp. 353-55. Anabaptists were held at Landshut (1528) for having "said in public bath that one reads in the gospel that when God was on earth only persons were baptized who first had the

faith," and proving it by the Great Commission; *WtQ:Bayern II*, #14-15, pp. 21f. See also *Z*, p. 31; *WtQ:Hessen*, #5 (Marburg, 1528), #10 (Fulda, 1530), #17 (Vacha, 1531), #45 (Marburg, 1536?), #145 (Friedewald, 1555-56). A statement by Gabrielites who joined the Hutterites in 1545 begins with baptism based on Matt. 28 and Mark 16; *Z*, pp. 250f. See also *WtQ1938*, pp. 236f. At an examination of various people at Erlangen, 1527, Hans Ritter said: 1) the Lord commanded, "Go ye . . ."; 2) man must submit under God as the animals under man; they went to flowing water, filled a hat, and poured; *WtQ1934*, p. 16. On the centrality of the Great Commission for Marpeck, see "Confession of Faith Composed at Strasburg, December, 1531 - January, 1532," XII *MQR* (1938) 3:167-203, 193. At the Bern Disputation the Anabaptists insisted the Great Commission applied to everyone who confessed Christ's name; Matthijssen, Jan P., "The Bern Disputation of 1538," XXII *MQR* (1948) 1:15-33.

    8. *Beck*, p. 64.

    9. *WtQ1938*, p. 15 (Hans Hut), p. 92 (Hans Schlaffer), p. 112. B. Hübmaier wrote to the authorities that he knew no other order but preach, believe, baptize: *Egli*, II, 449. When at St. Gall, Uolimann was summoned before the Town Council on April 25, 1525, for going on his own authority with baptism and the supper, he said the original order was teaching, believing, baptizing; and this lasted to the time of Tertullian and Cyprian when they began to baptize sick children. Heath, Richard, *Anabaptism from its Rise at Zwickau to its Fall at Münster* (London: Alexander & Shepheard, 1895), p. 39. (Heath's book contains interesting material in spite of its erroneous central thesis.) See also *WtQ:Hessen*, #17 (Vacha, 1531); *WtQ: Bayern II*, #75 (Regensburg, 1540), pp. 107-08. We read in Menno Simons: "Here we have the Lord's commandment concerning baptism, as to when according to the ordinance of God it shall be administered and received; namely, that the Gospel must first be preached, and then those baptized who believe it, as Christ says: Go ye into all the world, and preach the gospel to every creature; he that believeth and is baptized shall be saved, but he that believeth not, shall be damned. Thus has the Lord commanded and ordained; therefore, no other baptism may be taught or practiced forever. The Word of God abideth forever." "Foundation of Christian Doctrine" (1539), in *The Complete Writings*, p. 120.

    10. *WtQ1934*, #44 (Sept. 20, 1527), p. 34 (Hans Spitelmair).

    11. *Z*, pp. 269f.

    12. *WtQ1934*, #82 (Baiersdorf, 1528), pp. 78-94; #353 (April 27, 1534, Ansbach), pp. 338-40.

    13. Ludwig Hetzer marked converts with a cross on the forehead, reading the Great Commission; *WtQ1934*, #137, #138, #139 (July 6, 1528), pp. 124-29, 125.

    14. "The mature Christian" could be termed an Anabaptist ideal. One answered at Erlangen (Jan. 17, 1529): "8. He hoped it was yet the truth which God's word clearly shows, as it stands written, Mark 16, how the Lord Jesus Christ says: Go into all the world, preach the gospel to every creature, whoso believeth and is baptized he shall be saved; whoever doesn't believe, he shall be damned, says the Lord. By such a text I hope God's word is no heresy when he has spoken and commanded as I have done and taught; so

should you also do and teach, as Christ himself has done and also let himself be baptized in the 30th year." *WtQ1934*, p. 132.

15. Note Calvin's treatment of the matter in "Brième Instruction pour armer tous bons fidèles contre les Erreurs de la Secte des Anabaptistes," XXXV *CR* (1868) cols. 45-142, 58. Calvin did not restrict the command to the early period, but took the position that spreading the Gospel to new areas was the responsibility of Christian governments. Warneck, Gustav, *Abriss einer Geschichte der protestantischen Missionen* (Berlin: Martin Warneck, 1913), pp. 18-19.

16. Melanchthon, quoted in Warneck, Gustav, *op. cit.*, p. 13.

17. They emphasized Matt. 10:1-15 rather than Matt. 28:19, but had the whole world in prospect. On the Franciscan movement as a world mission, see Benz, Ernst, *op. cit.*, p. 66.

18. Horsch, John, *Mennonites in Europe* (Scottdale, Penna.: Mennonite Publishing House, 1942), p. 315. By the same author, *The Hutterian Brethren, 1528-1931* (Goshen, Ind.: Mennonite Historical Society, 1931): applicants for baptism and church membership were instructed in their duty to be willing to go to the provinces as missioners, p. 29, fn. 36; the oldest missionary hymn, 23 verses of 8 lines each, was composed by the Hutterites, pp. 27f. Hans Hut testified that he was baptized by Hans Denck in terms of Mark 16 and the last of Matthew; how seriously he took the instruction is recorded in his great evangelistic trips; *WtQ1934*, #57 (1527), pp. 41-44. See also the statement of Georg Nespitzer (Jörg von Passau) at Ansbach; *WtQ1934*, #206 (July 12, 1530), pp. 186-88: Hut baptized him while Jörg read the Great Commission, "Go to all creatures. . . ." Würzlberger, who based his testimony throughout on the Great Commission (Regensburg: May, 1528), reported his election as apostle by the congregation; he also said he was no *Wieder*täufer but considered him a *Wider*täufer who baptized against the word of God (i.e., infants) ; *WtQ:Bayern II*, #18, #22, #25. At the end he said it was "certainly a pitiful thing that they wouldn't let him stay fast by the truth. He didn't want to live otherwise than as a true Christian," p. 39.

19. Latourette, Kenneth S., "New Perspectives in Church History," XXI *Journal of Religion* (1941) 4:432-43, 438f. Professor Latourette has elsewhere listed six reasons for the failure of the Reformers in the matter of the Christian mission, and concluded: "several of the early leaders of Protestantism disavowed any obligation to carry the Christian message to non-Christians. Thus Luther and Melanchthon believed that the end of the world was so imminent that no time remained to spread the Gospel throughout the world. The New Testament command to 'preach the Gospel to every creature' Luther held had been binding only upon the original Apostles, and he maintained that the proclamation of the Christian message throughout the earth as a preliminary prophesied by the New Testament to the end of the age had long before been accomplished." *A History of the Expansion of Christianity* (New York and London: Harper & Bros., 1937-45), III, 25.

20. Contrast Butzer's position: "The Christians don't need to do anything else than what they've previously done; each stands up for the gospel in his appointed place, and the Kingdom of God will grow." Warneck, Gustav, *op. cit.*, p. 18.

21. *WtQ1938*, p. 95 (Hans Schlaffer).

22. *WtQ1930,* #947 (Dec. 4, 1590) , p. 658.

23. *Beck,* p. 39, fn. 2 (instructions to Georg Zaunring) .

24. The Anabaptists said the *Schriftgelernten* ("scribes") have no *creütz*: they were as though the goldsmith only talked to the metal and didn't take it into his shop: *WtQ1938,* p. 74 (Leonhard Schiemer) .

25. *The Christian Approach to the Moslem* (New York: Columbia University Press, 1942) , p. 66. Ernst Benz has pointed out that there was, nevertheless, some missionary effort in the Balkans supported by Luther and Melanchthon; "Kirchengeschichte als Universalgeschichte: Das Lebenswerk von K. S. Latourette," I *Saeculum* (1950) 4:487-507; p. 498, fn. 5.

26. *Von dem Geist der Widerteuffer* (Wittenberg, 1544) , p. Eiij + 1.

27. *Ibid.,* p. fij.

28. *Ibid.,* no pagination.

29. "Ein Brieff D. Mart. Luthers Von den Schleichern und Winckelpredigern" (1532) , *WA* XXX, 3:519.

30. *WA* XXX, 3:521. The Anabaptist failure to stay put in fixed stations in life was the chief complaint of Theodor Beza (1519-1605) , who also denied the continuing authority of the Great Commission: *ML* (1913) I, 215. Luther said that after the visit to the manger the shepherds went back to their flocks and didn't wander around in the woods like the Anabaptists; Buchwald, Georg, *Predigten D. Martin Luthers* (Gütersloh: C. Bertelsmann Verlag, 1925-26) , I, 175 (Dec. 26, 1528) ; again, II, 76 (Dec. 27, 1530) .

31. Warneck, Gustav, "Mission unter den Heiden: 2, protestantische," *Real.-3* (1903) XIII, 130-31.

32. "Wider die himmlischen Propheten" (1525) , *WA* XVIII, p. 97.

33. Warneck, Gustav, "Mission unter den Heiden," quotation on p. 128.

34. Gratz, Delbert L., *Bernese Anabaptists* (Goshen, Ind.: Mennonite Historical Society, 1953) , p. 17.

35. *Der Widertoeuffern ursprung/ fürgang/ Secten/ wäsen/* etc. (Zürich: Christoffel Froschower, 1541) , p. 148b.

36. Hartmann, Julius, *Johannes Brenz, Leben und ausgewaehlte Schriften* (Elberfeld: K. L. Fridericks, 1862) , p. 106.

37. Warneck, Gustav, *Geschichte der prot. Missionen,* p. 17.

38. "Bucers Widerlegung des Bekenntnisses von Pilgram Marbeck" (1532) , No. 303:21 in Rott, Jean, ed., *Elsässischen Täuferakten, I,* not yet published.

39. "Bekandtnuss und verantwortung Hansen Schlaffers . . . ," *WtQ1938,* p. 111.

40. *WtQ1930,* #113 (April 14, 1563) , p. 1057 (Paul Glock) .

41. Ecke, Karl, *Schwenckfeld, Luther, und der Gedanke einer apostolischen Reformation* (Berlin: Martin Warneck, 1911) , pp. 90f. Capito wrote that Schwenckfeld stood for "the service of the church, that is preaching and provision of the sacraments, not at all their elimination; and then to wait with two or three . . . until the Holy Spirit come again as on Pentecost at Jerusalem." *WtQ1930,* #65 (May 21, 1534) , pp. 990f. See "Epistles, Anabaptist," by Friedmann, *ME* (1956) II, 230-33.

42. *WtQ1930,* pp. 990f.

43. The church was where "two or three are gathered together," *unpartheyisch;* Report on the Tübingen Colloquy (May 28, 1535) , *CSchw,*

V, 336. It was founded in the freely preached evangel, Christ with us to the end of the world (Matt. 28:20) ; "Was die warhafftig Christlich Kirch sei" (c. 1530) , *CSchw*, V, 57.

44. "Freiwilligkeitskirche" was a term used by their enemies, in part justified by their championing of Erasmus against Luther in the controversy about the Free Will. See article by Wray, F. J., "Free Will," *ME* (1956) II, 387-89. Pilgram Marpeck and Peter Ridemann were Augustinian, Hübmaier and Denck and Menno more Erasmian. "Freiwilligkeitskirche" also conveys their significance as voluntary religious associations in lands controlled by Roman Catholic and Protestant state churches; see *GHW/M*, p. 87.

45. *WtQ1938*, pp. 178-79 (Jakob Huter). See also p. 238: "There it stands, in the first place one shall preach, then comes believing, thirdly, those that believe, baptize [them]. The children cannot believe, they know nothing of God, of Christ, therefore the baptism isn't used for them during childhood." (The Five Articles, c. 1547). "Question. 'What do you hold concerning infant baptism?' Answer. 'I consider it nothing else than a human institution.' Qu. 'By what then will you prove, or establish your baptism?' Ans. 'By Mark xvi'." Confession of an Anabaptist at Antwerp, 1551; Braght, T. J. van, *op. cit.*, I, 436-37. Infant baptism is refuted on the basis of the text, "preach and baptize," for they must first have the faith; *WtQ1930*, #169 (April 9, 1557) , p. 143. Permitting infant baptism indicates that the full value of mature decision are not known (Mark 16:16 !) ; *Egli*, #1201 (June 4, 1527) , II, p. 547. The answer of Christ *De baptismo parvulorum* is Matt. 28, then Mark 16; *WtQ1934*, #228 (Hans Hechtlein, 1530) , pp. 200-01. The two main influences launching Hans Hut on his great evangel seem to have been studying Matt. 28, Mark 16, and Acts 19:1-7 on infant baptism, and Müntzer's "Hoch verursachte schutzrede . . ."; Neuser, Wilhelm, *Hans Hut. Leben und Wirken bis zum Nikolsburger Religionsgespräch* (Berlin: Hermann Blanke, 1913) , pp. 12-13, fn. 40; p. 15, fn. 63. Thomas von Imbroich, who greatly influenced Campanus, is recorded to have said (May 5, 1558) : "They asked him why he did not have his children baptized? He answered: 'The Scripture teaches nothing of infant baptism; and they who will be baptized according to God's word must first be believers ! ' " Braght, T. J. van, *op. cit.*, II, 139. Felix Manz, in his "Protestation und Schutzschrift" (1524) , had informed the Town Council that infant baptism was introduced into the church artificially (*kündtlich*) , while the true scriptural basis of baptism was the Great Commission; *WtQ:Zürich*, #16, pp. 23f.

46. *Beck*, p. 67.

47. *Beck*, #795 (August, 1525), p. 377.

48. Article by Neff, "Beck," in *ML* (1913) I, 148-49. However, see Friedmann, Robert, "Christian Sectarians in Thessalonica and Their Relationship to the Anabaptists," XXIX *MQR* (1955) 1:54-69.

49. From a letter of Paul Glock; *WtQ1930*, #114 (April 14, 1563) , p. 1068. Among important missioners were Klaus Felbinger (? - 1560) , *ME* (1956) II, 320-21; Onophrius Griesinger (? - 1538) , *ME* (1956) II, 579-80; see article on Hutterite missioners, *ME* (1956) II, 866-67. Peter Walpot followed Ridemann as head of the great Hutterite missionary effort; he was also no mean theologian; see article, "Handbüchlein wider den Prozess . . . ," *ME* (1956) II, 645-46. Paul Glock (? - 1585) was a leader of the Hutterites

in the generation after the formative period of Anabaptism, and in principle falls outside this study; his epistles and travels, however, represent Hutterite missionary activity at its highest; see article, *ME* (1956) II, 525-26.

50. *WtQ1930*, #113 (April 14, 1563), p. 1061. Hans Schmidt said he was commissioned "to be a light to the world" (Matt. 5:14); #947 (Dec. 4, 1590), pp. 652f.

51. This proof text was also roundly stated by Jakob Huter in his "Brief an den Landeshauptmann in Mähren." Further, he said: "And we say and wish that the whole world were like us, and we want to lead and convert everyone to this faith. Then would all war and injustice come to an end." *WtQ1938*, p. 163.

52. Wiswedel, Wilhelm, *Bilder und Führergestalten aus dem Täufertum* (Kassel: J. G. Oncken Verlag, 1928, 1930, 1952), III, 40. So also Blaurock: *ML* (1913) I, 227-34, 230. This was also the proof test for religious liberty among the Swiss Brethren: Correll, Ernst, *Das Schweizerische Täufermennonitentum* (Tübingen: J. C. B. Mohr, 1925), p. 42.

53. For the way in which persecution, banishment, and exile spread the movement, see article, "East Prussia," in *ME* (1956) II, 123-25; also, by Irving B. Horst, "England," *ME* (1956) II, 215-21. For a summary on the expansion, with a map showing concentrations of Anabaptism in 1550, see Bender, on "Europe," *ME* (1956) II, 255-61. On the uses of banishment by magisterial Protestantism against dissenters, see article, "Exile," in *ME* (1956) II, 279-81.

54. For this office, "Apostel der Täufer" (Acts 2:38-41), the Brethren again reconstituted an order common in the Early Church. The highest responsibility in the community was to be sent out to lead the heathen to Christ; article by Loserth, *ML* (1913) I, 438-40.

55. For an example of missioners calling out large numbers to Moravia, see *Z*, p. 171. Peter Ridemann reported to Hans Amon on what he found in the groups of Württemberg and Hesse, see *Z*, pp. 193f. For examples of the way various areas were affected by the missioners' work, note the detailed articles under geographical rubrics in *ML* and *ME*; e.g., "Alsace," "Amsterdam," "Austria," "Baden," "Basel," "Bavaria," "Belgium," "Bern," "Chur," "Cleve," etc. For reports to Peter Walpot on missionary travels, see *WtQ1930*, #122 (Sept. 30, 1566), pp. 1086f.

56. On the loss of discipline due to the advent of economic refugees, see Horsch, John, *The Hutterian Brethren*, p. xvi.

57. *Infra*, III: 78.

58. The Word to all creatures seemed to imply a new creation, a new community not built with stones but by the Word; Hege, Christian, "Pilgram Marbecks Vermahnung," in Neff, ed., *op. cit.*, p. 245. Jörg von Passau wrote in a letter (1529): "Nachdem der almechtig ewig got uns erofnet hat sein geheimnus nach seinem veterlichen willn, wie ir dan ermanet seit durch das evangelium, das euch gepredigt ist, in allen creaturen, die uns weisen den weg der gerechtigkeit, dardurch wir komen zum ewigen reich durch Jesum Cristum." *WtQ1934*, p. 169.

59. After Zwingli's "Vom Tauf, Widertauf und Kindertauf . . . ," an edict of the Zürich Town Council forbade the corner meetings and suggested that the foreign enemies of infant baptism might earn their penny elsewhere; Loserth, Johann, and Beck, Josef R., "Georg Blaurock und die

Anfänge des Anabaptismus in Graubündten und Tirol," VII *Vorträge und Aufsätze* (1899) 1-30, 3. On return after expulsion, Blaurock was whipped into exile; *Egli*, #1110 (June 5, 1527), II, 530. On BLAUROCK, see Neff in *ML* (1913) I, 227-34; *ME* (1955) I, 354-59; Moore, John Allen, *Der Starke Jörg* (Kassel: J. G. Oncken Verlag, 1955); Jecklin, Fritz, "Jörg Blaurock vom Haus Jakob," XXI *Jahresbericht der hist.-antiq. Gesellschaft* (1891), 20 pages in reprint.

60. *Egli*, #646 (Feb. 18 and 25, 1525), I, 289.

61. *Egli*, #837 (Oct. 8, 1525), I, 395.

62. On Blaurock's capacity as a powerful missioner, see *Beck*, pp. 79f; Z, p. 49.

63. *Z*, p. 56.

64. *Egli*, #824 (Sept. 20, 1525), I, 391; report of a convert of Teck's, #953 (April 11, 25, May 2, 1526), I, 457-58; also, #1357 (Jan. 21, 1528), II, 586.

65. "Märtyrersynode," *ML* (1938) 32:53-56; Schowalter on "Märtyrer," *ML* (1938) 31:44-48, 32:49.

66. *ML* (1941) 35:204-05.

67. *ML* (1937) II, 187-88; *ME* (1956) II, 598-99.

68. *ML* (1913) I, 384-86; *ME* (1956) II, 1-2.

69. *ML*. (1937) II, 618.

70. *ML* (1913) I, 469; *ME* (1956) II, 93-94.

71. *ML* (1913) I, 648; *ME* (1956) II, 333.

72. *Beck*, pp. 310-12.

73. See Friedmann on "Gelassenheit," *ME* (1956) II, 448-49. This was the key word in Karlstadt; Barge, Hermann, *Andreas Bodenstein von Karlstadt* (Leipzig: Friedrich Brandstetter, 1905), I, 35f. "I testify that we gain assurance through suffering that we are sons of God. I testify also that we go to heaven in suffering. Through suffering and persecution a man enters into the poorness in spirit of which Christ said: 'Blessed are the poor in spirit, for theirs is the kingdom of heaven'." Quotation, I, 295.

74. Stauffer, Ethelbert, *loc. cit.*, p. 578. When Andreas Neff, a leading Schwenckfelder, made submission, C. S. heard of it and wrote (Sept. 29, 1545), praying God might give him grace to be strong and carry through "ritterlich"; *WtQ1930*, #136, p. 103f; #139, p. 109. There are four weapons of the true *Ritter* of Christ: faith, hope, love, and *Gelassenheit*. See Friedmann, Robert, "Concerning the True Soldier of Christ: A Hitherto Unknown Tract of the Philippite Brethren in Moravia," V *MQR* (1931) 2:87-99, 91.

75. *WtQ1938*, p. 88 (Hans Schlaffer).

76. Ludwig Hetzer, quoted in Weis, Frederick Lewis, *The Life and Teachings of Ludwig Hetzer* (Dorchster, Mass.: Underhill Press, 1930), p. 110.

77. "Die viert epistel vom Jakob Huetter, an die gmain Gottes in Mähren," in *WtQ1938*, pp. 150-59, 154.

78. The effectiveness of the Hutterite missioners among the depressed classes is portrayed in #634, #667, #716, #721 in *WtQ1930*. It is Bossert's final conclusion that the Schwenckfelders won more preachers and women from the nobility, while the Anabaptists drew mostly from the peasants; p. xii. Accounts of those fleeing to Moravia, debts and small goods, indicate their station as tradespeople and craftsmen; #261 (Nov. 9, 1569), p. 249; #262 (Oct. 27, 1569), p. 250. Properties inventoried sometimes indicate a

fair degree of prosperity; *WtQ1934,* #27 (1527), pp. 23-24. On the general problem of the relation of Anabaptism ("Handwerker Christentum"?) to social forces, see Loesche, Georg, "Archivalische Beiträge zur Geschichte des Täufertums und des Protestantismus in Tirol und Voralberg," 47 *Jahrbuch der Gesellschaft für die Geschichte des Protestantismus im ehemaligen und im neuen Österreich* (1926), p. 3. The flooding in of economic refugees accentuated the problems of organization within the Moravian communities, and many new colonists returned to their former stations when conditions were better or when persecution threatened the life in Moravia. One motif may have been a kind of reaction against city life and commercial complexities, and idealization of "die Bedürfnislosigkeit"; Correll, Ernst, *op. cit.,* pp. 61-62. A definite form of confession and submission was provided for those who returned, would promise obedience, and re-establish themselves in the fabric of a stable society; *WtQ1930,* #198 (June 27, 1559), p. 185. See also the case of Hans Volmar of Geradstatten, who after re-baptism went to Moravia and then returned and submitted; *WtQ1930,* #64, p. 44; also Christmann Schmidt of Diegenbach, who was banished on return, #70, p. 47. Konrad Wirtemberger of Zaisersweiher, who returned but refused to conform, was expelled and exiled; *WtQ1930,* #68, p. 46. Appollonia of Horrheim and husband came back from Moravia and submitted; *WtQ1930,* #73-74, p. 49. Very evidently the migration to Moravia was only an economic movement for many, and they found the life and discipline in the colonies too rigorous to bear. A fine new study on Anabaptism and economic groups is Peachey, Paul, *Die soziale Herkunft der Schweizer Täufer in der Reformationszeit* (Karlsruhe: Heinrich Schneider, 1954). See article by Friedmann on "Economic History of the Hutterian Brethren," *ME* (1956) II, 143-45; also, Neumann, Gerhard J., "Nach und von Mähren," reprinted from *ARG* (1957) 1:75-90.

79. *WtQ1934,* #12 (1527), p. 15. One of the men was Hans Ritter, who accompanied Hans Hut on many trips.

80. *WtQ1930,* #231 (Feb. 5, 1563), p. 227; see poor relief records, pp. 231f. A General Rescript (July 13, 1538) mentioned journeymen going up and down in the land and wandering off to Moravia.

81. *WtQ1930,* #241, pp. 234f. A typical process of confiscation against persons who had been in Moravia for some years included the following items: 1) Are there children, how old, and are they also Anabaptist? 2) If no other kin are eligible, who has a just claim to the goods and property? See #251 (Dec. 24, 1565): questions about goods and money of Anabaptists who had gone 28 years before to Moravia. See also #263 (Oct. 7, 1570): judgment on an estate; the daughter had married an Anabaptist and lived in Moravia, and her part was put in escrow.

82. *WtQ1934,* p. 18. Proof was given by the authorities that a man should not wander, but stay with his wife and children; #150 (Feb. 1, 1529), pp. 143-46. Note Calvin's opposition to the "bare-footed evangel" of the Libertines, which was as much social as ecclesiastical; Müller, Karl, "Calvin und die 'Libertiner'," XL *ZKG* (1922) N.F. III:83-129. Luther, himself a good *Hausvater,* stated the family as one of the orders of "natural" responsibility *(Schöpfungsordnungen)*, against the wandering *Schwärmer* as well as against Roman celibacy.

83. So was it reported of a wanderer examined by Johannes Brenz;

WtQ1930, #169 (April 9, 1557), p. 146. A familiar phrase in court records was "wife and children not of his faith," which may have been due to the father's effort to protect them from the authorities but could have derived also from the fact that the father had traveled widely in guild circles and broken loose from the established religion.

84. *WtQ1938,* p. 214 (Ulrich Stadler).

85. *WtQ1934,* #254 (April 30, 1531), p. 231: "di armen fruma leut auf apostolisch ire guter gemein halten," on the basis of the Great Commission.

86. Correll, Ernst, *op. cit.,* p. 18.

87. *Supra,* p. 38.

88. *Z,* p. 105.

89. *Z,* p. 112.

90. *Z,* p. 134; *WtQ1934,* pp. 144f.

91. *Z,* p. 157.

92. *Beck,* p. 99. See also *supra,* p. 91.

93. *Beck,* p. 226. In 1556, during the dispute among the Swiss Brethren on the incarnation, many came over to the Hutterites who stood on Reformation ground. Melchior Waal served as missioner among the Swiss to 1559, and from 1561 for the Hutterites; Wolkan, Rudolph, ed., *Geschicht-Buch der Hutterischen Brüder* (Vienna and Macleod, Alta.: Carl Fromme G. m. b. H., 1923), pp. 304, 311, 391. Testimony of a group coming over, stating their complaint against the Swiss; *WtQ1938,* pp. 265f. Many were won by Hans Schmidt, Hutterite "Diener des Worts" in Württemberg, who wrote among other tracts, "Warumb man in das Märherland ziehen soll"; pp. 267, 269-70.

94. On the occasion of the splits, see *Beck,* pp. 113f. Ascherham was essentially a spiritualizer, and later wrote that he had never opposed infant baptism and during a long series of acrimonious polemics permanently alienated both enemies and friends; p. 250. On Gabriel Ascherham (? - 1545), see *ML* (1913) I, 87-88; *ME* (1955) I, 174-76; also "Gabrielites," *ME* (1956) II, 429. On the followers of Philipp Weber, see article by Loserth, "Philipper," *ML* (1952) 38:367-68.

95. A notable effort was made in 1538; *Z,* p. 181.

96. On Stadler and his group, see *Beck,* p. 133; *WtQ1938,* p. 212f.

97. *WtQ1938,* p. 226.

98. *Z,* p. 102. On RIDEMANN, see article by Köhler, Walther, in *RGG - 2,* IV, 2030.

99. Rideman, Peter, *op. cit.:* the Great Commission is stated as the first thing sacrificed by those who baptize children (p. 70).

100. *Z,* pp. 176f. While imprisoned in Hesse, 1540, he composed his great *Rechenschaft* and, not knowing what his end might be, wrote his beautiful "unpartheyisch" admonition to the Brethren; pp. 212f.

101. *Beck,* p. 41, fn.

102. "Die viert epistel vom Jacob Huetter . . . ," *WtQ1938,* pp. 150-59, 152.

103. *WtQ1934,* #66 (Dec. 23, 1527), p. 61. Storch sent out 12 apostles through Germany, p. 9.

104. See article by Neff, "Jakob von Campen," *ML* (1913) I, 324-25. Deventer, Zwolle, Amsterdam, and Leiden were among the most important

centers of missionary effort; Cornelius, C. A., *Die Niederländischen Wieder-täufer während der Belagerung Münsters 1534 bis 1535* (Munich: Kgl. bayer. Akademie, 1869), p. 4. The names of missioners were listed by Vos in *DB* (1917) 98-100.

105. Bouterwek, K. W., "Zur Wiedertäufer-Literatur," I *Zeitschrift des Bergischen Geschichtsvereins* (1869) 3:280-344, 294. In the day of wrath the devil will be overthrown from his present reign: "In sum, the people of God which is left, which shall be unspotted and pure in all obedience, will stand to arms throughout the whole earth" (p. 311).

106. *Ibid.,* p. 310.

107. Quoting Rothmann, with discussion; Heyer, Fritz, *op. cit.,* p. 68. On the importance of the Great Commission in Rothmann's thought, see Detmer, Heinrich, and Krumbholtz, Robert, ed., *Zwei Schriften des Münsterischen Wiedertäufers Bernhard Rothmann* (Dortmund: Fr. Wilh. Ruhfus, 1904), pp. 12, 19.

108. Bouterwek, K. W., *loc. cit.,* p. 347.

109. Bainton, Roland H., "The Immoralities of the Patriarchs According to the Exegesis of the Late Middle Ages and of the Reformation," XXIII *Harvard Theological Review* (1930) 39-49, p. 45, fn. 28.

110. See chapter on Hut in Brush, John, *Radical Eschatology of the Continental Reformation;* MSS in Sterling Library, Yale University, Ph.D. thesis, 1942. Further, *supra,* p. 28.

111. *WtQ1934,* #206, #227, #242.

112. "Die Chronik von Clemens Sender," XXIII *Die Chroniken der Deutschen Städte* (Leipzig: S. Hirzel, 1894), p. 192.

113. "Urgicht . . . 16. September 1527," in Meyer, Christian, "Zur Geschichte der Wiedertäufer in Oberschwaben: 1. Die Anfänge des Wiedertäuferthums in Augsburg," I *Zeitschrift des Historischen Vereins für Schwaben and Neuberg* (1874) 207-56, 223.

114. Article by Hegler, in *Real.-3* (1900) VIII, 489-91.

115. Neuser, Wilhelm, *op. cit.,* pp. 26f. He traveled so widely that his trips cannot be traced, and also sent out apostles who were especially effective among the handworkers.

116. Article by Loserth, *loc. cit.,* p. 371: Matt. 24, Mark 13, Luke 17 — the last things.

117. "7 Urteile der Wiedertäufer," #234 (1530); *WtQ1934,* p. 212.

118. *WtQ1934,* p. 131.

119. *WtQ1934,* p. 65; this is from the Nikolsburger Articles (1527) which here express Anabaptist sentiments. Also, *WtQ1938,* p. 225 (Stadler).

120. Heyer, Fritz, *op. cit.,* p. 54. One rose to challenge the preacher in church and defend the corner preacher; *Egli,* II, 581. Sattler held his meetings in field and woods; II, 589-91. The court at Marbach, July 10, 1539, heard one say they met "by the oak in Esslingen wood," on Sunday morning while others were in church; *WtQ1930,* #99, p. 71. Part of any pledge of submission was to avoid the small corner meetings; if those who submitted fell back, their property was forfeit. On their general practices in worship, see Miller, Paul M., "Worship Among the Early Anabaptists," XXX *MQR* (1956) 4:235-46.

121. Heyer, Fritz, *op. cit.,* p. 16.

122. *WtQ1938,* p. 225 (Stadler).

123. *WtQ1938*, p. 165 (Huter).

124. "Meditation on the Twenty-fifth Psalm" (c. 1537), *The Complete Writings*, p. 81.

125. Jacob Huter, in writing to the lords against persecution, reported in moving language on the sick and helpless and orphans among them: *WtQ1938*, p. 162.

126. See Reublin's report on Sattler's death, *WtQ:Zürich*, #224, pp. 250-53; also *GHW/M*, pp. 136f.

127. On the general place of hymnology in the movement, see Correll, Ernst, "The Value of Hymns for Mennonite History," IV *MQR* (1930) 3:215f; Ramaker, A. J., "Hymns and Hymn Writers Among Anabaptists of the Sixteenth Century," III *MQR* (1929) 2:93f; Bender, Harold S., "The Hymnology of the Anabaptists," XXXI *MQR* (1957) 1:5-10; article on "Hymnology," *ME* (1956) II, 869f.

128. Written by Swiss Brethren in prison at Passau, 1535-1537. *Infra*, V:49.

129. This is the stock phrase describing the martyrs in the Greater Chronicle: *Beck*, p. 1.

130. The threefold baptism; *WtQ1938*, pp. 77f (Leonhard Schiemer).

131. The cup Jesus drank; *WtQ1934*, p. 51 (Huter).

132. *WtQ1938*, p. 203 (*Rechenschaft* at Trieste, 1539).

133. Müller, Lydia, *Der Kommunismus der mährischen Wiedertäufer* (Leipzig: M. Heinsius Nachf., 1927), p. 59. On a famous case of persecution at Schwäbisch-Gmünd, see "Wolfgang Esslinger," *ME* (1956) II, 252.

134. *WtQ1938*, p. 155 (Huter).

135. *WtQ1930*, #947 (Dec. 4, 1590), pp. 658-59, 662.

136. On Hutterite educational contributions, see article by Friedmann, in *ME* (1956) II, 149-50; Wiswedel, Wilhelm, "Das Schulwesen der Huterischen Brüder in Mähren," XXXVII *ARG* (1940) 1:38-60.

137. *WtQ1938*, p. 67 (Schiemer).

138. *WtQ1938*, p. 154.

139. Holl, Karl, "Luther und die Schwärmer," section 7 of *Gesammelte Aufsätze zur Kirchengeschichte* (Tübingen: J. C. B. Mohr, 1923), I, 429. Also: "Dan warhaftig innerlich wort ist ewige und almechtige kraft Gottes gleichfermig in menschen wie in Got, und vermag alle ding," *WtQ1938*, p. 214 (Stadler).

140. See quotations of observers: *Beck*, p. xx.

141. Clemen, Otto, "Das Prager Manifest Thomas Münzers," XXX *ARG* (1933) 73-81, 75. It was with Joachim of Fiore that suffering became eschatological, signifying in mysterious fashion an effective opposition to the Great Church: Benz, Ernst, *op. cit.*, p. 298.

142. It must be admitted that Menno and his associates represented to a degree a reaction against all eschatology; nevertheless, they looked for the Thousand Years of Peace which should be ushered in with Christ's coming: *Beck*, p. xviii.

143. Johnson, John W., "Balthazar Hubmaier and Baptist Historic Commitments," IX *Journal of Religion* (1929) 50-65, 54f.

144. Article by Loserth, *ML* (1937) II, 353-63, 360.

145. On their social expectancy, *WtQ1938*, p. xvi.

146. See article on "Apokatastase," *ML* (1913) I, 77.

147. Stauffer, Ethelbert, *loc. cit.*, quoting and discussing Menno, p. 566. On the Martyr Church as the type of Stephen, see Benz, Ernst, *op. cit.*, pp. 335f.

148. Loserth, Johann, and Beck, Josef R., *loc. cit.*, quotation on p. 38.

149. Bossert, Gustav, Jr., "Michael Sattler's Trial and Martyrdom in 1527," XXV *MQR* (1951) 3:201-18, 215.

150. Quoted in Lindsay, A. D., *The Essentials of Democracy* (Philadelphia: Univ. of Pennsylvania Press, 1929), p. 76. On the general question of Anabaptist social ideas, see Peachey, Paul, "Social Background and Social Philosophy of the Swiss Anabaptists, 1525-40," XXVIII *MQR* (1954) 2:102-27, 120.

151. *Supra*, p. 79.

152. Robert Kreider has given evidence that Russian Mennonitism, when tolerated, "moved in the direction and exhibited many of the characteristics of the VOLKSKIRCHE or what the English call the 'parish pattern of the church'." See "The Anabaptist Conception of the Church in the Russian Mennonite Environment, 1789-1870," XXV *MQR* (1951) 1:17-46, 18. This was still limited, presumably, to those of the blood and language; missionary work atrophied and the culture religion of an enclave was maintained. See Pannabecker, Samuel Floyd, *The Development of the General Conference of the Mennonite Church of North America in the American Environment;* MSS at Sterling Library, Yale University, Ph.D. thesis, 1944, p. 36: exclusiveness and growth of agrarian life coincide with the loss of missionary enterprise; p. 618: however, the foreign missionary enterprise was the first outside program to commend itself to the church in America, suggesting an earlier affinity.

153. Payne, Ernest A., *The Anabaptists of the Sixteenth Century and their Influence in the Modern World* (London: Carey Kingsgate Press, 1949); Bainton, Roland H., "The Enduring Witness: the Mennonites," IX *Mennonite Life* (1954) 2:83-90.

CHAPTER 5

THE CHANGING REPUTATION
OF THE ANABAPTISTS

1. Whitney, James P., *History of the Reformation* (London: S.P.C.K. and New York: Macmillan Co., 1940). First ed., Macmillan Co., 1907.

2. Smith, Preserved, *The Age of the Reformation* (New York: Henry Holt & Co., 1920), p. 244.

3. Lindsay, T. M., *A History of the Reformation* (New York: Charles Scribner's Sons, 1941). First published, 1907. The chapter on Anabaptism is in Bk. V, Vol. II, Ch. 2.

4. *Ibid.*, p. 431, fn. His notation on the difference between articles on Anabaptism in the second (1877) and third (1896) editions of Herzog's *Realencyclopädie für protestantische Theologie und Kirche* is revealing.

5. *Ibid.*, p. 443. "The Anabaptists would have nothing to do with

a State Church; and this was the main point in their separation from the Lutherans, Zwinglians and Calvinists. It was perhaps the *one* conception on which parties among them were in absolute accord. The real Church, which might be small or great, was for them an association of believing people. . . ."

6. *Ibid.*, p. 441. "For the whole Anabaptist movement was medieval to the core. . . ." p. 445: "The Swiss Anabaptists were in no sense disciples of Zwingli. They had held their distinctive principles and were a recognized community long before Zwingli came from Einsiedeln, and were the lineal descendants of the medieval Waldenses." For discussion of this classification, see *infra*, p. 153.

7. See the author's *The Free Church* (Boston: Starr King Press, 1957).

8. For a more competent treatment of the Anabaptists in a general survey, see Ch. 8 of Williston Walker's *The Reformation* (New York: Charles Scribner's Sons, 1917). "But though in many things thus representative of earlier tendencies, these extreme movements were even more children of the sixteenth century Reformation. They were called into being by it. They were not demonstrably in organic continuity with the medieval anti-Roman sects . . ." (p. 337). Chapter 39 of Henry S. Lucas' *The Renaissance and the Reformation* (New York and London: Harper & Bros., 1934), was until recently the most reliable textbook treatment of the Anabaptist movement. Vol. II, "The Reformation," of *The Cambridge Modern History* (New York: Macmillan Co., 1918), adds nothing to the discussion.

9. Vedder, Henry C., *The Reformation in Germany* (New York: Macmillan Co., 1914), p. 345. Ch. 10-13 in Vedder's *A Short History of the Baptists* (Philadelphia: American Baptist Publication Society, 1907), are much better done.

10. Allen, J. W., *A History of Political Thought in the Sixteenth Century* (London: Methuen & Co., 1928) ; see *supra*, pp. 101f.

11. Horsch, John, "The Character of the Evangelical Anabaptists as Reported by Contemporary Reformation Writers," VIII *MQR* (1934) 3:123-35.

12. It is refreshing to be able to report that certain of the most recent surveys show familiarity with the sources and a far better understanding of Anabaptism. See Bainton, Roland H., *The Reformation of the Sixteenth Century* (Boston: Beacon Press, 1952), Ch. 5; Dillenberger, John P., and Welch, Claude, *Protestant Christianity* (New York: Charles Scribner's Sons, 1954), pp. 58-67. Harold J. Grimm's *The Reformation Era: 1500-1650* (New York: Macmillan Co., 1954) is excellent on the Anabaptists. He concludes: "It was Grebel's conception of a free church, consisting of freely committed and practicing believers, as opposed to the VOLKSKIRCHE, or inclusive state church of the Catholics and most Protestants, which formed the basic doctrine of the Anabaptists" (p. 266).

13. *Infra*, p. 158.

14. *Supra*, pp. 3f.

15. Published in Wittenberg by Nickel Schirlentz; microfilm from Columbia University Library (UTS). Found also in *Der Ander Teil/ der Bücher D. Mart: Luth:/* (Wittenberg: Georg Rhaw Erb, 1551), pp. 302f. Menius, a persecutor, was himself ten years later driven from office and imprisoned as a follower of Georg Major. On MENIUS, see article by Kawerau

in *Real.-3* (1903) XII, 577-81; Schmidt, Gustav L., *Justus Menius* (Gotha: Fr. Andreas Perthes, 1867) ; Paul Schowalter in *ML* (1938) 32:75-77. Menius was also Superintendent over the Hausbreitenbach Condominium, and supported the harshness of the Duke of Saxony over against the tolerance of the Landgrave of Hesse; see *Supra*, I:163.

16. *Der Ander Teil*, pp. 350f.

17. Schmidt, G. L., "Ungedruckte Briefe von Justus Menius," N.F. II *Zeitschrift des Vereins für thüringische Geschichte und Altertumskunde* (1882) #7, 243-64.

18. Melanchthon in a letter of September 29, 1559, printed in *CR* IX, 926-30, 927. In 1551 appeared a less-known writing by Menius, *Von den Blutfreunden aus der Widertauff*, printed in Erfurt by Gervasius Sthürmer.

19. Of special importance is *Ein Bedencken/ der Luneburgeschen, ob/ einer oberkeit gezime die Wiederteuffer, odder andere Ketzer zum rech/ten glauben zu dringen* . . . (Hamburg: Fr. Rhodum, 1537) ; for the advice of the Lüneburgers to Philipp in support of the death penalty, see *WtQ:Hessen*, p. 105.

20. In the same exchange, *Ein Sendbrieff Hans Huthe,/ etwa ains furnemen Vor/ steers im Widertauf/ferordenn* (1528) ; both were printed at Augsburg by A. Weyssenhorn.

21. *Der Ander Teil*, pp. 400f.

22. Published in translation by C. J. H. Fick (Hermannsburg, 1860) . On RHEGIUS, see Ulhorn, Gerhard, *Urbanus Rhegius* (Elberfeld: R. L. Friderichs, 1861) ; article in *Real.-3* (1905) XVI, 734-41.

23. Items of note may be listed as follows: *Die Historia Thome Mün/tzers,/ des anfengers der Düringischen Auffrhur/ seer nützlich zu lesen* (1525) ; *Vnderricht Philip. Melancht./ wider die Lere der/ Widerteuffer auss/ dem latein verdeutschet, durch/ Just. Jonas* (1528) ; *Das weltliche Oberkeit den/ Widerteuffern mit leibliche Straffe zu wehren/ schüldig sey* (1534) ; *Etliche propositiones wi/der die Lere der Widerteuffer gestelt* (1535) ; *Wider das gottleslerlich vñ/scheudlich buch/so zu Münstei im druck newlich ist ausgangen/ Etliche Propositiones* (1535) ; *Verlegung etlicher vnchrist/licher Artikel/ welche die Widerteuffer furgeben* (1536) . The second in the list indicates no printer (President White Library) ; the other items may be found reprinted in the order given in *Der Ander Teil*, pp. 473f, 382f, 281f, 391f, 282f. On MELANCHTHON, see Neff's article in *ML* (1938) 32:66-69; article by Paul Kirn in *Real.-3* (1903) XII, 513-48; Hildebrandt, Franz, *Melanchthon: Alien or Ally?* (Cambridge, Eng.: University Press, 1946) ; Oyer, John S., "The Writings of Melanchthon Against the Anabaptists," XXVI *MQR* (1952) 4:259-79.

24. Note also the works: *Dass vn/ser Christus Jesus warer Gott sey/ Zeug/neuss der heyligen geschrifft, Wi/der die newen Juden vñ Arria/ner, vnter Christlichen namen,/ welche die Gottheyt Christi ver/leugnen* (Nürnberg: Fr. Peypus, 1526) ; *Von der/ Erbsund, das sye der Christen Kynder gleich als/ wol verdamb als der heyden./ Vnd von dem heyligen Tauff ob er die Erbsund hynweg nem.* (Nürnberg: Fr. Peypus, 1527) . On ALTHAMER, see Kolde, Theodor, "Andreas Althamer, der Humanist und Reformator in

Brand.-Ansbach," I *Beiträge zur bayrischen Kirchengeschichte* (1895) 1-25, 65-89, 98-127; by the same author, article in *Real.-3* (1896) I, 413-14; also, article by Neff in *ME* (1955) I, 79-80. For Althamer's conduct in a hearing, see "Julius Lober," *ML* (1937) II, 675-77. Other Lutheran opponents were Johannes Brenz (1499-1570), whose moderation on religious persecution offended Melanchthon; see *ML* (1913) I, 264-66; *ME* (1955) I, 418-20; Andreas Osiander (1498-1552), who changed from persecution to toleration as a result of the Copernican revolution: *ML* (1951) 37:312-13; Jakob Andreae (1528-90), who preached 33 sermons in Esslingen, 1566-67, against "Papists, Schwenckfelders, and Anabaptists," eight of them particularly aimed at refuting Ridemann's *Rechenschaft:* see "Formula of Concord," *ME* (1956) II, 355; "Andreae" in *ME* (1955) I, 119-20. On Johannes Bugenhagen, see *Supra,* I:99.

25. *Der Widdertauffer lere vñ geheimnis* . . . . p. cij.

26. *Von dem geist der Widerteuffer,* p. Bij; no pagination for second paragraph.

27. Friedmann, Robert "Conception of the Anabaptists," IX *CH* (1940) 4:341-65, 344. From the Böhmer seminar we mention the works of Karl Ecke, Wilhelm Neuser, C. Sachsse, Lydia Müller, Annemarie Lohmann.

28. According to Karl Holl, Thomas Müntzer introduced the authentic modern note — that religious reform is impossible without social reform at the same time — when he said economic change was necessary because the hard-working peasants didn't have time to read the Bible. "Luther und die Schwärmer," in *Gesammelte Aufsätze zur Kirchengeschichte* (Tübingen: J. C. B. Mohr, 1923), I, 445. The characteristic Anabaptist attitude to the state brings Holl to the judgment: "In this, our German concept is sharply distinguished from the sect influenced English-American. We value the union with the state, the furthering and deepening of the [national] community, as a good which ranks higher than the free movement of the individual" (p. 466). The passage in Müntzer appeared in the *Ausgetrückte emplössung des falschen Glaubens der ongetrewen Welt/* . . . (Mühlhausen, 1524) (Mühlhausen i. Thür.: Dannersche Buchdruckerei, 1908), edited by Jordan: "Da werden denn die armen dürfftigen leut also hoch betrogen, das es kein zung genug erzelen mag, mit allen worten vnd wercken machen sie es ya also, das der Arm man nicht lesen lerne vorm bekümernuss der narung, vnd sie predigen vnuerschempt der arm man soll sich von den Tyrannen lassen schinden vnd schoben, wenn will er denn lernen die schrifft lesen?" (p. 6).

29. Heyer, Fritz, *Der Kirchenbegriff der Schwärmer* (Leipzig: M. Heinsius Nachf., 1939).

30. *Infra,* p. 154.

31. *Supra,* p. 13.

32. Report of the Second Disputation at Zürich (Oct. 26-28, 1523), *CR* LXXXIX, 641. The Disputations afford a primary source worthy of special note in Anabaptist history, but beyond the scope of this study. Several reports are well known; John Howard Yoder is writing a doctoral dissertation on the ideas of the Anabaptists and Reformers as revealed in these documents. See *infra,* p. 159.

33. *CR* XC, 355f.

34. *CR* XCI, 188f.

35. *CR* XCI, 577f.

36. Printed at Zürich by Christopher Froschouer. On Zwingli, see *supra*, I:57-59.

37. Both works were printed at Zürich by Froschouer, who later went with Hübmaier to Nikolsburg. With Menius' two best-known works, these are the most frequently used writings about the Anabaptists. On BULLINGER, see Cornelius Bergmann in *ME* (1955) I, 467-68; Heer and Egli in *Real.* - *3* (1897) III, 536-49; Paulus, N., "Heinrich Bullinger und seine Toleranzideen," XXVI *Historisches Jahrbuch* (1905) 576-87.

38. On CALVIN, see Bohatec, Josef, *Calvins Lehre von Staat und Kirche* (Breslau: M. & M. Marcus, 1937) , sec. III: "Die Abgrenzung der calvinistischen Kirchenauffassung gegen die anabaptistische;" article by Neff, *ME* (1955) I, 495-98; McNeill, John T., *The History and Character of Calvinism* (New York: Oxford University Press, 1954) ; article by R. Stähelin, *Real.* - *3* (1897) III, 654-83. In August, 1540, Calvin married (at Strassburg) Idelotte von Büren, widow of an Anabaptist from Lüttich, Joh. Storder; *ML* (1913) I, 300-01.

39. *CR* XXXV, 45-142; see his *Psychopannychia* (Orleans, 1534) , and especially the second edition of 1544; *CR* XXXIII, 165-232; also, *Contra la secte phantastique et furieuse des Libertins, que se nomment spirituels* (Geneva, 1545) ; *CR* XXXII, 145-252; Müller, Karl, "Calvin und die 'Libertiner'," N.F. XL *ZKG* (1922) 3:83-129.

40. *Supra*, V:37.

41. On Egli's significance as editor of sources, see *infra*, p. 157.

42. On Erhard: see article by Loserth, *ML* (1913) I, 606-08; as supplemented by Friedmann, *ME* (1956) II, 243-44.

43. On Fischer: see *ML* (1913), I, 646-48. Like Erhard's writings, Fischer's are found in the United States only in the Mennonite Historical Library at Goshen College, Goshen, Indiana. For other Roman Catholic polemicists, see article on Georg Eder (1523-1556), *ME* (1956) II, 147; on Johann Faber (1478-1541), *ME* (1956) II, 285-86; Rembert on Joh. Cochlaeus (1479-1552), *ML* (1913) I, 365-67, and *ME* (1955) I, 632; on Johann Eck (1486-1543), *ML* (1913) I, 501-02, and *ME* (1956) II, 141. See "Catholicism and Anabaptism," *ME* (1955) I, 532-34, with bibliography of Roman Catholic polemical writers.

44. Article by Neff, *ML* (1913) I, 333-34.

45. See Schottenloher, Karl, *Philip Ulhart: Ein Augsburger Winkeldrucker und Helfershelfer der 'Schwärmer' und 'Wiedertäufer'* (1523-1529) , 4 *Historische Forschungen und Quellen* (1921) .

46. *Z*, p. xxv, fn. 2.

47. Hege, Christian, "Pilgram Marbeck's *Vermahnung*," in Neff, Christian, ed., *Gedenkschrift zum 400. Jährigen Jubiläum der Mennoniten oder Taufgesinnten, 1525-1925* (Ludwigshafen: Konferenz der Süd-deutschen Mennoniten E.V., 1925) , p. 178.

48. *Supra*, Ch. 2. See Rembert, Karl, *Die 'Wiedertäufer' im Herzogtum Jülich* (Berlin: R. Gaertners Verlag, 1899) , p. 207.

49. The cornerstone of the *Ausbund* was a section of fifty-one hymns from Swiss Brethren of the Auspitz Colony, imprisoned in Passau, Bavaria, 1535-1537. Many of the early leaders and martyrs, including Felix Manz, Georg Wagner, Leonhard Schiemer, Hans Schlaffer, Georg Blaurock, and Hans Hut, had given songs to the movement. Later were added hymns

from the Dutch Mennonites' *Het Offer des Heeren* (1562/63) and *Ein schön Gesangbüchlein geistlicher Lieder,* along with five hymns from the Bohemian Brethren. There may have been a first edition no longer extant, about 1570 or 1571; one dated 1583 is known, and is probably the first edition complete. There have been more than 30 editions in Europe and America, and the book is still used by the Old Order Amish. See article by Hege in *ML* (1913) I, 97, and *ME* (1955) I, 191-92; also Bender, Harold S., "The First Edition of the Ausbund," III *MQR* (1929) 2:147-50.

50. Tieleman Jansz van Braght (1625-64) edited in 1660 a record of martyrdom which has gone through many editions: *Bloedig Tooneel of Marteluursspiegel der Doopsgezinde en weerloose Christenen.* The latest edition, in English, was published at Scottdale, Penna., in 1950. Like the *Ausbund,* it indicates the central significance of a theology of suffering in the eschatology of the Anabaptists, and is of basic importance for understanding the movement: see Stauffer, Ethelbert, "Märtyrertheologie und Täuferbewegung," LII *ZKG* (1933) 545-98, 554, 559; Swartzendruber, A. Orley, "The Piety and Theology of the Anabaptist Martyrs in van Braght's Martyrs' Mirror," XXVIII *MQR* (1954) 1:5-26, 2:128-42; article on "Märtyrerbücher," *ML* (1938) 32:49-53. The historical dependability of the Martyrs' Mirror was discussed by Samuel Cramer in *DB* (1899) 63-164, (1900) 184-210. A valuable critical edition is *A Martyrology of the Churches of Christ Commonly Called Baptist* (London: Hanserd Knollys Society, 1850-53), edited by Edw. B. Underhill.

51. *Supra,* Ch. 4.

52. On Mennonite historiography, article by Hege in *ML* (1937) II, 96-101; see extensive article, *ME* (1956) II, 751-69.

53. *ME* (1956) II, 814-15.

54. Appearing during the decade 1839-1849, they comprised the five-volume *Geschiedenis der Doopsgezinden:* 1839 — Friesland, 1842 — two volumes on Groningen, Overyssel and Ost-Friesland, 1847 — two volumes on Holland, Zeeland, Utrecht and Gelderland. Also of interest is his *Geschiedkundig naar den Waldenzischen Oorsprong van de Nederlandsch Doopsgezinden* (1844). His publishers were W. Eekhoff and J. B. Wolters, Leeuwarden and Groningen. On ten Cate (1807-1884), see article by J. Loosjes in *ML* (1913) I, 335-36; *ME* (1955) I, 526-27.

55. His "Ketzer-Geschichte," the third part of *Chronica, Zeÿtbüch und Geschichtbibel* (Strassburg: Balthassar Beck, 1531), is of special worth. On FRANCK, see article by Neff, *ML* (1913) I, 668-74; Krahn and van der Zijpp in *ME* (1956) II, 363-67; Bischof, Hermann, *Sebastian Franck und deutsche Geschichtsschreibung* (Tübingen: Ernst Riecker, 1857); Hegler, A., *Geist und Schrift bei Sebastian Franck* (Freiburg: J. C. B. Mohr, 1892); Oncken, Hermann, "Sebastian Franck als Historiker," 82 *HZ* (1889) 385-435; Reimann, Arnold, *Sebastian Franck als Geschichtsphilosoph* (Berlin: Alfred Unger, 1921); Kommoss, Rudolf, *Sebastian Franck und Erasmus von Rotterdam* (Berlin: Dr. Emil Ebering, 1934); article by Hegler in *Real.-3* (1899) VI, 142-50; Räber, Kuno, *Studien zur Geschichtsbibel Sebastian Francks* (Basel: Helbing & Lichtenhahn, 1952); Teufel, Eberhard, "Die Deutsche Theologie und Sebastian Franck im Lichte der neueren Forschung," N.F. XI *Theologische Rundschau* (1939) 304-15, N.F. XII (1940) 99-129; by the same author, *"Landräumig": Sebastian Franck, ein Wanderer an Donau, Rhein*

212   The Anabaptist View of the Church

und Neckar (Neustadt a.d. Aisch: Degener & Co., 1954). On his *Chronika,*
see *ME* (1955) I, 587-89.

56. See his *Kirchen- und Ketzer-Historie* (Frankfurt a/M: Thomas
Fritsch, 1700) : shortly before its appearance, Arnold had become famous
for *Die erste Liebe, eine Darstellung des äusseren und inneren Lebens der
ersten Christen* (Frankfurt, 1696), printed in usable edition by Buchhandlung der Evang. Gesellschaft at Stuttgart, no date, edited by A. C. Lämmert.
Arnold was the first church historian to attempt justice to Julian the
Apostate, who then became a man who had detected the hypocrisy of the
various intolerant sects and defended freedom of conscience; Seeberg, Erich,
Gottfried Arnold: die Wissenschaft und die Mystik seiner Zeit (Meerane i.
Sa.: E. R. Herzog, 1923), pp. 83-84; he also considered Philip the Arabian
the first real Christian emperor, a man who made no show of it as did
Constantine (p. 78, fn. 1). On Arnold, see article by Neff in *ML* (1913) I,
85-86; Friedmann in *ME* (1955) I, 164-65; Schröder, William Freiherr von,
Gottfried Arnold (Heidelberg: Carl Winters Univ.-Buchh., 1917).

57. Von Mosheim followed a familiar line of thinking in his published
works, *De rebus Christianorum ante Constantinum magnum commentarii*
(Helmsstedt: C. F. Weygand, 1739), his dissertation, and other writings. He
published many rare items on the "heretics," and esp. on Servetus in *Ander-
weitiger Versuch einer vollständigen und unpartheyischen Ketzergeschichte*
(Helmsstedt: C. F. Weygand, 1748-50); his writings were especially read
and treasured in England and America (!). On von Mosheim, see *ML*
(1940) 34:170; Bonwetsch in *Real.-3* (1903) XIII, 502-06.

58. Füsslin, Johann Konrad, *Neue und unpartheyische Kirchen- und
Ketzerhistorie der mittlern Zeit* (Frankfurt and Leipzig: C. G. Hilschern,
1770-74). He is sometimes called "the Swiss Gottfried Arnold"; note also
his *Beyträge zur Erläuterung der Kirchen-Reformations-Geschichten des
Schweizerlandes* (Zürich: Conrad Orell & Co., 1741-53). On Füsslin, see
ML (1937) II, 22; *ME* (1956) II, 427-28.

59. *ME* (1956) II, 535.

60. *ME* (1956) II, 690.

61. *ML* (1940) 34:180.

62. *Ein Apostel der Wiedertäufer* (Leipzig: S. Hirzel, 1882), pp. iv, 30.

63. Ritschl, Albrecht, *Geschichte des Pietismus* (Bonn: Adolph Marcus,
1880), I, 22-36. On Ritschl, see article in *Real.-3* (1906) XVII, 22-34.

64. The Waldensian sources of Anabaptism (?) have been proposed
by Keller, Kühler, Rembert, Nikoladoni, etc. See *Supra*, II:103.

65. Friedrich Engels apparently started this style of interpretation
(1850); Peachey, Paul, *Die soziale Herkunft der Schweizer Täufer in der
Reformationszeit* (Karlsruhe: Heinrich Schneider, 1954), p. 12. See Kautsky, Karl, *Communism in Central Europe in the Time of the Reformation*
(London: T. Fisher Unwin, 1897); Bax, E. Belfort, *Rise and Fall of the
Anabaptists* (Swan Sonnenschein & Co., 1903). For a more sound study
emphasizing the social and economic aspects, see Pascal, R., *The Social
Basis of the German Reformation* (London: Watts & Co., 1933). For an
interesting contemporary study of the Left Wing, emphasizing the eschatology and social views of the revolutionaries, see Hordern, William, *Christianity, Communism, and History* (New York and Nashville: Abingdon
Press, 1954).

66. *The Social Teaching of the Christian Churches* (New York: Macmillan Co., 1931) , II, 639f. The German edition appeared in 1912. Troeltsch depended largely upon secondary sources, but his historical sense was sound; he was not precommitted to hostile sources, nor was he afraid to discuss objectively the logic of free religious association. Note the study by Walther Köhler: *Ernst Troeltsch* (Tübingen: J. C. B. Mohr, 1941) .

67. Troeltsch, Ernst, *op. cit.*, II, 729f. Note footnote 440, II, 949, praising Hegler's original research in *Geist und Schrift bei Sebastian Franck* pp. 1-10. See also "Die Täufer und Spiritualisten," in "Protestantisches Christentum und Kirche in der Neuzeit," in P. Hinneberg's *Die Kultur in der Gegenwart* (Leipzig and Berlin: B. G. Teubner, 1922) .

68. Article by Köhler in *RGG - 2*, V, 1915-17, 1915.

69. For an interesting example from the Reformed tradition, by the translator of Menno Simons, see Verduin, Leonard, "On Detesting Anabaptists," *Calvin Forum* (1948) 183-86; also, by the same author, "Menno Simons' Theology Reviewed," XXIV *MQR* (1950) 1:25-32. According to Verduin, Menno was nearer to the truth than most of his contemporaries on the matter of discontinuity between the church and popular culture.

70. *Geschichte des Münsterischen Aufruhrs* (Leipzig: T. O. Weigel, 1855) , three books, third not published; appendices are esp. important. Note also *Die Münsterischen Humanisten und ihr Verhältniss zur Reformation* (Münster: Theissingische Buchh., 1851) . On Cornelius, see *ML* (1913) I, 372-74; *ME* (1955) I, 714-15.

71. See also *Die Reformation und die älteren Reformparteien* (Leipzig: S. Hirzel, 1885) ; *Johann von Staupitz und die Anfänge der Reformation* (Leipzig: S. Hirzel, 1888) ; *Zur Geschichte der Altevangelischen Gemeinden* (Berlin: E. S. Mittler & Sohn, 1887) ; "Die Anfänge der Reformation und die Ketzerschulen," IV *Vorträge und Aufsätze aus der Comenius-Gesellschaft* (1897) 1 and 2. On Keller, see *ML* (1937) II, 480.

72. On Egli, see article by C. Bergmann in *ML* (1913) I, 508-09; *ME* (1956) II, 163.

73. On Beck, see *ML* (1913) I, 149; *ME* (1955) I, 258-59.

74. On the *DB*, see *ME* (1956) II, 87.

75. See Dosker, Henry Elias, "Recent Sources of Information on the Anabaptists of the Netherlands," V *Papers of the American Society of Church History* (second series, 1917) 49-71. On Cramer, see *ML* (1913) I, 377-81; *ME* (1955) I, 731-32.

76. Wolkan, Rudolph, ed., *Geschicht-Buch der Hutterischen Brüder* (Vienna and Macleod, Alta.: Carl Fromme G. m. b. H., 1923) ; Zieglschmid, A. J. F., ed., *op. cit.* Unfortunately the utility of the latter volume is seriously limited by peculiar typography. Zieglschmid also edited *Das Klein-Geschichtsbuch der Hutterischen Brüder* (1947) , which covers a period later than that of our study.

77. Rideman, Peter, *Rechenschaft unserer Religion, Lehr und Glaubens, von den Brüdern, so man die Hütterischen nennt, ausgangen. . . . 1565* (Ashton Keynes, Wilts., Eng.: Cotswald-Bruderhof, 1938) ; *Account of Our Religion, Doctrine, and Faith* (London: Hodder & Stoughton/Plough Publishing House, 1950) . Several pamphlets have been published by the colonies which joined the Hutterites after World War I under the leadership of Eberhard Arnold, and have in Hutterite fashion migrated from Germany to

England, and lately to Alto Paraguay.

78. The statement of the *Verein*'s plan is found in *WtQ1930*, pp. v-vi. Further items to date are *WtQ1934, WtQ1938, WtQ:Hessen, WtQ:Baden/ Pfalz, WtQ:Bayern II, WtQ:Zürich.* See explanation of the Swiss phase of the project, in *WtQ:Zürich*, pp. v-ix. Note also Bender, Harold S., "Recent Progress in Research in Anabaptist History," VIII *MQR* (1934) 1:3-17, and the report on the postwar status of the series in XXIII *MQR* (1949) 1:48-52. The volumes on Denck by Baring and Fellmann belong to the series; see *Supra,* I:102.

79. *GHW/M;* bibliography, pp. 285f. The volume has also been published by the SCM Press in London, 1957.

80. See article by C. Bergmann, *ML* (1913) I, 451-56. Various articles have appeared in the *ME* on Disputations. See names of cities: i.e., "Frankenthal Disputation," *ME* (1956) II, 373-75; "Emden Disputation," *ME* (1956) II, 201-02.

Selected Bibliography

Source Books and Bibliographies

Bainton, Roland H., *Bibliography of the Continental Reformation: Materials Available in English* (Chicago: American Society of Church History, 1935).

Beck, Josef, ed., *Die Geschichts-Bücher der Wiedertäufer in Oesterreich-Ungarn* (Vienna: Carl Gerold's Sohn, 1883); XLIII *Fontes Rerum Austriacarum* (Hist. Comm. Kaiserl. Akad. der Wiss. in Wien), 2te Abth.

Bender, Harold S., *et. al.*, ed., *The Mennonite Encyclopedia* (Scottdale, Penna.: Mennonite Publishing House, 1955—). Articles by HSB on "Historical Libraries," *ME* (1956) II, 749-51, and "Historiography," *ME* (1956) II, 751ff. Also, "Bibliographies," *ME* (1955) I, 334-37.

Bossert, Gustav, ed., *Quellen zur Geschichte der Wiedertäufer, I: Herzogtum Württemberg* (Leipzig: M. Heinsius Nachf., 1930); XIII *QuFRG*.

Braght, T. J. van, *A Martyrology of the Churches of Christ Commonly Called Baptist* (London: Hanserd Knollys Society, 1850-53); 2 volumes, edited by Edward B. Underhill.

Catalogus der Werken over de Doopsgezinden en hunne Geschiednis aanwezig in de Bibliotheek der Vereenigde Doopsgezinde Gemeente te Amsterdam (Amsterdam: J. H. de Bussy, 1919).

Cramer, Samuel, and Pijper, F., ed., *Bibliotheca Reformatoria Neerlandica* (s' Gravenhage: Martinus Nijhoff, 1903-14); 10 volumes.

Egli, Emil, ed., *Actensammlung zur Geschichte der Zürcher Reformation in den Jahren 1519-1533* (Zürich: J. Schabelitz, 1879); 2 volumes.

Franz, Günther, *et. al.*, ed., *Wiedertäuferakten, 1527-1626* (Marburg: N. G. Eltwert'sche Verlagsbuchhandlung, 1951); IV *Urkundliche Quellen zur hessischen Reformationsgeschichte*.

Friedmann, Robert, "Die Briefe der österreichischen Täufer," XVI *ARG* (1929) 30-80, 161-87; translated and condensed as "The Epistles of the Hutterian Brethren," XX *MQR* (1946) 3:147-77.

Geisberg, Max, ed., *Das Wiedertäuferreich* (Munich: Hugo Schmidt Verlag, 1929); 16 facsimiles.

Hege, Christian, and Neff, Christian, ed., *Mennonitisches Lexikon* (Frankfurt/M and Weierhof/Pfalz: privately published, 1913, 1937, 1938 —); 2 volumes, with sections 31 *et. seq.*

Horsch, John, ed., *Catalogue of the Mennonite Historical Library* (Scottdale, Penna.: Mennonite Publishing House, 1929).

Krahn, Cornelius, "The Historiography of the Mennonites in the Netherlands: A Guide to Sources," XIII *CH* (1944) 3:182-209.

Krebs, Manfred, ed., *Quellen zur Geschichte der Täufer, IV: Baden und Pfalz* (Gütersloh: C. Bertelsmann Verlag, 1951); XXI *QuFRG*.

Menno Simons, The Complete Writings of . . . (Scottdale, Penna., Herald Press, 1956); translated by Leonard Verduin and edited by John Christian Wenger, with a biography by Harold S. Bender.

Müller, Lydia, ed., *Glaubenszeugnisse oberdeutscher Taufgesinnter* (Leipzig: M. Heinsius Nachf., 1938) ; XX *QuFRG.*

Muralt, Leonhard von, and Schmid, Walter, ed., *Quellen zur Geschichte der Täufer in der Schweiz, I: Zürich* (Zürich: S. Hirzel Verlag, 1952) .

Schornbaum, Karl, ed., *Quellen zur Geschichte der Wiedertäufer, II: Markgraftum Brandenburg* (Leipzig: M. Heinsius Nachf., 1934) ; XVI *QuFRG.*

Schornbaum, Karl, ed., *Quellen zur Geschichte der Täufer, V: Bayern, II. Abteilung* (Gütersloh: C. Bertelsmann Verlag, 1951) ; XXIII *QuFRG.*

Schottenloher, Karl, *Bibliographie zur Deutschen Geschichte im Zeitalter der Glaubensspaltung, 1517-1585* (Leipzig: Karl W. Hiersemann, 1933-39) ; 5 volumes.

Williams, George Huntston, and Mergal, Angel M., ed., *Spiritual and Anabaptist Writers* (Philadelphia: Westminster Press, 1957) .

Wolkan, Rudolph, ed., *Geschicht-Buch der Hutterischen Brüder* (Macleod, Alta., and Vienna: Carl Fromme G. m. b. H., 1923) .

Zieglschmid, A. J. F., ed., *Die älteste Chronik der Hutterischen Brüder* (Philadelphia: Carl Schurz Memorial Foundation, 1943) .

Works of General Significance

Bainton, Roland H., "The Left Wing of the Reformation," XXI *Journal of Religion* (1941) 2:124-34.

Bender, Harold S., "The Anabaptist Vision," XIII *CH* (1944) 3-24.

Bergfried, Ulrich, *Verantwortung als Theologisches Problem im Täufertum des 16. Jahrunderts* (Wuppertal-Elberfeld: A. Martini & Grüttefien, 1938) .

Bergmann, Cornelius, *Die Täuferbewegung im Kanton Zürich bis 1660* (Leipzig: M. Heinsius Nachf., 1916) .

Bouterwek, K. W., "Zur Wiedertäufer-Literatur," I *Zeitschrift des Bergischen Geschichtsvereins* (Bonn, 1864) 3:280-344.

Brons, A., *Ursprung, Entwickelung und Schicksale der Taufgesinnten oder Mennoniten* (Norden: Diedr. Soltau, 1844) .

Burckhardt, Paul, *Die Basler Täufer* (Basel: R. Reich, 1898) .

Burrage, Champlin, *The Church Covenant Idea* (Philadelphia: American Baptist Publication Society, 1904) .

Burrage, Henry S., *The History of the Anabaptists in Switzerland* (Philadelphia: American Baptist Publication Society, 1882) .

Correll, Ernst, *Das Schweizerische Täufermennonitentum* (Tübingen: J. C. B. Mohr, 1925) .

Dosker, Henry Elias, *The Dutch Anabaptists* (Philadelphia: Judson Press, 1921) .

Ecke, Karl, *Schwenckfeld, Luther, und der Gedanke einer apostolischen Reformation* (Berlin: Martin Warneck, 1911) ; abridged and without notes, Gütersloh: C. Bertelsmann Verlag, 1952.

Egli, Emil, *Die St. Galler Täufer* (Zürich: Friedrich Schulthess, 1887) .

Egli, Emil, *Die Züricher Wiedertäufer zur Reformationszeit* (Zürich: Friedrich Schulthess, 1878) .

Evans, Austin Patterson, *An Episode in the Struggle for Religious Freedom: the Sectaries of Nuremberg, 1524-1528* (New York: Columbia University Press, 1924) .

Friedmann, Robert, "Conception of the Anabaptists," IX *CH* (1940) 4:341-65.
Hege, Christian, *Die Täufer in der Kurpfalz* (Frankfurt/M: Hermann Minjon, 1908).
Hegler, Alfred, *Beiträge zur Geschichte der Mystik in der Reformationszeit* (Berlin: C. A. Schwetschke & Sohn, 1906); Erg. Bd. I *ARG*.
Hershberger, Guy F., ed., *The Recovery of the Anabaptist Vision* (Scottdale, Penna., Herald Press, 1957).
Heyer, Fritz, *Der Kirchenbegriff der Schwärmer* (Leipzig: M. Heinsius Nachf., 1939); 56:2 *SVRG*.
Horsch, John, "The Faith of the Swiss Brethren," IV *MQR* (1930) 241-66; V (1931) 7-27, 128-47, 245-54.
Horsch, John, *The Hutterian Brethren, 1528-1931* (Goshen, Ind.: Mennonite Historical Society, 1931).
Horsch, John, *Mennonites in Europe* (Scottdale, Penna.: Mennonite Publishing House, 1942).
Hulshof, Abraham, *Geschiedenis van de Doopsgezinden te Straatsburg van 1525 tot 1557* (Amsterdam: J. Clausen, 1905).
Kühler, W. J., *Geschiedenis der Nederlandsche Doopsgezinden in de Zestiende Eeuw* (Haarlem: H. D. Tjeck Willink & Zoon N. V., 1932).
Loserth, J., "Der Communismus der Mährischen Wiedertäufer in 16. und 17. Jahrhundert," 81 *Archiv für österreichische Geschichte* (1895) 135-322.
Loserth, J., ed., *Quellen und Forschungen zur Geschichte der oberdeutschen Taufgesinnten im 16. Jahrhundert* (Vienna and Leipzig: Carl Fromme G. m. b. H., 1929).
Lüdeman, H., *Reformation und Täufertum in ihrem Verhältnis zum christlichen Princip* (Bern: W. Kaiser, 1896).
Mellink, A. F., *De Wederdopers in de Noordelijke Nederlanden, 1531-1544* (Groningen and Djakarta: J. B. Wolters, 1954).
Müller, Lydia, *Der Kommunismus der mährischen Wiedertäufer* (Leipzig: M. Heinsius Nachf., 1927); 45 *SVRG*.
Neff, Christian L., ed., *Gedenkschrift zum 400. Jährigen Jubiläum der Mennoniten oder Taufgesinnten, 1525-1925* (Ludwigshafen: Konferenz der Süd-deutschen Mennoniten E. V., 1925).
Newman, Albert Henry, *A History of Anti-Pedobaptism* (Philadelphia: American Baptist Publication Society, 1897).
Peachey, Paul, *Die soziale Herkunft der Schweizer Täufer in der Reformationszeit* (Karlsruhe: Heinrich Schneider, 1954).
Rembert, Karl, *Die 'Wiedertäufer' im Herzogtum Jülich* (Berlin: R. Gaertners Verlag, 1899).
Smith, C. Henry, *The Story of the Mennonites* (Newton, Kansas: Mennonite Publication Office, 1950); third edition, revised and enlarged by Cornelius Krahn.
Smucker, Donovan E., "Anabaptist Historiography in the Scholarship of Today," XXII *MQR* (1948) 2:116-27.
Stauffer, Ethelbert, "Märtyrertheologie und Täuferbewegung," LII *ZKG* (1933) 545-98; translated, without last paragraphs, in XIX *MQR* (1945) 3:179ff.
Trechsel, Fr., *Die Protestantischen Antitrinitarier vor Faustus Socin* (Heidelberg: Karl Winter, 1844); 2 volumes.

218   The Anabaptist View of the Church

Troeltsch, Ernst, "Die Täufer und Spiritualisten," in "Protestantisches Christentum und Kirche in der Neuzeit," in P. Hinneberg's *Geschichte der christlichen Religion: Die Kultur der Gegenwart* (Leipzig and Berlin: B. G. Teubner, 1922).

Van der Zijpp, N., *Geschiedenis der Doopsgezinden in Nederland* (Arnhem: Van Loghum Slaterus, 1952).

Wappler, Paul, *Die Stellung Kursachsens und des Landgrafen Philipp von Hessen zur Täuferbewegung* (Münster: Aschendorffsche Buchhandlung, 1910).

Wappler, Paul, *Die Täuferbewegung in Thüringen von 1526-1584* (Jena: Gustav Fischer, 1913).

Wessel, J. H., *De Leerstellige Strijd tusschen Nederlandsche Gereformeerden en Doopsgezinden in de Zestiende Eeuw* (Assen: Van Gorcum & Co., 1945).

Westin, Gunnar, *Der Weg der freien christlichen Gemeinden durch die Jahrhunderte: Geschichte des Freikirchentums* (Kassel: J. G. Oncken Verlag, 1956).

Wilbur, Earl Morse, *A History of Unitarianism* (Cambridge, Mass.: Harvard University Press, 1945); volume I.

Wiswedel, W., *Bilder und Führergestalten aus dem Täufertum* (Kassel: J. G. Oncken Verlag, 1928, 1930, 1952); 3 volumes.

Special Studies

Bainton, Roland H., *Concerning Heretics . . . An anonymous work attributed to Sebastian Castellio* (New York: Columbia University Press, 1935).

Bainton, Roland H., *David Joris: Wiedertäufer und Kämpfer für Toleranz im 16. Jahrhundert* (Leipzig: M. Heinsius Nachf., 1937); Erg. B. VI ARG.

Barge, Hermann, *Andreas Bodenstein von Karlstadt* (Leipzig: Friedrich Brandstetter, 1905); 2 volumes.

Bender, Harold S., *Conrad Grebel (c. 1498-1526), The Founder of the Swiss Brethren* (Goshen, Ind.: Mennonite Historical Society, 1950).

Benz, Ernst, *Ecclesia Spiritualis* (Stuttgart: W. Kohlhammer Verlag, 1934).

Brandt, Otto H., *Thomas Müntzer: Sein Leben und seine Schriften* (Jena: Eugen Diedrichs Verlag, 1933).

Cornelius, C. A., *Geschichte des Münsterischen Aufruhrs* (Leipzig: T. O. Weigel, 1855); 3 books, 3rd not published.

Coutts, Alfred, *Hans Denck (1495-1527): Humanist and Heretic* (Edinburgh: Macniven and Wallace, 1927).

Detmer, Heinrich, *Bilder aus der religiösen und sozialen Unruh in Münster während des 16. Jahrhunderts* (Münster: Coppenrathsche Buchh., 1903-04); 3 volumes.

Friedmann, Robert, *Mennonite Piety Through the Centuries* (Goshen, Ind.: Mennonite Historical Society, 1949).

Hegler, Alfred, *Geist und Schrift bei Sebastian Franck* (Freiburg: J. C. B. Mohr, 1892).

Holl, Karl, "Luther und die Schwärmer," in Vol. I of *Gesammelte Aufsätze zur Kirchengeschichte* (Tübingen: J. C. B. Mohr, 1923), I, 420-77.

Horsch, John, *Menno Simons* (Scottdale, Penna.: Mennonite Publishing House, 1916).

Keller, Ludwig, *Ein Apostel der Wiedertäufer* (Leipzig: S. Hirzel, 1882).

Krahn, Cornelius, *Menno Simons (1496-1561)* (Karlsruhe: Heinrich Schneider, 1936).

Linden, Friedrich Otto zur, *Melchior Hofmann, ein Prophet der Wiedertäufer* (Haarlem: de Ervon F. Bohn, 1885).

Littell, Franklin H., "The Anabaptist Doctrine of the Restitution of the True Church," XXVI *MQR* (1950) 1:33-52.

"The Anabaptist Theology of Missions," XXI *MQR* (1947) 1:5-17.

"The Anabaptist Concept of the Church" in Hershberger, Guy F., ed., *The Recovery of the Anabaptist Vision* (Scottdale, Penna.: Herald Press, 1957), pp. 119-34.

"The Anabaptists and Christian Tradition," IV *Journal of Religious Thought* (1947) 2:167-81.

"Spiritualizers, Anabaptists, and the Church," XXIX *MQR* (1955) 1:34-43.

"Wiedertäufer, Schwärmer, Christen?" XVIII *Junge Kirche* (1957) 5/6: 128ff; in English, "Who were the Anabaptists?" II *Brethren Life and Thought* (1957) 2:13-20.

Loesche, Georg, "Archivalische Beiträge zur Geschichte des Täufertums und des Protestantismus in Tirol und Voralberg," 47 *Jahrbuch der Gesellschaft für die Geschichte des Protestantismus in ehemaligen und in neuen Osterreich (1926).*

Loserth, Johann, *Doctor Balthasar Hubmaier und die Anfänge der Wiedertaufe in Mähren* (Brünn: R. M. Rohrer, 1893).

Mau, Wilhelm, *Balthasar Hübmaier* (Berlin: D. Walter Rothschild, 1912).

Nestler, Hermann, *Die Wiedertäuferbewegung in Regensburg* (Regensburg: Josef Hobbel, 1926).

Neuser, Wilhelm, *Hans Hut. Leben und Wirken bis zum Nikolsburger Religionsgespräch* (Berlin: Hermann Blanke, 1913).

Nicoladoni, Alexander, *Johannes Bünderlin von Linz und die oberösterreichischen Täufergemeinden in den Jahren 1525-1531* (Berlin: R. Gaertners Verlag, 1893).

Peachey, Paul, "Anabaptism and Church Organization," XXX *MQR* (1956) 3:213-28.

Sachsse, Carl, *D. Balthasar Hubmaier als Theologe* (Berlin: Trowitsch & Sohn, 1914).

Schiedung, Hans, *Beiträge zur Bibliographie und Publizistik über die Münsterischen Wiedertäufer* (Münster: Heinrich Bornkamm, 1934).

Schultz, Selina Gerhard, *Caspar Schwenckfeld von Ossig (1489-1561)* (Norristown, Penna.: Board of Publication of the Schwenckfelder Church, 1946).

Weis, Frederick Lewis, *The Life and Teachings of Ludwig Hetzer* (Dorchester, Mass.: Underhill Press, 1930).

Wenger, John C., articles on Pilgram Marpeck, in XII *MQR* (1938) 137ff, 167ff, 205ff, 269ff.

Wenger, John C., "Pilgram Marpeck, Tyrolese Engineer and Anabaptist Elder," IX *CH* (1940) 24-36.

Abbreviations

WtQ:Bayern II .... Schornbaum, Karl, ed., *Quellen zur Geschichte der Täufer, V: Bayern, II. Abteilung*

WtQHessen: .... Franz, Günther, *et. al.*, ed., *Wiedertäuferakten, 1527-1626*

WtQ:Zürich .... Muralt, Leonard von, and Schmid, Walter, ed., *Quellen zur Geschichte der Täufer in der Schweiz, I: Zürich*

Z .... Zieglschmid, A. J. F., ed., *Die älteste Chronik der Hutterischen Brüder*

ZKG .... *Zeitschrift für Kirchengeschichte*

ZTK .... *Zeitschrift für Theologie und Kirche*

Index

Certain names are printed in small capital letters in the Index, in the text of the book, and in the Footnotes. This means that the person concerned played a key role in relation to Anabaptism, and that a bibliographical aid to further study will be found in the Footnotes. A special signature has been used for reference to information in the Footnotes: A Roman number followed by colon and Arabic number. The Roman number refers to the chapter of the book, the Arabic number to the footnote where detail may be found.

as a missionary community, 126f
educational contributions, IV:136
Hymns of the Anabaptists, IV:127

Italian reformers, I:77

JOACHIM OF FIORE: influence on radical movements of, 52f, II:16
Jörg von Passau: missioner, IV:66
JORIS, David: prophet, 40, I:195
Jud, Leo: reformer, I:57
Julian the Apostate: esteemed by primitivist historians, V:56
Justinian Law: applied to the Anabaptists, xiv

KARLSTADT, Andreas Bodenstein von, II:80:
at Orlamünde, 10
opponent of the Mass, 68f
Kautsky, Karl: socialist writer, 153
Kautz, Jakob: spiritualizer, 22, I:112
Keller, Ludwig: historian, 153, 156, V:71
Kessler, Johannes: friend, opponent, 12

Laity:
in radical revolt at Wittenberg, 5f
in league at Orlamünde, 10
in congregational reform at Zürich, 14
congregationally o r g a n i z e d at Waldshut, 17
Pilgram Marpeck, great lay leader, 24f
its decline a mark of the "Fall," 68
of key importance in Anabaptist "third type," 79
by believers' baptism coming under discipline, 85
lay region redeemed by Anabaptism, 91
under the Great Commission, 112
redeemed in his vocation, 113f
Langenmantel, Eitelhans: leader and missioner, IV:69
Lasco, John à : opponent, I:206
Left Wing of the Reformation:

as classifying category, 45, I:213
primitivism of all groups in, 47
various groupings in, I:7
Lord's Supper (*Abendmahl*) :
Anabaptist opposition to the Mass, 68
a major aspect of the restitution of the True Church, 98f
simile from the Didache, 101, III:101
LUTHER, Martin, I:8:
opposition to Puritan reforms at Wittenberg, 5f
polemicist, 7
in reaction to Peasant Revolt, 7f

Maccabean Christians: religious revolutionaries, a definite type in the Left Wing, 28
Märtyrer-Spiegel, 150, V:50
Magistrate: his function affirmed by the Anabaptists, 101f
Mandates, Imperial: vs. the Anabaptists, I:162
MANZ, Felix, I:61:
with Grebel at Zürich, 13
hymn of martyrdom, II:66
MARPECK, Pilgram, I:119:
leader of South German Brethren, 24
dispute with Schwenckfeld, 25
Martyr, the:
Church of the Martyrs, obedient to the Magistrate, 105
his suffering a motif of the restitution of the True Church, 117
as prototype of the true Christian, 119
Martyr/Missionary Synod (1527), 122, IV:65
theology of martyrdom: suffering as power, 132f
Mass, the:
validity of, denied by Anabaptists, 68
contrasted with Lord's Supper, 98f
MELANCHTHON, Philipp, V:23:
temporarily influenced by Zwickau prophets, 4
polemicist, 144

DUE	DUE	DUE
		APR 14 '81
		APR 12 '83
		MAR 20 1985
	JAN 26 '77	NOV 24 1986
	APR 1 '77	DEC 03 1996
APR 24 '63	NOV 16 78	NOV 20 1998
MAY 30 '63	JAN 30 79	NOV 17 '98
JUN '65	MAR 2 79	MAR 19 2003
JUN 4 '65	MAR 23 79	DEC 03 2003
FEB	APR 3 79	MAR 25 2007
APR 22 '72	april 9	OCT 26 2011
NOV 14 '72	APR 26 79	
DEC 17	MAY 8 79	FEB 2 '81
SEP 2 74	DEC 17 74	MAR 2 '81
NOV 24 75		MAR 6 '81
DEC 15 '75		MAR 31 '81
DEC 22 78		
OCT 22 78		
NOV 29 78		
DEC 13 78		